KT-389-081

BEHAVIOUR IN SCHOOLS

Theory and practice for teachers

LOUISE PORTER

OPEN UNIVERSITY PRESS

WITHDRAWN FROM THE LIBRARY
KA 0271127 3

For Gerard, who continues to tolerate my actual and mental absences while I write.

Open University Press
Celtic Court
22 Ballmoor
Buckingham
MK18 1XW

email: enquiries@openup.co.uk
world wide web: www.openup.co.uk

and
325 Chestnut Street
Philadelphia, PA 19106, USA

First published 2000
Reprinted 2001, 2002

Copyright © Louise Porter, 2000

All rights reserved. Except for the quotation of short passages for the
purposes of criticism and review, no part of this publication may be
reproduced, stored in a retrieval system, or transmitted in any form or
by any means, electronic, mechanical, photocopying, recording or
otherwise, without prior written permission of the publisher or a licence
from the Copyright Licensing Agency Ltd. Details of such licences
(for reprographic reproduction) may be obtained from the Copyright
Licensing Agency Ltd of 90 Tottenham Court Road, London, W1P 0LP.

KING ALFRED'S COLLEGE
WINCHESTER

371.5
POR

0271123

A catalogue record of this book is available from the British Library.

ISBN 0 335 20668 9

Library of Congress Cataloguing-in-Publication Data

Porter, Louise, 1958–
    Behaviour in schools : theory and practice for teachers / Louise Porter.
        p. cm.
    Includes bibliographical references (p.) and index.
    ISBN 0-335-20668-9 (pbk).
    1. School discipline. 2. Classroom management. 3. Behaviour modifica-
    tion.
    I. Title.

I.B3012. P65 2000
371.39'3—dc21   99-059115

Printed and bound in Australia.

Contents

Contents

Contents

Contents

Figures

Tables

Acknowledgments

I am grateful to Dr Colin MacMullin for his inspiration and guidance about the structure of the degree topic that formed the basis for this text and, in particular, guided my review in his specialty area of children's social skills.

I am similarly grateful, once again, to Dr Phillip Slee. He generously supplied me with comprehensive references on school bullying and guided my exploration of that literature.

Finally, I thank my students whose willingness to be enthused and challenged demonstrates the power of knowledge.

Part One
The theories

There is an old saying that states: 'If you want to get ahead, get a theory.' Yet most teachers are practical people who 'want to get on with it' and do not want to 'waste' time theorising. The trouble is, 'getting on with it' can involve doing the same unsuccessful thing over and over—not because you are incompetent, but because the ideas (the theories) that drive your responses are not helping.

Like Lewis (1997), I believe that inservice training sessions seldom result in lasting change—in part because the imperative to 'get on with it' means that session leaders usually propose only a loosely structured set of practices, with little theory as a rationale for their use. When you enact the resulting recommendations, you do not have a coherent series of beliefs to explain failure and to suggest what else you could do. So, naturally, you revert to what you *do* know.

The more organised your ideas, the more effective you can be in your responses to difficult or disruptive behaviour. Thus, although the notion of examining theories can sound dry, this text begins by describing theories as these will form the menu from which you will choose your own discipline methods and style. Once you are familiar with their underlying philosophy and recommended practices, you can build a coherent set of ideas that helps you describe, explain and predict student behaviour and how you can respond to it. In short, you will have generated your own 'theory'. Nothing can be more relevant, useful and empowering than that.

1 Introduction

If you have the end in view of . . . children learning certain set lessons, to be recited to a teacher, your discipline must be devoted to securing that result. But if the end in view is the development of a spirit of social co-operation and community life, discipline must grow out of and be relative to such an aim.

Dewey (1943: 16–17)

Key points

- Theories allow us to organise our ideas and therefore to be clearer about our practices. They empower us.
- The theories covered in this text differ in their goals for school discipline, ranging from the *managerial* function of maintaining order so that learning can occur, to four *educational* functions of teaching students self-discipline, emotional self-control, cooperation and integrity.
- With any of these goals as their basis, the theories differ in terms of the relative status of teachers and students.

Issues with language

It is important to mention at the outset some problems with the language that pertains to behaviour management in schools. The first is that the term 'management' itself has overtones of controlling others—of doing something *to* them, rather than working *with* them (Kohn 1996). It is a term that carries with it a great deal of baggage, being associated with a reward-and-punishment system of behaviour modification. Even the term 'discipline'—which might seem preferable—has connotations of punishment. This is because our society has such a long tradition of controlling forms of discipline that the two terms are mistakenly used interchangeably.

A second issue with language is that terms such as 'misbehaviour' or 'inappropriate behaviour' do not specify to whom those acts are 'inappropriate' (Kohn 1996). They imply that teachers' judgment on this issue is sacrosanct. Similarly, when a student's behaviour interrupts or disrupts the class, we often call this 'disruptive behaviour' as if that were its intent (even though we admit that we cannot read minds), or we label it 'problem behaviour'. This goes a step further when we say that an individual student has behaviour problems—or, worse still, *is* a behaviour problem.

The implication is that, when there is a disruption in a classroom, the offending students are to blame—there is something wrong with *them*. The job then becomes one of diagnosing the personal deficiency. Under this clinical model, the resulting diagnosis is regarded as the only 'right' definition of the situation and, because only professionals can confer diagnoses, they are seen to be the experts while parents and students are less powerful at best and, at worst, are regarded as dysfunctional or 'sick'.

Furthermore, this deficit or clinical orientation means that we expend energy on diagnosing young people's difficulties, in the expectation that finding out what causes them will suggest how to 'fix' them, without realising that what started a difficulty might not be the same factor that is maintaining it.

The final issue is that the terms 'discipline' and 'behaviour management' have an interventive bias, neglecting the fact that by far the largest and most crucial component of any discipline program is the prevention of difficulties.

Proposed definitions

Keeping in mind these issues of language, I shall refer to 'behaviours that result in a disruption' or, anticipating the discussion later in this chapter about the goals of discipline, will call these acts 'inconsiderate' or 'thoughtless'.

As to behaviour management or discipline, I include in those terms both proactive measures for preventing disruptions—usually through meeting students' educational, emotional and social needs—and also interventions that are aimed at returning students to considerate behaviour.

Why discipline young people?

As a teacher, you have two functions. The first is the instructional one of covering the curriculum, ensuring that individual students master the content, and promoting favourable attitudes to the specific subject and to learning in general (Doyle 1986). Your second function is a managerial one that promotes order through instituting procedures and limits, and responding to disruptive behaviour (Doyle 1986).

- *Order.* The first goal of the various approaches to school discipline is to establish and maintain order to create an environment in which learning is not only possible but probable. This is the *managerial* goal of discipline (Doyle 1986). Your instructional and managerial roles are intertwined: if the curriculum is relevant and attractive to students, they will be motivated to become involved and cooperate in a lesson (Doyle 1986). In turn, they are less likely to be disruptive and you will therefore have fewer management challenges. In short, high-quality academic work will achieve order. However, although order is necessary, it is not sufficient to promote high achievement (Doyle 1986).
- *Compliance.* Although the authoritarian theories often mention self-discipline, they actually mean only that students will comply with teachers' externally imposed discipline. However, discipline has a broader purpose than this. Rodd (1996: 6) says that behaviour management is 'the professional responsibility to socialise young children and help them learn to become responsible, competent fully functioning members of their culture and society according to their developmental capability'. Thus many of the theories of discipline in schools espouse one or many educational goals as well.
- *Self-discipline.* The first educational goal is to teach students self-discipline. The authoritarian theories regard this as teaching them to 'internalise' or learn the behaviours that we expect of them so that they can be trusted to make wise decisions about their behaviour, whether they are being supervised or not; the humanists contend that this is mere compliance and instead aim to teach students to construct their own values and behave according to those (Kohn 1996). Given the disparity in definitions of this goal, I have called the first 'internalised compliance' and the second 'autonomous ethics'.
- *Emotional regulation.* A second educational goal of discipline is to teach students to express their feelings appropriately, without getting themselves distressed and without upsetting the other people around them (Gartrell 1998). This goal is

not only so that students' emotional outbursts do not interfere with others, but also to safeguard students so that they learn to deal with setbacks without becoming so upset that they feel unable to cope (Porter 1999a).

- *Cooperation.* A third goal is to teach students to cooperate with other people (Hill & Hill 1990; Johnson & Johnson 1991; Rogers 1998) whereby they are given sufficient knowledge and experience to propose solutions to critical social issues (Knight 1991). The humanists extend the notion of cooperation beyond the here and now to teaching young people to balance their own needs against the needs of their communities (Goodman 1992).

- *Integrity.* A final potential goal is to teach young people to have the integrity to make ethical choices and the confidence to act on their values, so that they exercise their social responsibilities as well as their rights (Gartrell 1998; Ginott 1972; Glasser 1998a; Gordon 1970, 1974, 1991; Greenberg 1992a, 1992b; Knight 1991; Porter 1999a; Rogers 1951, 1978; Rogers & Freiberg 1994). Although this is a long-term aim, it begins when you teach the moral principles behind students' decisions, and encourage them to empathise with other people.

Which behaviours need a response?

Bill Rogers (1997, 1998) divides behavioural difficulties in schools into primary and secondary behaviours. Primary behaviours comprise:

- behavioural *excesses*, such as when a behaviour lasts beyond the normal developmental stage or occurs more frequently than normal (Herbert 1987);
- behavioural *combinations* that comprise a number of behaviours, each of which on its own would not present major management problems but which, together, can become disruptive, such as with the attention deficit disorders;
- *mistimed* behaviours which are appropriate elsewhere, but not at the time and place where they are occurring. For example, it may not be appropriate to applaud wildly at assembly when the school's team victory is announced, whereas the same behaviour is acceptable during the match.

Doyle (1986) distinguishes between behaviours that minimise a student's learning, such as disengagement, and those that disrupt the flow of the activity for the whole group (disruptive behaviours). Primary disruptive behaviours include: unsafe acts, property damage, aggression, disruptive off-task behaviour, disengagement, demeaning the task, and violations of a behavioural agreement (Charles 1999; Doyle 1986; Grossman 1995; Rogers 1998). The humanists define these or other acts as unacceptable if they violate an individual's rights (Gordon 1970, 1974, 1991). Those affected may be students themselves (such as when their behaviour impedes their own learning or leads to ostracism by peers), the teacher or other students in the class. The extent to which any given behaviour disrupts the activity will also determine whether you will regard it as unacceptable.

Secondary behaviours are students' negative response to your attempts at correction (Rogers 1997, 1998). These include defensiveness, arguing with you, answering back, baiting you and becoming angry. They are typical responses to an assertive message (see Chapter 6). Sometimes these behaviours cause more difficulties than the original or primary behaviour, so it is crucial that you have the knowledge and skill to respond in ways that are less likely to provoke these secondary reactions from students (Rogers 1998).

How to discipline: Overview of the theories

The next question is how to discipline students. That has a longer answer, one that takes up the rest of this text. Nevertheless, to begin to answer it, the following are some key points about each theory. At this introductory stage, you might not yet know the names of some of the theories, but you will probably find that you recognise some of their practices at work in schools.

The limit-setting approaches

These approaches incorporate Canter and Canter's 'assertive discipline' (1992) and Jones' 'positive discipline'. They believe:

- Teachers have the right to impose order on students.
- Students 'need' adults to make it clear what we expect of them (Charles 1999).
- Positive and negative consequences for individuals and the group as a whole will ensure that students comply with teachers' expectations.

Applied behaviour analysis (ABA)

You might recognise applied behaviour analysis (ABA) by the earlier name of behaviour modification. Its main tenets are:

- Behaviour continues because it works. It earns students something that they want.
- If you want a behaviour to cease, then you must stop it from working. You can do this either by rewarding an alternative behaviour, or by punishing the target behaviour.

Cognitive-behaviourism

As the double-barrelled title suggests, cognitive-behaviourism retains some of the beliefs of ABA, but takes account of individuals' thinking (cognitions) as well.

- This theory agrees that behaviour is controlled by its consequences, but also by students' emotional state, self-esteem, motivation, social setting and developmental level.
- Therefore, intervention is directed both at the consequences (rewards and punishments) of behaviour and at students' thinking and feeling.
- Students have a more active role in determining behavioural goals and overseeing the discipline program.

Neo-Adlerian theory

Many modern writers have based their ideas on those of Alfred Adler, who wrote at the beginning of this century. The best-known of the modern writers are the authors of the Systematic Training for Effective Teaching (or Parenting) packages (STET and STEP) (Dinkmeyer et al. 1980, 1997; Dinkmeyer & McKay 1989). In Australia, the best-known neo-Adlerian is Maurice Balson (1992, 1994) and, in early childhood, Jeannette Harrisson (1996). This theory:

- believes that students become disruptive when they grow discouraged. This discouragement arises from the feeling that they cannot belong in other ways;
- attempts to prevent this discouragement by building cooperative relationships in the classroom;
- advises that when students' behaviour disrupts, you should diagnose which of four goals is motivating the behaviour. These goals are: attention, power, revenge or withdrawal. Next, you are to find ways that students can meet their identified need in more appropriate ways.

Humanism

The humanist approach to school discipline arose originally from the progressive education movement, the founders of which included John Dewey and Maria Montessori, and continues with the current emphasis on constructivism in education which says that children actively construct their understandings of the world. Humanism believes that:

- students will learn when what they are learning meets their intellectual, social and emotional needs;
- the teacher must act as a facilitator who helps students to learn what interests them and what they need to know. When this occurs, few disruptions will result;
- when a student's behaviour violates someone's rights, you should solve the problem by listening, being assertive and collaborating with students to resolve the issue. This approach looks for a solution rather than punishing a culprit.

Choice theory

This is the new title for Glasser's 'control theory'. Drawing its philosophical base from humanism and cognitive theory, it believes:

- Individuals behave as they do out of choice. They believe that their chosen behaviour will help meet their needs.
- Therefore, you must make it possible for students to make better choices so that their behaviour meets their own needs without violating the rights of others.

Systems theory

Unlike all the previous theories, systems theory focuses on students' relationships, rather than on them as individuals. It believes that disruptive behaviours recur because present solutions are not working. Although this assertion is fairly obvious, its recommendations for how to change solutions may seem unorthodox to new initiates.

- Students get stuck in repetitive behaviour not because of their personal flaws, but because of how teachers and students relate to each other when a disruption occurs.
- Therefore, you can change troublesome behaviour by changing these student–teacher interactions.

- Systems theory attempts to change the teacher's half of the student–teacher interaction, as it recognises that it is difficult to change students' contribution to the relationship.

Philosophical assumptions of theories of school discipline

The above theories differ in their philosophical assumptions which, in turn, leads to differing teacher roles. It is important to make these assumptions explicit, because that enables them to be evaluated (Fisch et al. 1982).

Nature of childhood

The various theorists believe that children are either deficient in moral reasoning or cognitive skills and therefore need constant guidance and supervision, or that they are inherently moral and rational human beings who will behave accordingly when given the chance. A third view is that children are born with both capacities, and that their environment will influence which characteristics are expressed.

Conditions necessary for learning to occur

Edwards (1997) summarises three different views about how children learn and develop. The first is that children grow as a result of external stimulation over which they have little control. This implies that children and their environments need *managing*. A second view is that children develop from an inner unfolding, driven by biological maturation and curiosity. This implies that if children are free to direct themselves, their choices will be appropriate. Edwards calls this approach the *nondirective* approach, and attributes it mainly to Carl Rogers. The third view is the *leadership* approach which holds that children develop from an interaction between inner and outer influences. This implies that teachers should take a leadership role with students, showing them how to control their own lives and learning. The main proponent of the leadership approach is Bill Glasser (Edwards 1997).

Purpose of discipline

All theories aim to enhance student success in schools by promoting an orderly learning environment. However, some see this managerial role as an end in itself, while others see it only as a means of facilitating learning and so add any or all of the educational purposes that were listed earlier.

Reasons for disruptive behaviour

The authoritarian theories emphasise faulty external controls as the cause of student disruptions; the democratic theories say that disruptions occur when students' emotional or relationship needs are not being met.

Teacher–student status

Figure 1.1 places the theories of student behaviour on a continuum defined by the relative power of teachers and students. On the left are the authoritarian theories in which teachers have control over students, the most extreme of which is James Dobson (1992). Dobson believes that unless we punish children, they will not learn

Figure 1.1 The balance of power proposed by theories of student discipline

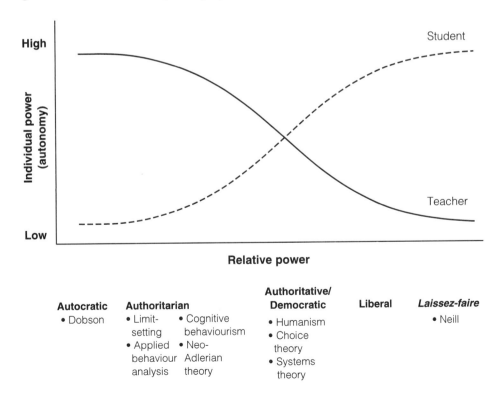

appropriate moral (by which he means sexual) standards of behaviour, and will be 'damned in hell'. His approach draws on biblical support rather than on evidence from the social sciences or education. This renders it a personal philosophy rather than a testable theory, so it is not included in this text.

At the other end of the continuum is the permissive or *laissez-faire* approach which grants students a free rein, with very few adult-imposed restrictions (McCaslin & Good 1992). This approach has no modern adherents and, for that reason, it too is not covered in this text.

The middle ground is occupied by the democratic theories—humanism, choice theory and systems theory—that promote students' autonomy. The democrats argue that not only does no one have the *right* to force someone else to comply, but also that coercion does not *work*. Nevertheless, the democratic theories do not suggest that adults and children are the same. Teachers and students have equal *rights* to have their needs met, but different *roles*.

Disciplinary role of the teacher

Under the authoritarian theories, teachers set limits on students' behaviours and specify what will happen if those limits are violated. They use external controls.

In contrast, the authoritative or democratic theorists state that we must *teach* self-discipline, rather than imposing controls on students. Under this philosophy, you would be an authoritative leader: you would discuss your standards with students and teach them how to meet them (McCaslin & Good 1992), ensuring that they have the necessary information to make an informed choice about their actions.

Criteria for evaluating the theories

To guide your practice, you will need to evaluate these theories on the basis of some criteria. Your options include: blending attractive elements of each theory; choosing a theory with goals that match your own; examining the research evidence for the various approaches; or judging them according to ethical guidelines.

Eclecticism

When choosing a theory to guide your practice, it might be tempting to select elements of all the theories to arrive at an eclectic blend. To be eclectic means to select the best practices from various theories (Corey 1996). This can occur in three ways (Young 1992). The highest form is *synthetic eclecticism*, which is an attempt to synthesise or integrate compatible approaches, resulting in a more complex and comprehensive theory than any of the original theories alone. The second form, *technical eclecticism*, utilises one organising theory and borrows some approaches from other theories. The third form is *atheoretical eclecticism*, in which the practitioner lacks a theory base and so uses whatever methods 'seem like a good idea at the time'.

Atheoretical eclecticism is not an option for professionals. Corey (1996) describes it as sloppy and labels it the worst form of eclecticism, saying that it represents a haphazard picking of elements of theories without any overall rationale. It results in a recipe-like mindset that dictates 'if students do this, teachers should do that', but ultimately it will let you down as it cannot predict all student behaviours and will not help to explain those occasions when your methods fail or suggest what else you could do (Young 1992). You may respond to a new behaviour in a way that has worked in the past, when instead a new solution was necessary (Fisch et al. 1982). Corey (1996) maintains that this type of undisciplined approach can be an excuse for failing to understand the theories adequately, claiming that it allows users to pick and choose elements of theories that merely support their preconceived notions and biases.

Technical eclecticism is deceptive: it appears to make it possible to parcel together a few strategies; however if their underlying philosophies are at odds with each other, the various practices will in turn contradict and undermine each other, resulting in confusion for both your students and yourself.

Therefore, I recommend selecting only those methods that share similar philosophies, rationales and goals. You might be able to combine these elements from a number of compatible theorists to yield your own, more meaningful, synthesis. An integrated synthesis preserves the integrity of the original theories' philosophy, while leaving you free to employ a range of useful approaches rather than just those contained in the original theories. The hybrid will not create contradiction and confusion as long as the original philosophical principles have been preserved, while your commitment to a personally synthesised theory will be more effective than borrowing someone else's methods (Edwards 1997; Lewis 1997; Young 1992).

On the other hand, we have to be cautious about adopting an inflexible belief system that we come to regard as a higher form of truth rather than just one possible interpretation of reality (Fisch et al. 1982). A reified theory can bias our observations:

we become subject to the theory, instead of using it as a tool for understanding our subject. A useful theory, then, is one that provides focus and direction without blinding us to other issues and to the individuality of each case (Young 1992).

Research evidence of effectiveness

All the theories claim that they work, but there is no consensus on how to define effectiveness (Kyriacou & Newson 1982). Kohn (1996) observes that the usual assumption equates effective behaviour management with teacher dominance over the class, yet the constructivist approach to teaching upholds that teacher dominance detracts from the quality of students' learning. When considering whether the theories are effective, then, you need to ask: effective at what? In partial answer to this question, the box below lists the goals of each theory.

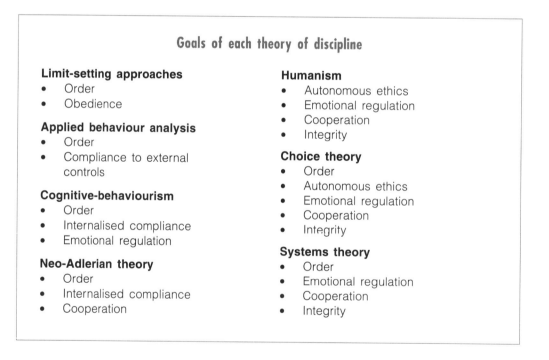

Goals of each theory of discipline

Limit-setting approaches
- Order
- Obedience

Applied behaviour analysis
- Order
- Compliance to external controls

Cognitive-behaviourism
- Order
- Internalised compliance
- Emotional regulation

Neo-Adlerian theory
- Order
- Internalised compliance
- Cooperation

Humanism
- Autonomous ethics
- Emotional regulation
- Cooperation
- Integrity

Choice theory
- Order
- Autonomous ethics
- Emotional regulation
- Cooperation
- Integrity

Systems theory
- Order
- Emotional regulation
- Cooperation
- Integrity

Furthermore, measures of effectiveness might address whether the students' behaviour improves but seldom ask whether there are other unwanted side-effects of the management methods (Emmer & Aussiker 1990).

Given the research difficulties, there is little empirical evidence for the superiority of any of the theories in promoting student learning and avoiding student disruptiveness (Doyle 1986). However, it may be that the democratic approaches lead to more voluntary observance of reasonable rules and engender more self-controlled, self-confident, independent and social children than the authoritarian approaches (Baumrind 1967; Berk 1997). (See also Chapter 9 for a full critique of the theories.)

Comprehensiveness

Each theory proposes an explanation for disruptive behaviour but not all explanations are equally useful for the purpose of helping students to change. Theories that are most likely to be useful are those that:

- are non-blaming, as blame causes people to become defensive and so depletes their emotional resources for making changes;
- describe how the behaviour can improve, rather than offering static explanations—say, about students' personalities or home backgrounds—that imply that the problem *cannot* change;
- suggest what to do, rather than what to think—solutions require action, rather than insight;
- focus on the present rather than the past, as the past cannot be changed;
- generate hope in both students and teachers that improvement can occur;
- respect individuals' rights—including the miscreant, onlooking students and teachers (Haley 1980; Molnar & Lindquist 1989).

Practical requirements

As you read about each theory, you will need to consider whether each one is practicable. Do you have the time and supports to institute its practices? Would you need additional training in order to use the theory? How could you receive this? Awareness of practical requirements also needs to take into account the constraints on best practice, including the immediate context of your classroom, with its physical setting and demands, and the collegial supports that are available to you within your school.

Educational value

You might like to consider how educational each of the theory's practices is, by asking whether the theories conform to what you know about how children learn and whether they teach students any useful skills.

Ethics

When assessing which theory best fits within a school setting, the issue of justice or ethics is fundamental. Ethics refer to your moral duty and obligation to do what is right, just and good rather than what is merely expedient, convenient or practical (Katz 1995).

Ethical decision-making

Ethical dilemmas arise when two possible courses of action both have benefits and costs and you must choose between them. It is important that such judgments are not arbitrary or capricious (Strike & Soltis 1992). Arbitrary judgments occur when decisions are made without considering all the evidence; capricious decisions are unsystematically formed, without due process (Strike & Soltis 1992).

Two strands must inform your ultimate decision: the ideals that underpin professionalism; and consideration of the consequences that may arise from your actions (Strike & Soltis 1992).

Ideals

The first, idealistic, approach requires that you behave towards others as you would wish them to act towards you (Strike & Soltis 1992). This approach rests on the principle of equal respect for all persons, which states that all individuals' interests, while different, deserve equal consideration. It might be enshrined in your profession's code of ethics, but this list of principles can be a general guide only, partly because behaving ethically involves more than just abiding by the letter of the law (Corey 1996), and partly because codes of ethics and legislation often specify minimum standards of conduct only, rather than optimal standards.

A shortcoming of relying on general principles is that it can discourage individual reflection on the specific circumstances of a dilemma, with the result that you might make judgments that stick rigidly to irrational or general principles but which are not responsive to individual circumstances (Coady 1994; Strike & Soltis 1992; Turnbull & Turnbull 1990).

Some basic moral ideals can be useful, however—particularly when, as in teaching, you serve a group (students) who have little power to advocate for themselves; when you are accountable to many consumers at once, including students, parents, the wider community, your school community and your own professional body; and when (as is often the case in education) evidence about the effectiveness of various practices is not compelling, in which case you must rely on your professional judgment (Katz 1995).

Consequences

The consequentialist aspect of decision-making requires you to examine the outcomes for all parties and to choose a course of action that produces better consequences than might otherwise have occurred. However, this assumes that you can predict these outcomes accurately, which is seldom possible. It also might ignore the need to redress past injustices, as the consequentialist approach focuses entirely on the future.

Therefore you will need to find a blend by considering potential consequences within a framework of ideals (Strike & Soltis 1992). Such an approach might generate the following ethical guidelines with respect to school discipline.

- You should do no harm.
- Students have a right to competent teaching.
- Individualised behaviour management programs require informed consent.
- Confidentiality for students and their families must be preserved.
- Students' independence must be supported.

These principles have some implications for the practice of discipline in schools.

A safe environment

You need to provide a setting that treats students humanely, is safe, responsive to human needs and enjoyable, and which imposes the fewest restrictions necessary (Alberto & Troutman 1999).

Competent service

It is crucial that you are sensitive to students' rights to freedom and dignity, while at the same time providing them with the most effective and ethical intervention (Rekers 1984). In order to evaluate whether an intervention is desirable, you need to:

- know about the theory that guides your practice;
- be aware of a range of treatment options; recognise your own limitations and

refer students to specialists if you are not equipped to deal with their difficulties (which also involves knowledge of appropriate services); and

- collaborate with other professionals who are working with any of your students.

Intensive training and ongoing supervision are also desirable, especially when you are dealing with complex behavioural difficulties (Alberto & Troutman 1999).

Student involvement in the program

You should collaborate with students about a behavioural program's goals and methods (Fawcett 1991).

Ongoing evaluation

When you institute an individual behaviour management program, you will need to evaluate the effect of your intervention so that you detect early any unwanted side-effects.

Consent

If all these criteria are met, then the crucial one of consent is more likely to be satisfied also. There are four types of consent: legal, competent, voluntary and informed (Rekers 1984). The first two are beyond the capacity of young children, in which case parental consent will be necessary, although older students may be asked to give their own consent as well. The third form, *voluntary* consent, requires that you cannot threaten students or their parents with any unfair consequences— such as school suspension or refusal to teach a student—if they withhold consent to the program (Rekers 1984), but neither can you promise extravagant benefits if they do participate in the program (Alberto & Troutman 1999). Last, informed consent acknowledges that your professional status may put parents or students under subtle pressure to consent, and so the onus is on you to ensure that what they are agreeing to represents best practice (Rekers 1984) and that you have considered a range of viable treatment options and have discussed these with them (Martin & Pear 1999).

Confidentiality

This is a dilemma faced in all interpersonal work. Confidentiality involves your duty to protect students' privacy; safeguarding their files or other records; keeping these records accurate, unbiased and fair; avoiding staffroom gossip about students and their families; and making available to the students or parents all information in their files. However, Geldard (1998) discusses the limits which apply to confidentiality, including the need to pass on information to other school staff or other agencies whose work with your students would be affected by their ignorance of key information; occasions when behaviour is illegal; or when it likely to result in injury to other students or to the individual students themselves. To balance students' and parents' needs for privacy with your professional obligations to disclose some information, you can discuss with them what information you will be disclosing and to whom, so that they are aware of who knows what about them.

Summary

Your approach to student discipline will depend on your beliefs about students and how they learn, your purpose of discipline, your explanations of disruptive behaviour, and how much autonomy you trust students to exercise. These beliefs will yield a view of your role as controlling or guiding.

Once you are aware of your beliefs and are familiar with a range of theories of student behaviour, you can generate a repertoire of congruent responses. Then you will be empowered: you will not only know *what* to do, but *why*.

Discussion questions

1 Think about your own goals for maintaining discipline in a class. Which of the managerial and educational goals do you emphasise most?
2 Which behaviours are a high priority for you to correct? Are there behaviours that you would include in a list of difficult behaviours but which are not mentioned in this chapter?
3 Think about the approaches you presently use or are familiar with for responding to students' disruptive behaviour. Which ones are most effective at meeting the goals you specified when answering question 1? Which practices seem ineffective?
4 With which of the theories mentioned in this chapter are you already familiar? Which do you use, and which have you (so far) found unattractive? How do your personal beliefs influence your preferences?

5   If you are already teaching, do you have either a formal or informal discipline plan to guide you in responding to students' behaviour? If you have been teaching for some years, how have this plan, your beliefs, ideas and practices evolved over time?

2   The limit-setting approaches

An assertive teacher [is] one who clearly and firmly communicates her expectations to her students, and is prepared to reinforce her words with appropriate actions. She responds to students in a manner that maximizes her potential to get her own needs to teach met, but in no way violates the best interest of the students.

Canter & Canter (1992: 14)

Key points

- The assertive teacher has a right and a duty to enforce order so that teaching and learning can be accomplished.
- To encourage their cooperation, you will develop warm relationships with students.
- To maximise their ability to abide by them you will teach students the rules.
- Positive recognition and incentives build cooperation.
- You will apply graded consequences for serious or repeated disruptions.

Introduction

Lee and Marlene Canter (1992) and Fredric Jones (1987a, 1987b) define successful classrooms as those that are under firm teacher control. Jones' suggestions were derived from systematic observations and comparisons of classrooms where teacher control was assured versus those where it was not, while Canter and Canter's approach was born from an attempt to answer the practical problems that they encountered in their own work and, later, in the classrooms of teachers to whom they consulted (Canter & Canter 1976). Both approaches are skills-based, requiring you to practise the techniques to become skilful at using them (Jones 1987a).

Philosophical assumptions

The limit-setting approaches emphasise that, as a teacher, you have both a right and a responsibility to establish order in classrooms so that you can teach and students can learn.

Nature of childhood

The question of the particular needs of children is not addressed by either theory. Canter and Canter (1992) assume that children want and need clear limits on their behaviour so that they know what they have to do to be successful (Charles 1999), and that they have a right to encouragement when they do attain your standards.

Conditions necessary for learning to occur

Learning requires order. Aside from this statement, Canter and Canter detail no other conditions required for learning. This lack of an underlying philosophy about childhood and how learning occurs leads to a unitary purpose of discipline.

Purpose of discipline

The purpose of discipline is a largely managerial one of creating order—that is, to maintain an effective and efficient learning environment (Jones 1987a) through teaching obedience to authority. The goal of obedience is to provide psychological safety, to protect students from performing behaviour that they would regret later, and to allow them to build on their positive skills (Charles 1999).

Reasons for disruptive behaviour

Canter and Canter (1992) assert that students no longer respect teachers and education and that their homes lack stability, support and discipline. Consequently, children lack the self-esteem and self-control needed to choose responsible behaviour. Resulting behavioural problems in school continue because teachers lack the confidence to be clear about their expectations and consequences for infractions of rules.

Teacher–student status

The classroom belongs to the teacher. You have an unquestioned right to determine expectations and consequences for your students. This external control is intended to teach students how to exercise control over themselves, although no specific approaches are recommended for transferring control back to students.

Disciplinary role of the teacher

Your job is to establish order by defining rules and delivering positive consequences for compliant behaviour and negative consequences for rule violations. These management procedures must always be positive and gentle, developing cooperation without coercion (Jones 1987a).

Prevention of classroom problems

You will prevent classroom behavioural problems by establishing and maintaining order. To that end, as a limit-setting teacher, you would ensure that your teaching was of high quality, and that your body language, verbal response style (non-assertive, assertive or aggressive) and your relationships with students all confirmed your authority.

High-quality instruction

A good curriculum is necessary for maintaining order. You will maintain order through your lesson design and presentation, by giving corrective feedback, and by offering incentives for diligence and excellence, while your demeanour will establish that order in the first place (Canter & Canter 1992; Jones 1987b).

A crucial ingredient of high-quality instruction is momentum. If you provide lengthy help to individual students, then others are free to be disruptive, while those being helped can become dependent on your personal support (Charles 1999). Jones suggests, therefore, that when you give help, you should comment on something the student has achieved, give a straightforward suggestion or hint, and then leave. This will communicate your confidence that the student will be able to carry on independently. In short, you should 'be positive, be brief, and be gone' (Charles 1999: 118).

Body language

To establish order, as the limit-setting teacher you would use assertive body language. This conveys more powerfully than any other medium that you 'mean business' (Jones 1987a). Your self-assurance will convey to students that you expect them to respect your limits. This does not mean that you are overbearing, but instead are calmly confident and supportive. Effective body language can also restore order by giving a non-confrontational reminder to students about your expectations, without interrupting the teaching process.

- *Eye contact.* Even if a disruptive student does not return eye contact, your gaze communicates that you have noted the behaviour and disapprove of it.
- *Physical proximity.* When one or two students are being disruptive, you can step in close without necessarily saying anything. Physical proximity alone may bring the behaviour back into line. Room and desk arrangements need to facilitate quick access to students.
- *Tone of voice.* You should avoid sarcasm, abuse and intimidation, but instead should convey firmness (Charles 1999). Also, the appropriate use of humour is a very powerful way to soften a behaviour plan (Canter & Canter 1992).
- *Facial expressions and gestures.* More than anything else, your facial expressions and gestures can convey humour and confidence in yourself and in the students' cooperation (Charles 1999). Frowns and other expressions can cue students to stop inappropriate behaviour or can re-engage uninvolved students without interrupting the flow of a lesson. Touch can be used cautiously to encourage students, but should never be used to discourage disruptiveness.

Assertiveness

To set limits effectively, you need to be assertive. As an assertive teacher, you can choose how to respond to students' behaviour, rather than simply reacting. You are able to communicate your pleasure clearly to students when they are behaving appropriately and can state what you need when they are not (Canter & Canter 1976). As a result, students learn what is expected of them, feel good when their achievements are acknowledged, and respect the fair treatment that they receive from you (Canter & Canter 1976). Meanwhile, you benefit by having your needs met and achieving job satisfaction from discharging your professional duties well.

In contrast, timid teachers do not have their needs met because they do not state what they need clearly, or do not back up their words with action (Canter & Canter 1976). Students feel frustrated, manipulated and angry while timid teachers feel frustrated, inadequate and hostile towards students whom they 'cannot handle'.

Hostile or aggressive teachers, on the other hand, have their needs met but at the expense of students' self-esteem—by putting students down, issuing threats or administering harsh consequences (Canter & Canter 1976, 1992). Teachers feel guilty about being aggressive, while students comply, but only because they fear and dislike hostile teachers.

While acknowledging that no one is assertive all the time, the Canters' program aims to encourage teachers to be assertive more consistently.

Warm relationships with students

Warm, positive relationships in the classroom allow you to have an influence on students (Jones 1987a). When you respect students, they will respect your values, rules and opinions. You will need to get to know students and their interests, encourage them to get to know each other, greet students by name daily, have fun together, give individuals a few special minutes, make home visits by arrangement and always help students to do their work (within the specific guidelines already discussed) (Canter & Canter 1992; Jones 1987a).

The classroom discipline plan

The purpose of a classroom discipline plan is to avoid hasty, timid or hostile responses to student behaviour, so that your responses can be consistent and therefore predictable for students. A plan also enables you to get support from parents and school administrators. While the plan is designed to apply to all students, on occasions modifications are made for individuals whose behaviour is not improving under the class-wide plan. The plan consists of rules, positive recognition and consequences that result when students do not follow the rules.

Rules

General rules

General rules are guidelines about good behaviour and good work habits (Jones 1987a). Canter and Canter (1992) suggest these general rules: follow directions; keep hands, feet and objects to yourself; no teasing or name calling; no swearing. These rules are observable, and they apply throughout all classroom sessions. (Behaviour outside the classroom is dealt with by a school discipline plan and does not affect the classroom plan.) Students can contribute to determining rules (Canter & Canter 1992; Jones 1987a), although you will need to guide them in not making their expectations too strict.

Specific rules

These detail the procedures that students need to observe when carrying out specific activities; also they specify standards for students' work (Jones 1987a).

Teaching the rules

You cannot assume that students will know the rules and so should not simply announce them and expect that students will understand them. Instead you will have to teach the rules, describing them and explaining what they mean, why they are in place, and what will happen if students violate them. You could direct younger children to rehearse rules and procedures. Having checked that students understand the rules, you should next describe the positive consequences that you will award for their observance.

Positive recognition

Positive recognition is 'the sincere and meaningful attention you give a student for behaving according to your expectations' (Canter & Canter 1992: 57). By recognising students when they conform to your standards, you will motivate them to repeat appropriate behaviour and so reduce disruptive behaviour, increase their self-esteem, create a positive environment for the class, and build positive relationships between you and each student. Positive recognition is especially crucial during the first days of working with a class, but remains a high priority all year as it conveys the message that the way to gain your attention is to obey rather than to disrupt.

The first form of positive recognition is praise, which must be simple, direct, personal, genuine, specific and descriptive. Your plan might also include positive recognition in the form of calling parents, giving students awards, awarding special privileges, and delivering tangible rewards. You can apply the more formal forms of recognition to the whole class as needed, rather than being in place permanently, whereas recognition of individuals' compliance is a permanent feature of the discipline plan. Older students may be embarrassed by public positive recognition, so instead it can be delivered in private. So that older students learn to feel good about themselves, you can follow your praise with a statement such as, 'You should be proud of yourself'. Another way to avoid a student's public embarrassment is giving the whole group bonus points for individuals' successes.

The criteria for earning a reward need to be reasonable and realistic for the students' ages (Canter & Canter 1992).

Group incentives

An incentive system is a program for delivering reinforcers for cooperative behaviour.

Informal systems

Your relationship with students is 'money in the bank' (Jones 1987a: 148): its quality determines how willing students are to cooperate with you. A warm relationship is necessary but not sufficient for discipline, however, and so you will also need to develop some formal systems for delivering reinforcers.

Formal systems

Jones (1987a) contends that incentive systems have to be cost-effective: while a particular plan might work, it may take up too much of your time to plan and execute, especially when tailored for individuals. Therefore, Jones devised a group incentive system based on 'responsibility training'. A simple incentive involves Premack's principle (otherwise known as 'Grandma's rule') which states that once you complete something distasteful, you can have something you like. Three elements are in operation here: the task, the reward, and monitoring to check that the reward has been earned.

These simple incentives can be difficult to operate for a whole class, because a few individuals will abuse them. For this reason, you will also need more complex incentive systems. Two elements are added: bonuses and penalties. A complex system involves rewarding the whole class for orderly behaviour by giving them some time to do a favourite activity, which is both fun (so that students want to do it) and educationally valuable (so that you can justify the time it takes).

On the issue of penalties, there is a difference of opinion between the two theorists: Canter and Canter (1992) advise you not to impose fines for misbehaviour, while a central feature of Jones' system is penalties for individual misbehaviour. Jones uses a stopwatch to time any student's infraction of a rule (even one as basic as individual students having to sharpen a pencil because they did not have a sharp one ready ahead of time). The time it takes for individual students to correct their behaviour is subtracted from the time the group is allowed to engage in the preferred activity. Thus, the whole class is penalised if a single individual breaks a rule (Edwards 1997; Jones 1987a; 1987b). The exception is when students lose self-control altogether, in which case you will remove them from the room rather than penalising the whole class.

Jones (1987a) gives detailed advice on fine-tuning the incentive system to suit individual students and particular situations. This is beyond the scope of this text, although I refer you to Jones (1987a) for more detail.

Enforcing the limits

The limit-setting sequence follows an invariant series of steps, which are terminated when students correct their behaviour. The process is based on firmness as well as kindness, even when students are being nasty to you (Jones 1987a). Your calm demeanour helps students accept responsibility for their own behaviour and models the maturity and self-possession that you want them to learn.

- *Monitoring the classroom.* You must stand where you can see most of the students easily, and need to listen for disturbances that you cannot see.
- *Terminate instruction.* Disruptive behaviour entertains students so it has its own rewards. Therefore, you should not ignore it because it is not your attention that is maintaining the behaviour but the fun it is generating for the miscreant and the whole class (Jones 1987a). Instead, you should stop teaching, and begin the following steps to quell the behaviour.
- *Face and name the disrupting student.* First, face the most disruptive student squarely and gain eye contact, to convey the expectation that he or she will cease the disruption.
- *Move in.* If the ringleading student does not turn her body fully back to her work in response to your direct gaze, then it is clear that she is not committed

to returning to work. In that case, you will move unhurriedly to her desk and stand in front of it for the count of two slow breaths. This pause gives both you and the student time to calm down and gives the student time to think about her behaviour.

- *Prompt.* Lean with one palm on the student's desk and state exactly what you want the student to do. Stay in that posture for two breaths.
- *Camp out in front.* If this does not provoke a return to work, slowly move in closer by leaning on both palms placed on the student's side of the desk. At no time should you offer academic help, as disruption is not the correct procedure for seeking or gaining help.
- *Camping out from behind.* If two students continue to talk while you are camping out in front of a student's desk, then move around behind to place yourself physically between them.
- *Move out.* At whatever stage the student resumes work, watch for two breaths (fifteen seconds) and then thank the student genuinely for cooperating. Then move in on an accomplice and repeat the moving out sequence, even if the second student is already back on task.
- *Return to instruction.* Finally, return to your former position, and pause to watch the disruptive students for two breaths before resuming your instruction. If a disruptive student issues a cheap shot while you are moving out, recycle the limit-setting steps, beginning with moving in.
- *Responding to back talk.* During the limit-setting steps, students may back-talk by asking for help, denying responsibility for the disruption (which is sometimes paired with blaming someone else), accusing you of causing the problem through your poor teaching, inviting you to leave, insulting you, using profanity, crying, giving compliments, saying something irrelevant, or pushing you aside (Jones 1987a). Regardless of the content of these plays, they are all attempts to gain control. You must stand your ground impassively without saying anything. To reaffirm your resolve, you may lean on your elbows rather than palms, and wait.

Conclusion: The limit-setting sequence

Jones (1987a) details variations on this sequence, such as how to respond when students say something that is genuinely funny while you are camped out at their desk, what to do when you are already behind students when they disrupt, and when not to use the sequence at all.

Negative sanctions (consequences)

You will need a backup system of a series of progressive negative sanctions in case limit-setting fails. Negative sanctions suppress severe disruptions and buy time for you to consult parents and the school administration (Jones 1987a). Any backup system of sanctions will be over-used if it stands alone. It can only repair order, not establish it, and so will be effective only in the context of the earlier steps of your overall management plan.

The chosen sanctions cannot add to your workload and must be cost-effective, as the process of management cannot become more important than teaching. Canter and Canter (1992) contend that consequences are not punishments (which are something teachers *do* to students) but are a natural outcome of students' behavioural choices: they are something that students do not like but they are not physically or psychologically harmful. The students must not be humiliated or embarrassed.

Consequences do not have to be severe, as it is their inevitability, not their severity, that has an impact. They must be delivered in a calm, matter-of-fact manner, when you do not threaten, but only remind students about the consequences if they continue to behave inappropriately. You must follow a consequence with positive recognition when students return to appropriate behaviour.

Canter and Canter (1992) advise you to apply consequences in a step-wise manner for repeated infractions on the same day, and to start each new day with a clean slate. The first infraction is met with a warning, comprising your assertive message or a request for appropriate behaviour. The limit-setting sequence would constitute this first warning. The second and third infractions earn a consequence such as a brief time-out period, or a one-minute wait after class. For the fourth infraction on the same day (in primary school) or in the same lesson (in secondary school), you would contact the parents or have the students ring them themselves. The final consequence (for the fifth violation) is being sent to the principal, with this having been planned in advance so that you know what support you will receive from the principal. This sanction is also invoked for dangerous behaviour that needs an immediate intervention. Canter and Canter (1992) call this the 'severe clause'.

To keep track of individual students' behaviours and their consequences, you are advised to write these on a clipboard rather than on the blackboard so that students are not publicly humiliated.

Students will need an 'escape mechanism' that allows them to tell their story later, but not while a lesson is in progress. This may mean that you allow them to write down what they wanted to say, which you discuss together later.

Obtaining support

No teacher can work successfully with each and every student: sometimes, support from parents and the school administration is necessary. In the first instance, you should deal with the behaviour yourself but then call on the school administration and parents as the need arises, and finally invoke social welfare agencies and the criminal justice system if necessary.

The first step for achieving this is to advise parents and administrators of your classroom discipline plan and to make routine and positive contact with all parents early in the school year (Canter & Canter 1992; Jones 1987a). You can do this by form letters or through phone calls to all parents or only to those whose sons or daughters are most likely to present difficulties (Jones 1987a). Sending students' work home can also promote contact with their parents.

Once a behavioural problem arises, you will document the steps you have taken to handle it. You should contact parents at the first sign of the sort of difficulty that you would like to know about if *you* were the child's parent (Canter & Canter 1992). When calling, state your specific concerns, describe what action you have taken so far, listen to the parent's view of the problem and suggestions for handling it, agree on what you will each do to solve it, and arrange for a follow-up call. Make sure that you express confidence that the behaviour can be mended.

School administrators can be supportive by providing counselling or arranging for counselling of the parent or student, setting up a meeting with the parent and the school, and instituting in-school suspensions.

Summary

Canter and Canter (1992) and Jones (1987a, 1987b) detail a discipline plan that requires you to set limits on students' behaviour so that order is maintained and teaching and learning can occur. You are advised to be assertive both in word and manner, while being warm and supportive with students. You must teach rules and reward compliance with personal and formal recognition and incentives.

If disruptive behaviour occurs, you must enforce the limits, and invoke backup sanctions if this fails. To help you tailor the plan to suit individual needs, you can counsel students (outside class time), beginning with asking them if something is the matter, as you cannot assume that you know why they are misbehaving. You can offer to help in some way—such as by moving a student away from a troublesome peer, giving academic help, or renewing your commitment to giving positive recognition.

You are empowered to seek support from parents and the school administration when faced with intractable disciplinary problems. Finally, Canter and Canter (1992) caution you to use the discipline plan as a tool rather than as a law and to adjust it to individual students' circumstances as required.

Case study

Adam is seven. He has difficulty with reading, spelling and writing, although he enjoys and is capable at maths. During non-maths lessons, you have noticed that he spends a considerable amount of time off-task, when he frequently disrupts the other students. This is worse in the afternoon than in the morning.

He is in a composite class of six- and seven-year-olds. He spends most of his play time with the younger children. Frequently a pair which includes Adam is apprehended during play times doing such things as harassing passers-by from an out-of-bounds area of the playground which is close to the street, rifling through rubbish bins for food or cans to swap for other items with students, or engaging in fights in and around the toilets.

He seems bemused by the trouble he gets into, usually saying when challenged that he doesn't know why he behaves in these inappropriate ways, that he couldn't remember a given behaviour was against the rules, or that the other child was at fault for suggesting the activity.

Until a recent assessment, it was believed that Adam behaved as he did because of low academic ability. However, a battery of tests has shown his overall ability (IQ) to be average, with his maths skills in the high–normal range and his reading and spelling skills, while delayed, still within the lower range of normal limits. Teaching staff are now at a loss to find a new explanation for his behaviour.

A limit-setting response

If you worked under the limit-setting system, you might take the following steps in response to Adam's behavioural difficulties.

Step 1: Adopt an assertive demeanour. You might start with realising that you have been non-assertive with Adam, sometimes virtually pleading with him to 'pull his socks up', but also at other times expressing some frustration at his behaviour and being punitive and almost hostile. Therefore, you will practise verbal assertion and make your body language convey more confidence in your handling of Adam, so that he learns that he has to take you seriously.

Step 2: Reduce Adam's dependence on supervision. You have been taking responsibility for Adam's behaviour by reminding him to bring required equipment to school or to do his homework, and by giving him excessive one-to-one guidance in class about his work. To teach Adam to work independently, you should give him only brief instructional help. You will do this in the three steps Jones recommends, namely: 'be positive, be brief and be gone'. The aim of this is to convey to Adam that you are confident that he can work alone successfully.

Step 3: Foster a warm relationship. Your frustration and near-hostility to Adam will have harmed your relationship with him. Therefore, make some time to be alone with Adam to get to know him better and take an interest in what he enjoys. Until now, when Adam has worked appropriately, you have felt relieved that this has freed you to work with other students; from now on, increase your rate of positive recognitions of Adam's appropriate behaviour.

Step 4: Teach the rules. Adam clearly knows about the rules, but not how to observe them. In a class meeting, instruct all the students about what the rules are, why they are in place, how to abide by them, and the positive and negative consequences of infractions and the reasons for these. Give Adam and all students the opportunity to check their understanding of the rules and to role-play how to observe them.

Step 5: Distinguish between in-class and out-of-class infractions. Stop being responsible for infractions of the rules in the playground. This is the responsibility of the school as a whole, guided by its discipline policy. Meanwhile, in class, you will consistently enforce the limits that you taught the group in step 4.

Step 6: Use the limit-setting sequence. Respond to Adam's off-task or disruptive behaviour in a sequence of graded steps suggested by Jones (1987a). Do not ignore this type of behaviour: suspend instruction whenever Adam or any other student is disengaged or being disruptive. Routinely and calmly enact the steps of facing and naming the student, moving in, giving a prompt, camping out in front (or behind, as required) and moving out.

Step 7: Use incentives. If Adam is just one of many disruptive students, set up a group incentive program; if Adam is the only student whose behaviour is seriously disruptive, establish an individual program, giving Adam the incentive of being allowed to spend time on a preferred activity.

Step 8: Invoke negative sanctions (consequences). If Adam disrupts repeatedly in the same day, invoke a series of consequences. The limit-setting sequence will be considered as a warning; you can impose subsequent consequences such as time out from the class or staying back briefly at the end of a lesson.

Step 9: Obtain support. If Adam displays any further infractions on the same day, call his parents. Also, together with the principal, plan what you will do if Adam needs to be sent to the principal in the future. The two of you might decide that this final consequence will involve a conference with the principal, perhaps in conjunction with the parents.

Step 10: Revise the plan. If earlier steps prove unsuccessful, in consultation with Adam's parents and the principal, revise your plan for responding to Adam's behaviour. The plan will refine, adapt and add to the interventions that you have already tried. Monitor the plan and conduct follow-up meetings to discuss and reach agreement on any changes that might increase the plan's effectiveness.

Discussion questions

1   Do you agree with Canter and Canter's assertion that children *need* adults to exercise control over them?

2   Do you see any pitfalls in the assumption that external controls will teach children to exercise self-discipline?

3   Do you see any alternatives to being either timid or hostile? Is assertiveness as defined by the limit-setting theorists the only option?

4   What forms of positive recognition do you routinely use (or plan to use) when you teach? Are they individual or given to the class as a whole? How effective are they?

5   Would you feel comfortable using Jones' limit-setting sequence? What steps, if any, would you want to modify?

6   What do you think about the use of negative sanctions? Are they necessary? Effective? Practicable? Under what conditions would you apply negative sanctions?

7   Write your own case study. What responses would a limit-setting approach recommend for that student? What effect would the practices have on the student? On onlookers? On you?

Suggested further reading

For a detailed description of assertive discipline:

Canter, L. and Canter, M. 1992 *Assertive discipline: positive behavior management for today's classroom* Lee Canter & Associates, Santa Monica, CA

This edition is strictly limited to participants in assertive training courses. Instead, their 1976 volume, *Assertive discipline: a take charge approach for today's educator*, covers similar material and may be more widely available.

For a detailed description of Fredric Jones's approach:

Jones, F.H. 1987a *Positive classroom discipline* McGraw-Hill, New York
——1987b *Positive classroom instruction* McGraw-Hill, New York

3 Applied behaviour analysis

A major concern within the behavioural approach to teaching is with the identification of things and events which children find rewarding and to structure the teaching environment so as to make access to these rewards dependent upon behaviour which the teacher wants to encourage in his class.

Wheldall & Merrett (1984: 19)

Key points

- Behaviour is controlled by the response it receives (its consequence). Thus, if you want to increase the rate of a behaviour, you must follow it with a positive consequence, and if you want to reduce its rate, you must follow it with a negative consequence.
- The environment (antecedents) can also make behaviours more or less likely to occur.
- Reinforcers and punishments vary in intrusiveness (which is the extent to which they interrupt teaching) and restrictiveness (the extent to which teachers apply external controls to students).

Introduction

As its title implies, applied behaviour analysis (ABA) focuses on behaviour rather than thinking or feelings, even though it acknowledges that these exist. This is because behaviourists believe that we cannot change students' thinking and feelings. Instead, ABA aims to change the conditions that surround a behaviour, so that a desirable behaviour is strengthened by receiving a favourable response from others, and an undesirable behaviour is either no longer provoked by its circumstances or is no longer maintained by the positive response it receives.

Philosophical assumptions

Behavioural understandings of individuals arose in opposition to the likes of Freudian theory which postulated that all of us seek to gratify our drives for sex and aggression—that is, all of our behaviour comes from within (Alberto & Troutman 1999).

Nature of childhood

Children are behaving beings, and so their actions are governed by the same rules that apply to the behaviour of adults, which is to say that outside forces shape their actions. Even developmental theory which links children's behaviour to their stage of development is questioned by behaviourists (Alberto & Troutman 1999).

Conditions necessary for learning to occur

Skinner (1989) states that learning is not an act: it is changing how we act (acquiring a new behaviour). Individuals may begin a new behaviour by imitating others, and that behaviour is then maintained by its consequences. Therefore, consequences shape learning.

Purpose of discipline

Behaviourists would define the main purpose of discipline as a managerial one of establishing, maintaining or reinstating order so that students can be successful at learning. It seeks to do so by teaching students to comply with outside controls.

Reasons for disruptive behaviour

Behaviour, appropriate or otherwise, is more likely to recur when it receives a positive response—that is, when the behaviour works. Therefore, to change inappropriate behaviour, you must change the response it receives.

Teacher–student status

From Wheldall and Merrett's statement (1984) that opened this chapter, it is clear that you remain in control of students. You manipulate their external environment to alter the probability that they will behave in certain ways. However, latest applications of ABA do consult students about their actions, the conditions that give rise to them, and their effects on others. The more student involvement there is, the less authoritarian ABA becomes in practice.

Disciplinary role of the teacher

Watson (1913, in Heward & Cooper 1987: 7) wrote that the goal of ABA is 'the prediction and control of behaviour'. This, plus the opening quote, gives a succinct description of your disciplinary role: to structure your responses to students' behaviour in such a way that they are more likely to behave in desirable ways and less likely to display undesired behaviour.

Unlike the cognitive and humanist theories that are summarised in coming chapters, which see your job as being to arrange the environment so that students can learn or construct their own knowledge, behaviourism emphasises direct instruction. This is because ABA adherents contend that, under the constructivist educational approach, teachers have too little control over what students are learning (Alberto & Troutman 1999).

Behaviourist principles

Behaviour can be of two types: reflexes, such as eye-blinking (which are termed *respondent* behaviours); and all other behaviours (termed *operant* behaviours), which are voluntary.

Principle 1: Consequences

All voluntary behaviour (as distinct from reflexes) is controlled by its consequences. These consequences will *reinforce* the behaviour (result in its increase); *punish* (result in a decrease in the behaviour); or will be *neutral* in their effects (the behaviour rate will be unchanged).

Principle 2: Antecedents

It is not enough to explain behaviour by describing its consequences only. You must also note the conditions under which the behaviour occurs. These are the *antecedents*. Antecedents can greatly increase the likelihood that a given behaviour will occur, and so you must understand these conditions in detail so that you can enact preventive measures (Bailey & Pyles 1989; Horner 1994).

There are many advantages of altering the antecedents rather than the consequences. It can be easier to change the antecedent, and also more humane and ethical than allowing students to get into trouble unnecessarily. Changing the antecedent can remove the need for an intervention, and is also more likely to ensure that behaviour improvement is maintained (Bailey & Pyles 1989).

Thus addressing antecedents is the first step in a behavioural program, followed by altering the consequences only if the first step is unsuccessful. You can address general antecedents by ensuring that students have a comfortable working environment, with adequate space and materials, an effective instructional program that maximises their engagement, and a high level of natural reinforcers (Wolery et al. 1988). More specific and individualised manipulation of antecedent conditions may be suggested by affirmative answers to any of the following questions (adapted from Bailey & Pyles 1989):

- Are there any circumstances under which the behaviour does *not* occur?
- Are there any circumstances under which the behaviour *always* occurs?
- Does the behaviour occur at certain times of the day?
- Does the behaviour occur only with certain people?
- Could the behaviour be related to any skills deficit?
- Could the behaviour be a result of any form of physical discomfort (including allergies or food sensitivities) or side-effects of medication?
- Does the behaviour allow students to gain attention, which may imply that there is insufficient attention (an antecedent) in the normal teaching situation?
- Does the behaviour allow students to escape learning, in which case some aspect of the content or teaching process is aversive to them and acts as an antecedent for the behaviour?
- Does the behaviour occur as part of a chain of behaviours?
- Does the behaviour occur as a result of having another ongoing behaviour terminated?

Principle 3: Defining target behaviours

The behaviour that is of concern and that becomes the focus of intervention is termed the *target* behaviour. You must define this precisely in behavioural terms rather than diagnostic ones—that is, in terms of what actually *happens* (for instance, student A hits student B during library session) rather than by labelling the behaviour or the student (e.g. student A is aggressive). The behaviours must be observable and measurable, which means that you can quantify their frequency and duration. Your definition of the target behaviour must be complete or comprehensive so that you can discriminate the behaviour from others that are not the focus of intervention.

This principle is in contrast to, say, a circular definition of a problem, in which students are said to behave impulsively because they are hyperactive, and are diagnosed to be hyperactive because they are impulsive (Alberto & Troutman 1999). The behaviourist is interested simply in what events occur—because these can be verified; behaviourists are not interested in generating 'explanatory fictions' that cannot be tested, or in designing complex interventions when more simple and immediate ones would be effective (Alberto & Troutman 1999: 23).

Principle 4: Observation and recording

To establish how often the behaviour occurs, under what conditions, and what response it engenders, you will need to observe systematically and to record the antecedent conditions and consequences that surround the behaviour. You can then use this information to plan an intervention and to check whether it is having an effect. This data collection is essential to the accuracy and success of any behaviour modification program, because intuitive judgments about improvement or lack of change may be inaccurate and because your own discouragement and mood fluctuations can bias your observations.

When observing and recording, you can focus on:

- the *frequency* of the behaviour, which is the number of times it occurs;
- its *rate*—that is, the number of times the behaviour occurs within a specified time period;
- the *accuracy* of the behaviour—for instance, the number of items the student gets right on a series of tests over time;
- the *duration* of each instance of the behaviour;

- its *intensity*;
- its *latency*, which refers to the amount of time it takes for a student to begin a task once instructed.

You can record every instance of the behaviour, which is termed *frequency* or *event recording*. Another method is *interval recording*, in which you divide the observation period into time intervals, and note whether the behaviour did or did not occur during, throughout or at the end of each interval. Intervals need to be short enough that success will be demonstrated by the undesired behaviour occurring in fewer and fewer intervals, or desired behaviour occurring more often.

The observation method that you choose will depend on the type of target behaviour, the context in which it is occurring, and the amount of time you have available for making observations. As a classroom teacher, you may not be able to use the more intensive observation and recording procedures because of their heavy demands on your time and so for accurate observation, you might have to call in an observer.

Principle 5: Establishing behavioural objectives

Having observed the target behaviour and the conditions under which it occurs, you then define in positive terms what modified form the target behaviour will take as a result of successful intervention—that is, your objective will state what students *will* be doing rather than what they *will not* be doing (Zirpoli & Melloy 1997). This is called the *terminal* behaviour. When defining terminal behaviour, you will specify to whom the objective applies, what students are expected to do, under what conditions, and how well they have to perform the task before the program is deemed to have been successful (Wolery et al. 1988).

Principle 6: Increasing behaviour

Behaviour is strengthened by reinforcement—that is, by delivery of a consequence which the behaver values. This is the defining characteristic of reinforcement: that it *increases the rate of behaviour*. This means that reinforcement is defined by its effects, not by what an outsider may assume will be reinforcing.

When an action results in the *presentation* of a consequence, and as a result the behaviour occurs more often in the future, it has been *positively* reinforced. When the action results in the *removal* of something negative and the behaviour subsequently increases in frequency, then it has been *negatively* reinforced. An example of negative reinforcement is allocating no homework if students complete their work in class. (Many people confuse negative reinforcement with punishment, but these are very different: negative reinforcement *increases* a desirable behaviour by removing something negative; punishment *decreases* an undesirable behaviour.)

Principle 7: Decreasing behaviour

Behaviour can be reduced or weakened by *punishment*. Again, what seems to be a punishment may not be so for a given individual. As with reinforcement, punishment is defined simply by its effect, not by your intentions. To reduce undesirable behaviour, you can deliver an aversive consequence (Type 1 punishment) or withdraw a positive one (Type 2 punishment).

Behaviour can also be decreased by removing the specific consequence that maintains it. This is termed *extinction* and is discussed again later in this chapter.

Principle 8: Contingency

You must deliver the consequence when the behaviour occurs, and not when the behaviour is not displayed—in short, presentation of the consequence must be *contingent*, or dependent, on the behaviour (Lattal & Neef 1996).

Principle 9: Least intrusive methods

A key axiom of ABA is that you must use the least invasive, intrusive and aversive methods that are available but which will still be successful. You must use reinforcement first and, if punishment becomes necessary, you should choose the least aversive form.

Principle 10: Individualisation

Any technique may or may not work for a given student and, therefore, the key to effectiveness is to individualise your intervention for each student (Wolery et al. 1988). You need to collect detailed data to document the effects of every intervention. For this reason, ABA is mainly used for intervening with individual students, rather than a whole class, as it will be impractical to design specific reinforcers and consequences for every student individually.

Developing new behaviour

If students do not display a behaviour very often, they do not receive reinforcement very often either, and so they are not likely to learn a new behaviour. In this case, you must develop the new behaviour by reinforcing improvements, while at the same time using the process of extinction (which is described in later sections) to decrease inappropriate acts.

Modelling

If you reinforce one student's behaviour, those who are observing this are more likely to display the same behaviour as long as they:

- are capable of performing it;
- respect the student who has been reinforced;
- regard themselves as similar to him or her in significant ways;
- receive reinforcement themselves for the behaviour (Kerr & Nelson 1998).

Prompts and fading

You can give students prompts to help them complete a task, and then gradually withdraw these (in a process called *fading*) until students can complete the task alone. You may be familiar with Axelrod's (1977) example of the teacher writing most of a letter of the alphabet, and then using dashes and dots to write less and less of it until students can write the letter without any visual prompts at all.

Shaping

Shaping is the process of reinforcing small improvements in the target behaviour until students are performing it at a desirable level. You can use it when students do not often perform the target behaviour (Wolery et al. 1988). At first, you give reinforcement for a less than optimal performance, and gradually raise the standards that you expect students to achieve until they are able to produce an acceptable quality of work or standard of behaviour. Each new standard must be only a small improvement on the last and must be within the students' capabilities.

Chaining

When students cannot complete a task that comprises many steps, you can break it down, or *task analyse* it, into a series of small steps that they can achieve serially. To do this, you will need to know the students' abilities so that the steps are manageable for them.

Forward chaining

In this process, you reinforce students for completing the first step successfully, and then for completing the first two, then three, and so on. In this way, over time, students acquire all the steps and so learn the complete task.

Backward chaining

For some tasks, if students were to do the first step it might seem out of context and irrelevant and so they would not be motivated to complete it. Instead, you can prompt them through the earlier steps but reinforce them only when they complete the *last* of these independently. Next you require them to complete the final two steps before you deliver a reinforcer, then the last three, and so on. In this way, students also receive inherent reinforcement for completing the task, which can increase motivation.

Contracting

Along with students, you can negotiate, write and evaluate an agreement that when they display a certain behaviour to a specified level, you will award a specified reinforcer. Likewise, you will specify what constitutes failure and what consequences that will attract. Students should have a right to renegotiate and to correct failure. Last, you need to institute a reliable means of record-keeping (Wolery et al. 1988). All this may take some time to set up, although it has many of the advantages of self-regulation—namely, that students oversee and are accountable for their own compliance and so are more motivated to adhere to the agreement (Olympia et al. 1994).

Increasing existing behaviour

To increase the rate of a behaviour, you can arrange for the delivery of reinforcers which, by definition, strengthen the behaviour. You can deliver reinforcers naturally both at the beginning and the end of a behavioural intervention. At the beginning, increasing natural reinforcers so that they occur at a high enough rate to influence students' behaviour positively can avoid the need for an intervention. At the end of an intervention, you should again strengthen natural reinforcers so that the behaviour itself becomes intrinsically rewarding, allowing you gradually to withdraw (or fade) external rewards altogether. In this way, reinforcement becomes less restrictive than when students administer it themselves, or when you deliver it. (Restrictiveness refers to how much external control is imposed on students.)

Types of reinforcers

Intrusiveness is the extent to which interventions interfere with the educational process. The types of reinforcers, arranged in order from the least to most intrusive, include: social, activity, tangible, token, edible and sensory reinforcers.

Social reinforcers

These have three aspects: feedback, attention, and approval (Kerr & Nelson 1998). Feedback on its own is a weak reinforcer, although attention and approval can be powerful, as long as students value your judgment of them.

Praise is a common social reinforcer, and can be used alone or paired with other types of reinforcement. To be effective, it must be contingent on the desired behaviour, as well as specific, credible, high in quality and not over-used. It should not interrupt student attention (Wolery et al. 1988).

Caring touch can also be a social reinforcer. Students must feel in control of any touch they receive and must perceive it as safe. When choosing to touch students, you would need to consider issues of child protection and abuse, and ensure that you are not exposed to allegations of improper conduct (see Chapter 10).

Other social reinforcers include: appointing a child as student of the day or leader of an activity, and calling or writing to students' parent/s about their positive behaviour (Zirpoli & Melloy 1997).

Activity reinforcers

To encourage students to complete activities that they do not like, you can reward them with the chance to do an activity that they prefer. This is Premack's principle (Kerr & Nelson 1998), also known as 'Grandma's rule'. Preferred activities may include free time, time with you, an opportunity to hand out materials to the other students, use of the computer, feeding the class pet, bringing a toy to school, listening to music, or reading a story (Zirpoli & Melloy 1997).

At first you may have to give students access to the preferred activity after just one instance of the target behaviour, as a reinforcer can be ineffective if there is too long a delay in its delivery. As students develop more self-control, however, you can lengthen the delay between the behaviour and the reinforcing activity.

Tangible reinforcement

Tangible reinforcers are non-food items that students value for their own sake. They may include stars, stamps, stickers, points, toys or magazines (Zirpoli & Melloy 1997). Tangible reinforcers differ from tokens in that they are valued in themselves and are not traded in for any other reinforcer. Determining a reinforcer for each student separately can make using tangible reinforcers intrusive (Kerr & Nelson 1998).

Token reinforcers

Under a token reinforcement system, you would give students a portable and durable token (such as a poker chip) when they display target behaviours. Later, they can trade these tokens in for pre-negotiated backup reinforcers. Setting up a token program is detailed and demanding. You need to determine how many tokens each desired behaviour earns, the costs of the various backup reinforcers, procedures for exchanging tokens for them, and fines for misdemeanours. You will need a reliable recording system. The token system must seem fair to the students or they will stop working within it. The reinforcers will need fading out once the program has achieved success, which will take skilful handling in case the behaviour deteriorates again. Finally, an ethical issue with using token economies is the claim that students have a right to noncontingent access to many objects and activities, which therefore should not be used as backup reinforcers (Williams et al. 1989). This criticism can be overcome if the back-up reinforcer is a special privilege to which the students do not ordinarily have access, although this can be difficult to arrange in schools.

The major advantage of token programs is that tokens can be exchanged for a variety of reinforcers, which avoids the problems of deprivation and satiation (Axelrod 1977). The symbolic reinforcer can be delivered immediately, although the actual reinforcer itself is delayed. This may be sufficient for some students;

others may not be able to delay gratification until the backup reinforcer is delivered, however.

Edible reinforcers

Food is a reinforcer for everyone as it satisfies a basic physiological need. However, determining students' food likes and dislikes makes edible reinforcers difficult to establish. Issues such as nutrition (including issues of obesity and tooth decay), food sensitivities, the ethics of depriving students of food prior to training sessions, and parental preferences about their child's diet will affect your decision to employ edible reinforcers.

Tactile and sensory reinforcers

This class of reinforcers has been used mainly with people with severe and profound intellectual disabilities, especially to replace self-stimulation with a less dangerous or more appropriate form of stimulation.

Choice of reinforcers

Choosing from the range of reinforcers listed above, you will select a specific reinforcer for a particular student on the basis of which general reinforcers usually work (Martin & Pear 1999). Then you can ask individual students to write a list of their interests and preferences and select one of these, reserving the right to veto any items on the list if they are unsuitable. Once a reinforcer is in place, you will observe its effects and abandon it if it does not increase the frequency of the desired behaviour. You will need to make your chosen reinforcer relatively more attractive than naturally occurring alternatives. For example, some behaviour allows students to escape the learning task altogether and so your replacement reinforcer has to be even more powerful and quite immediate to overcome students' avoidance (Dixon et al. 1998; Zarcone et al. 1994).

Reinforcement schedules

A reinforcement schedule refers to how often students have to display the behaviour (or how much time must elapse) before you give them some reinforcement. In classroom settings, as opposed to research laboratories, it is not possible to be exact about schedules, but a few research results can be borne in mind:

- For discrete acts, you will reinforce students when they have displayed a specified number of target behaviours (Axelrod 1977). This is called a *ratio* schedule.
- For continuous behaviours (e.g. staying in their seats) you will reinforce students after a specified *time* period. This is called an *interval* schedule.
- Students will learn new behaviour more rapidly when they receive frequent reinforcement, but towards the end of training, you must gradually reduce the rate of reinforcement to natural levels so that gains are maintained.
- If behaviour improves but then deteriorates, this may mean that the reinforcement has become too inconsistent and infrequent (Foxx 1982).

Guidelines for administering reinforcers

Adherents of ABA contend that reinforcement produces behaviour change; students learn to identify the link between their actions and consequences; and they learn to value reinforcement (Alberto & Troutman 1999). These gains are more likely when you abide by the following guidelines for administering a reinforcement program (Kaplan & Carter 1995; Martin & Pear 1999; Wolery et al. 1988; Zirpoli & Melloy 1997):

- *Tell students in advance* exactly what behaviours you expect and what consequences will follow their observance or non-compliance. This also allows for delayed gratification—that is, for the use of less immediate reinforcers.
- Allow students to *choose* from a range of reinforcers, rather than selecting these yourself.
- Reinforce often at first so that behaviour is learned quickly (Zanolli & Daggett 1998), but gradually reduce reinforcement to natural levels as soon as possible so that new behaviour is maintained.
- Reinforcers work best when delivered *immediately*. Students with impulsive behaviour choose the most immediate reinforcer, even when it is less attractive (Neef et al. 1993), which implies that for these students in particular, you will need to deliver reinforcement immediately if it is to be more potent than competing reinforcers.
- Reinforcement must be *systematic*: its delivery must be contingent on the occurrence of the behaviour. That is, you must be careful to deliver the reinforcement if the behaviour is displayed, and not when the behaviour does not occur.

- If a reinforcer is to be effective in increasing behaviour, the student must have been *deprived* of it initially.
- A reinforcer will lose its reinforcing capacity if it is overused. This process is termed *satiation*. Thus, it will be necessary to vary reinforcers.
- Improvement and *generalisation* will be most easily assured if you employ reinforcers that are commonly and readily available in the environment.
- *Model* the behaviour that you want your students to display.

Methods for reducing behaviour rates

Having examined ways of increasing students' behaviours, next I shall describe ways to reduce their inappropriate actions. The two aspects are considered in this order for two reasons: first, it is more ethical to use the least restrictive methods for increasing student behaviours before reducing behaviours by more restrictive means; second, reinforcement gives students something else to do in place of an inappropriate behaviour that is being reduced.

In ABA, when a behaviour has been reduced, it is said to have been *punished*. This demonstrates that the term *punishment* has a specific meaning in ABA, one that is different from the lay use of the term. The lay use refers to the administration of some aversive consequence to a misbehaving individual. However, in this lay use, the behaviour may or may not in fact decrease. In the technical ABA definition, punishment is *any* consequence that *decreases* the likelihood that the behaviour will be repeated. It includes a broader range of interventions than that to which the lay use refers.

Nevertheless, whether we are talking about the lay or technical use of the term, Wheldall and Merrett (1984: 21) caution that:

> Contrary to popular belief, punishment plays only a minor and infrequent role in the behavioural approach, not least because what we believe to be punishing could, in fact, be reinforcing to the child.

The strategies for decreasing inappropriate behaviour can be ranked in order from the least to the most restrictive methods, which refers to how much external control is imposed on students:

1 discrimination training;
2 simple correction;

3 self-punishment;
4 differential reinforcement;
5 stimulus satiation;
6 extinction;
7 withdrawal of positive stimuli (Type 2 punishment);
8 overcorrection;
9 presentation of aversive stimuli (Type 1 punishment);
10 negative practice.

Discrimination training

While a behaviour may be appropriate in one setting, the same act can be inappropriate somewhere else. When you administer consequences differently in different circumstances, students will learn to discriminate the difference and will behave accordingly in those differing conditions. You can teach students to discriminate by offering cues about the differences between one circumstance and another, even if that is only to state: 'That won't work with me'. In this way, students achieve some measure of self-control (or learning).

Simple correction

Unlike overcorrection (to be discussed in a later section), simple correction, as the name implies, requires students simply to undo or correct the results of their behaviour (Wolery et al. 1988). The restrictiveness of this approach depends on the extent to which students correct their behaviour willingly when asked. If no other punishment is delivered, then it is one of the least restrictive (and intrusive) methods available.

Self-punishment

This is discussed in Chapter 4, although two conflicting points can be made here in advance of that discussion. An advantage of self-punishment is that it is less restrictive than adult-administered methods because students have agreed to it and are in control of it. A disadvantage is that self-punishment can have a negative effect on students' motivation because it highlights their errors and so may activate a fear of failure.

Differential reinforcement

Differential reinforcement procedures involve reinforcing a positive behaviour and simultaneously withholding reinforcement of an undesirable target behaviour (Vollmer et al. 1993; Wolery et al. 1988). It is less restrictive than other reductive methods as it focuses on reinforcement rather than punishment (Alberto & Troutman 1999; Sulzer-Azaroff & Mayer 1991). On the other hand, the extinction component can make differential reinforcement ineffective (Vollmer et al. 1993) for reasons discussed below.

There are four types of differential reinforcement. The first is differential reinforcement of *lower rates of behaviour* (DRL), in which you reinforce students when their undesirable behaviour occurs less frequently. You specify how many instances of the behaviour they may display within a specified time period, and if they do not exceed this number, then you deliver a reinforcer. Gradually, you decrease the number of behaviours that you permit, or increase the time period, until the behaviour occurs at a tolerable level. This approach can take time to achieve results and relies on careful measurement of the frequency of the behaviour. It has the advantage that students continue to receive reinforcement, although your focus is on undesirable behaviour rather than its positive alternatives (Sulzer-Azaroff & Mayer 1991).

While ceasing reinforcement of the target behaviour, you can reinforce incompatible behaviours such as staying seated when the target behaviour is out-of-seat behaviour (a process called differential reinforcement of *incompatible* behaviours—DRI), or you can reinforce alternative (not opposite) behaviours such as putting a hand up rather than calling out. This is differential reinforcement of *alternative* behaviours (DRA).

In real situations, it can be difficult to withhold all reinforcement of the target behaviour and always to reinforce its alternative, although perfect accuracy is not essential (Vollmer et al. 1999). DRI and DRA have the advantage of teaching students what *to* do, rather than what *not* to do, although reinforcement can be effective only if they display the behaviour often, and when the alternative behaviour serves a similar purpose to the targeted behaviour (Sulzer-Azaroff & Mayer 1991).

Less positive in its approach is differential reinforcement of *zero rates* of behaviour (DRO), in which you give students reinforcement for not displaying the target behaviour at all. Although this can achieve rapid results, it is less educational than the other methods as you do not teach any alternative replacement behaviours (Sulzer-Azaroff & Mayer 1991).

Stimulus satiation

Stimulus satiation involves giving students so much of the antecedent to the behaviour that they tire of it. An example is giving dozens of pencils to a student who frequently steals them from classmates. The theory predicts that the student will eventually become overloaded with pencils and will no longer choose to steal them.

Extinction

Extinction involves discontinuing the particular reinforcer that is maintaining the target behaviour, resulting in its reduced occurrence (Lerman & Iwata 1996). Success with extinction requires, first, that you are able to identify what is reinforcing the behaviour and, second, that you have control over whether or not it is delivered. An example is when teacher attention is reinforcing student misbehaviour, in which case ignoring the behaviour should result in its reduction (Alberto & Troutman 1999). Extinction procedures present a number of difficulties, however, including:

- It may not be possible for you to notice how your own actions are maintaining the student's behaviour. A consultant may be needed to observe your role in unwittingly reinforcing inappropriate behaviours.
- Successful extinction relies on your being able to identify the particular reinforcer for each student. However, this can be difficult to do as the same outward behaviour may have different reinforcers for different students (Iwata et al. 1994).
- The target behaviour may initially deteriorate, new aggressive behaviour may emerge, or students may become agitated as they try to regain the reinforcement they previously received (Alberto & Troutman 1999; Lerman & Iwata 1996; Lerman et al. 1999). When this occurs, it makes it difficult to tell whether the extinction procedure is failing, or whether it is working and just needs you to persist with it.
- If the behaviour is being maintained on a partial reinforcement schedule, it will be resistant to extinction, and so improvement may be slow to appear. You

might not be able to wait for the predicted improvement, as the behaviour may in the meantime become so intrusive or so dangerous that you must deal with it in other ways. One way to overcome this problem could be to reinforce the undesirable behaviour continuously before beginning a reductive method so that, once the program begins, students can easily recognise that there has been a change in the contingencies. However, this is not likely to appeal to many practitioners (Lerman & Iwata 1996) and has not been shown to have any consistent effect on extinction (Spradlin 1996) and so would appear to be an unattractive option.

- When extinction is used with groups of individuals—as in a classroom—you cannot control reinforcement that is being delivered by a student's peers and so it may never be possible to place the behaviour on an extinction schedule.
- Neither can you control the fact that other students may copy the target behaviour, as they observe that it is not attracting punishment.
- Extinction will not eliminate behaviours that are self-reinforcing (Axelrod 1977). For example, when students talk to each other, their conversation itself is reinforcing and has no additional reinforcer that you can withdraw. Another instance is when inappropriate behaviours allow students to escape work demands and so are being strongly reinforced (Mace & Wacker 1994; Zarcone et al. 1994), in which case extinction may be ineffective.
- Behaviour that has been extinguished in one setting is still likely to occur elsewhere. That is, gains made with extinction do not generalise readily (Alberto & Troutman 1999).

These limitations will make extinction inappropriate for certain behaviours, especially if they are dangerous, intolerable or contagious and therefore you do not want them to escalate. As an alternative, you can increase your rate of natural reinforcement using a fixed time schedule. This will give students a high rate of reinforcers so that they no longer need the reinforcement they have been receiving from engaging in the target behaviour (Vollmer et al. 1998).

Withdrawal of positive stimuli (Type 2 punishment)

As the name implies, withdrawal of positive stimuli means that you withdraw something the student likes when the undesirable behaviour is displayed, with the expectation that this will decrease the rate of the inappropriate behaviour. The two main types of this form of punishment are *response cost procedures* and *time out*. For each of these, there must be a high level of reinforcement in the natural situation, so that the punishing condition is noticeably less positive than the usual setting.

Response cost procedures

With these approaches, you fine or otherwise penalise students when the behaviour occurs. In practice, response cost procedures are used most effectively when combined with token economies because token economies can be flexible (Alberto & Troutman 1999). However, it can be difficult for you to take tokens away from students, so a points system may be more manageable as you can withdraw points at your discretion. Another difficulty with response cost approaches is establishing the magnitude of fines: if these are too severe and a day's gains can be wiped out with one misdeed, then the students will resist working for the tokens, points or stickers. Also, students who have been fined may soon become bankrupt of points or tokens, meaning that you cannot exact further punishment and so have no further influence over the behaviour. If fines are too lenient, on the other hand, they will have no effect as a punishment.

Time out from positive reinforcement

Following an unacceptable behaviour, you remove students' access to reinforcement (Axelrod 1977). It is important that the natural setting is very attractive, of course, so that removal from it is indeed a punishment rather than a reinforcer. The corollary of this is that reinforcement cannot be available in the time-out condition.

There are three types of time out (Alberto & Troutman 1999; Wolery et al. 1988). The first is *nonseclusionary* time out, in which students remain where they are but are deprived of reinforcers such as attention or materials. The second form is *exclusionary*, when you remove students from the activity but do not isolate them. The third is *seclusionary* time out, in which you confine students to an isolated area for a specified and brief period of time. The room must be of a reasonable size with adequate ventilation and lighting, it should be free of objects with which students could hurt themselves, it should allow you to monitor the student continuously, and it should not be locked (Gast & Nelson 1977, cited by Wolery et al. 1988).

Time out has some difficulties: with all forms, you need to be clear about its appropriate duration and exiting criteria. Other disadvantages depend on the type of time out: nonseclusionary and exclusionary time out can embarrass students, which may engender defiance. On the other hand, it is demanding to have to supervise seclusionary time out so that students remain safe and are not forgotten.

Overcorrection

The first form of overcorrection is *positive practice overcorrection*. In this approach, whenever students misbehave, you compel them to practise a more appropriate form of the behaviour. Foxx (1982) gives the example of a teacher who required a self-abusive student to hold an ice pack to his head whenever he hit himself. A second and more restrictive form is *restitutional overcorrection*, in which students repair the damage done, restoring it to a state that is a vast improvement on what existed before their destructive behaviour. An example is requiring students not only to clean off their own graffiti, but also to remove all graffiti in the school.

If delivering overcorrective procedures, you need to be firm and emphasise their educative nature. The activity itself must not become reinforcing. You should accompany overcorrection with verbal instruction, and if necessary force, to make students enact the appropriate behaviour. One problem is that a physically strong student may defy your directive and become unmanageable. Also, the time involved in the procedure and its aversive nature for both student and teacher point to caution in its use.

Presentation of aversive stimuli (Type 1 punishment)

This form of punishment involves administering an aversive consequence with the aim of reducing students' inappropriate behaviour. Aversive consequences include verbal and physical aversives.

Verbal aversives

Verbal reprimands can be very effective with mild behavioural difficulties, although they are less successful with more severe behavioural problems (Kerr & Nelson 1998). Verbal aversives can be more effective when you gain eye contact, stand close to the student, and deliver other aversive consequences at the same time.

Physical aversives

In discussing physical aversives, we must be aware of the reluctance of a significant sector of the community to endorse physical punishment, especially when delivered by professionals rather than parents. Where your school or departmental policies do not permit administration of physical aversives, you cannot use this approach.

Even where permitted, physical aversives would be a last resort, reserved only for extreme or dangerous behaviours (Alberto & Troutman 1999).

Negative practice

In contrast to overcorrection, with negative practice, you make students repeat their *inappropriate* behaviour on the assumption that fatigue or satiation will result. It may be that because you are now in control of its occurrence, the behaviour no longer has power over you, and so is no longer reinforcing for students. You may need to use force to make students repeat their negative behaviour over and over again, which provides a strong argument against the use of this procedure.

Disadvantages of punishment

Aversive consequences work quickly to produce a change in behaviour, they provide unambiguous cues that teach students to discriminate acceptable from unacceptable behaviour, and punishing individual students reduces the likelihood that others in the class will copy their unacceptable behaviour (Alberto & Troutman 1999). Having recognised these potential gains, however, I need to pre-empt the discussion of the humanists to consider the costs of punishment from the standpoint of both its advocates and detractors.

Ineffectiveness

Punishment is fundamentally ineffective because you cannot respond until students have behaved inappropriately, causing hurt or inconvenience to someone else. This is like shutting the stable door after the horse has bolted. The democratic writers suggest instead that a teacher who uses guidance rather than controlling methods will be able to prevent inappropriate behaviour and also therefore avoid the need to punish. This would be both more humane and more effective (see Chapters 6 and 7).

Second, punishment can increase the undesirable behaviour. In one study, increased punitive control raised students' misbehaviour from 9 per cent to 31 per cent (Jones & Jones 1998). Of course, in ABA terms, this is not punishment at all as, by definition, it has not reduced the troublesome behaviour; all other theorists find this explanation somewhat circular, however, and contend that such side-effects are so serious that they raise doubts about the practice of punishment, if not its theory.

Third, punishment has only a limited effect on learning. Students learn to behave appropriately not because it is the right way to act, but simply to avoid being punished. In short, they do not *learn* standards for their actions. So they then behave well only when someone is present who is likely to punish them (Rolider et al. 1991). Or they restrict themselves to only the safest of activities, fearing punishment for anything else (Gordon 1991).

Fourth, because punishment works best when applied to all infringements, you must be constantly vigilant to detect all instances of misbehaviour. Constant surveillance is, of course, impossible, and so you will not punish consistently, making punishment ineffective.

Fifth, punishment can be unfair because you cannot see all the circumstances of a misdeed, and so there is a high risk of:

- misinterpreting these and punishing the wrong person;
- not acknowledging that the student did not intend the consequences;
- failing to appreciate that the outcome has already frightened (punished) the student;
- not understanding students' perceptions of events and what they regard as a fair punishment.

Even if the misdeed were detected every time, and if the punishment were perfectly and fairly administered, its effects may be only temporary and may suppress the inappropriate behaviour but not necessarily replace it with a better one. Therefore, the punishment would need to be used for a long time.

Because punishment is regarded as a last resort, students usually have to break a rule repeatedly before teachers take action. This forces students to misbehave more often than they otherwise might, while their disruptiveness stretches unreasonably the tolerance of those around them.

Finally, Dreikurs and Cassel (1990) state that punishment is effective only for those who do not need it. Most students will respond to lesser methods; for those who do not, punishment seldom works either.

Effects on recipients

Punishment produces emotional side-effects such as fearfulness and frustration from not having one's needs met. Ginott (1972) claims that, whereas the purpose of punishment is to convince students to stop unacceptable behaviour, it is more likely to enrage them and make them ineducable. It can also make children sick and emotionally unstable (Gordon 1991). Some of these effects include accident-proneness, suicidal tendencies, 'neurosis', low self-esteem, shyness, poor peer relationships, increased worry and poor relationships with adults. Feeling that they have failed will lower students' self-esteem and perhaps give rise to more infringe-ments because they feel discouraged.

Punishment may provoke retaliation against the punisher, and imitation of the punisher's aggression (students bully others as they are being bullied).

Students may learn to avoid the circumstances in which they are punished or to avoid punishment at all costs. This means that they may withdraw at least emotionally, may tell lies rather than own up to a misdeed (Ginott 1972), or may tell tales on others to make themselves look good in comparison. None of these behaviours is attractive in children, and they tend to attract further punishment. As Ginott (1972: 151) says:

> Punishment does not deter misconduct. It merely makes the offender more cautious in committing his crime, more adroit in concealing his traces, more skillful in escaping detection. When a child is punished he resolves to be more careful, not more honest and responsible.

An opposite way in which students avoid punishments is to become submissive, compliant and a 'goodie-goodie'. These students become the 'teacher's pets', but at the same time they lack self-esteem because they and their peers despise their actions. Meanwhile, punishment may intimidate onlookers even though they themselves are never punished and might cause them to define a punished student as 'naughty' and, as a result, exclude that student from their friendship group.

Effects on administrators and society

Because punishment can work quickly at first, it can become addictive, causing teachers to forget to use more positive approaches (Martin & Pear 1999) or succumbing to increasing brutality (Ginott, in Edwards 1997). In this way, punish-ment can escalate into abuse (which is defined as causing physical injury).

Alternatively, when you are aware of this potential for abuse, you may instead threaten to carry out a more severe punishment, but never do so. This teaches students not to take you seriously and so, not surprisingly, they ignore you in future.

Or, says Ginott (in Edwards 1997), students might push you to see how far you will go, and to force you to back down from a threat that you have no power to enact. In the process students are assaulted verbally with blame and shame and you are unnecessarily stressed.

Finally, even if punishment does not harm individual children (which is uncertain), it certainly damages relationships, while violence in our homes or schools creates a violent society in which direct recipients and the wider community are unsafe. The disadvantages of punishments are summarised in the following box.

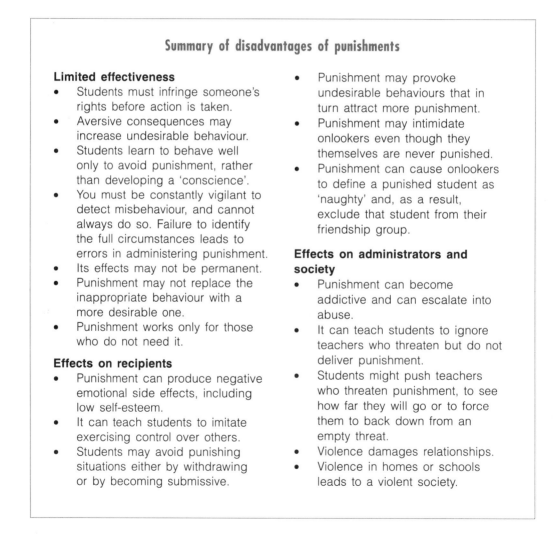

Summary of disadvantages of punishments

Limited effectiveness
- Students must infringe someone's rights before action is taken.
- Aversive consequences may increase undesirable behaviour.
- Students learn to behave well only to avoid punishment, rather than developing a 'conscience'.
- You must be constantly vigilant to detect misbehaviour, and cannot always do so. Failure to identify the full circumstances leads to errors in administering punishment.
- Its effects may not be permanent.
- Punishment may not replace the inappropriate behaviour with a more desirable one.
- Punishment works only for those who do not need it.

Effects on recipients
- Punishment can produce negative emotional side effects, including low self-esteem.
- It can teach students to imitate exercising control over others.
- Students may avoid punishing situations either by withdrawing or by becoming submissive.

- Punishment may provoke undesirable behaviours that in turn attract more punishment.
- Punishment may intimidate onlookers even though they themselves are never punished.
- Punishment can cause onlookers to define a punished student as 'naughty' and, as a result, exclude that student from their friendship group.

Effects on administrators and society
- Punishment can become addictive and can escalate into abuse.
- It can teach students to ignore teachers who threaten but do not deliver punishment.
- Students might push teachers who threaten punishment, to see how far they will go or to force them to back down from an empty threat.
- Violence damages relationships.
- Violence in homes or schools leads to a violent society.

Guidelines for administration of punishments

Some of the above cautions give rise to guidelines for the use of punishment.

- You should deliver a punishment immediately after the undesirable behaviour.
- Virtually every instance of the behaviour must be punished. This implies that if you are not able to detect most instances of the undesired behaviour, you should have serious doubts about attempting to use punishment to decrease it (Martin & Pear 1999). Perhaps, instead, some discrimination training is needed to teach students that certain behaviours can be performed in one circumstance but not in others.
- You will need to administer a punishment in a matter-of-fact manner so that your high emotion does not reinforce the inappropriate behaviour or interfere with your judgment about administering the program.
- Punishment should work quickly: if it does not, then you must abandon it.
- You will also need to fade out a punishment as soon as it has produced the desired result.
- At the earliest opportunity, you should replace a punisher with reinforcement for an alternative behaviour.

Generalisation

Behaviourism has had a disappointing record of maintaining behavioural gains over time and generalising these gains to other settings or other teachers. In most cases, generalisation does not occur naturally and so needs to be taught (Zirpoli & Melloy 1997). You can improve the likelihood that students will perform a newly learned behaviour in other settings and with other teachers by:

- teaching the behaviour in the setting in which it will be used (rather than in the classroom);
- using a variety of teachers;
- fading artificial prompts and cues so that naturally occurring cues come to control the behaviour;
- when artificial reinforcers have been used, shifting from continuous to intermittent reinforcement;
- developing objectives for, and reinforcing, generalisation itself.

Ethical issues with ABA

Martin and Pear (1999: 388) contend that: 'The history of civilisation is a continuous story of the abuse of power.' Ethical guidelines for intervening with students' behaviour were detailed in Chapter 1; suffice to say here that ABA is one of the few theories discussed in this text that specifically gives ethical recommendations for the use of its methods.

Fundamental to ABA philosophy is that you must provide students with the most effective intervention (Alberto & Troutman 1999; Rekers 1984). It is inhumane to allow students to underfunction out of fear of using approaches that work. Nevertheless, proponents of this theory acknowledge that its methods are powerful and so add some additional ethical guidelines to those introduced in Chapter 1 (Alberto & Troutman 1999; Axelrod 1977; Martin & Pear 1999; Wolery et al. 1988):

- *Attention to antecedents.* You should minimise the causes of disruptive behaviour by changing the antecedents that occasion it and by making natural conditions highly reinforcing so that students are motivated to behave appropriately.
- *High priority behaviour.* You should target only those behaviours that are a high priority, namely those that violate someone's rights, rather than acts that are merely inconvenient to others (Alberto & Troutman 1999). At the same time, however, interventions—or a lack of them—cannot be to the detriment of others (Martin & Pear 1999). Thus appropriate goals are essential for the ethical use of behaviourist methods (Alberto & Troutman 1999).
- *Functional skills.* Students need to learn skills that benefit them and are functional for them and, equally, they do not need to learn skills that are not functional in their lives (Alberto & Troutman 1999). An intervention aimed at teaching non-functional skills is not ethical. A corollary of this view is that an attempt *must* be made to replace a dysfunctional behaviour (such as hand biting) with a more functional one.
- *Least restrictive treatment.* A key axiom of ABA is the use of reinforcement as a first measure, with more restrictive methods employed only when reinforcement has failed. Punishment should be reserved only for those behaviours—such as self-abuse—that cannot be suppressed in other ways and it must always be followed by positive reinforcement to maintain the new desired behaviour.

    Advice differs on how severe a punishment should be. In line with the least restrictive principle, some writers say that you should use the gentlest available form of punishment first, and increase its restrictiveness only if the first method has failed (Axelrod 1977; Kerr & Nelson 1998). However, other writers advise that the initial punishment should be fairly intense (Foxx 1982; Martin & Pear 1999), because if the first punishment is ineffective and then has to be intensified, students might not notice the gradual increase in the punishment, with the result that the undesirable behaviour would persist (Martin & Pear 1999).

- *Advance preparation.* When planning an intervention that uses punishment, you will need to be clear about exactly what punishment is to be used, and for what behaviour. You will need to select a punishment individually for each case, and must abandon it if it is not reducing the behaviour.

Conclusion: Ethics

Each of us must determine the point where, for us, the result does not warrant the methods used to achieve it. Even advocates of ABA recognise that the use of punishment is clearly an issue; critics go further to claim that the use of controlling strategies *per se* is a still more fundamental question. Guess and Siegel-Causey (1985: 232) ask the final question:

> Does the prevalent behaviorally-based technology used with severely hand-icapped persons adversely affect the emergence of those human qualities that we are striving so hard to develop in them?

This question is relevant to students of all ability levels. It can also apply to the administrators as well as the recipients of behaviourist methods, as teachers can be as constrained and unspontaneous as the students on whom the methods are used (Guess & Siegel-Causey 1985; Kohn 1996).

Summary

Applied behaviour analysis contends that human behaviour is lawful—that is, it can be predicted by observing the events surrounding it. Behaviour that is followed by a consequence which the recipient values will increase in frequency; behaviour that is followed by a negative consequence will reduce; the conditions (antecedents) under which either positive or negative consequences occur will themselves acquire the power to change the rate of behaviour (Matthews, pers. comm.).

Applied behaviour analysis in schools begins by defining, observing and recording the outward behaviour of students. When you are attempting to change the rate of a behaviour, you will first try to change the conditions under which it occurs. These are called the antecedents. Next you will change the consequences that follow the behaviour so that the behaviour is no longer reinforced.

When administering consequences, you will begin with reinforcing appropriate behaviour to increase its occurrence, using a range of reinforcers from natural to edible, and will reinforce fewer instances of a negative behaviour (differential reinforcement). If all else fails, then you can use punishing or reductive procedures, under strict conditions. The following box gives the methods for delivery of consequences in order of how restrictive (or controlling) they are of students.

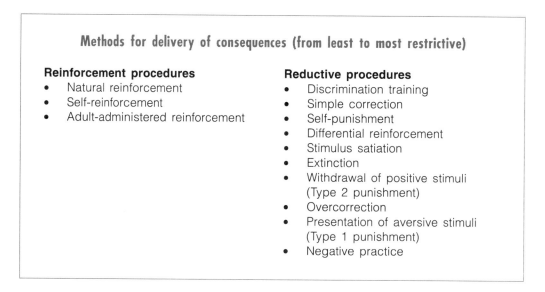

Methods for delivery of consequences (from least to most restrictive)

Reinforcement procedures
- Natural reinforcement
- Self-reinforcement
- Adult-administered reinforcement

Reductive procedures
- Discrimination training
- Simple correction
- Self-punishment
- Differential reinforcement
- Stimulus satiation
- Extinction
- Withdrawal of positive stimuli (Type 2 punishment)
- Overcorrection
- Presentation of aversive stimuli (Type 1 punishment)
- Negative practice

In addition, the types of reinforcers can be ranked by how much they intrude on the individual, the environment or the process of teaching.

Case study

Adam is seven. He has difficulty with reading, spelling and writing, although he enjoys and is capable at maths. During non-maths lessons, you have noticed that he spends a considerable amount of time off-task, when he frequently disrupts the other students. This is worse in the afternoon than in the morning.

He is in a composite class of six- and seven-year-olds. He spends most of his play time with the younger children. Frequently a pair which includes Adam is apprehended during play times doing such things as harassing passers-by from an out-of-bounds area of the playground which is close to the street, rifling through rubbish bins for food or cans to swap for other items with students, or engaging in fights in and around the toilets.

He seems bemused by the trouble he gets into, usually saying when challenged that he doesn't know why he behaves in these inappropriate ways, that he couldn't remember a given behaviour was against the rules, or that the other child was at fault for suggesting the activity.

Until a recent assessment, it was believed that Adam behaved as he did because of low academic ability. However, a battery of tests has shown his overall ability (IQ) to be average, with his maths skills in the high–normal range and his reading and spelling skills, while delayed, still within the lower range of normal limits. Teaching staff are now at a loss to find a new explanation for his behaviour.

An applied behaviour analysis application

If you were operating under ABA theory, you would perform the following steps to reduce Adam's behavioural difficulties.

Step 1: Observe the conditions. You will need to observe Adam in a range of settings for specified time periods and record in behavioural terms the conditions (antecedents) that occasion his inappropriate behaviour, and the consequences that follow it. In language-based activities, you might notice, for instance, that Adam remains on task for only two minutes, following which he chats to a neighbour or leaves his desk for spurious reasons such as wanting to sharpen an already sharp pencil. In so doing, he frequently speaks to or touches other students who in turn become distracted by him.

Step 2: Define a target behaviour. Next you would select the behaviour that is of most concern to you (termed the *target* behaviour) and define it operationally in precise terms. Let's say you are most concerned with Adam's off-task behaviour because it interferes with other students' learning. In that case, you will decide that your target behaviour is disruptive acts such as chatting to other students during desk activities or moving about the room unnecessarily.

Step 3: Define goals (the terminal behaviour). Next you would define what improvement you are aiming for in the target behaviour. Instead of distracting after two minutes in language-based activities, you could decide that you want Adam to remain on-task for five minutes, following which his distractions are not to disrupt the other students' learning. You will define what on-task means. For instance, does it include sharpening pencils, and how dull does a pencil have to be before it legitimately needs sharpening? (Note that you would probably avoid such debates by reminding Adam to sharpen his pencil at the beginning of each work period.) Your earlier observations of Adam's off-task behaviour will help to clarify what you will accept as being on-task and what you will not.

Step 4: Change antecedents. You will turn your attention to changing the antecedents. For example, Adam might distract his peers to gain the social contact that he cannot achieve in other ways. If so, you may need to improve his motor, language or social abilities to enable him to participate in social play and gain peer approval without having to display inappropriate behaviour at play time or in class. While this intervention is occurring, or if it makes insufficient difference to Adam's behaviour, then you would institute a behavioural intervention program that focused more directly on the target behaviour.

Step 5: Choose a recording method. You must record systematically to assess whether Adam's behaviour is improving. Of the recording methods that are available to you, you may be reluctant to use self-recording as it could distract Adam, given that he is easily attracted off-task. For continuous behaviour such as the target behaviour, event recording is unsuitable, and so you might decide to observe Adam for three five-minute periods during a desk exercise, and record for each minute of that five-minute span whether Adam was on-task throughout the minute interval or not. (It is likely that you will find this observation regime is incompatible with teaching other students, and so you will need to ask an assistant to observe and record for you, or will have to be less ambitious— and perhaps less accurate as a result—about what you expect yourself to observe.)

Step 6: Plan a reinforcement regime. Next, you will plan a reinforcement program because enhancing a positive behaviour is more ethical than attempting to reduce undesired behaviour. Your plan might be that if Adam is predominantly on task for two of the one-minute time slots, then you will administer a reinforcer. After one week, you will increase your demand to three one-minute intervals before he receives reinforcement, increasing by a minute per week until he must be on-task for five minutes to earn reinforcement.

When selecting a reinforcer, you could ask Adam about his likes and then choose one of these to be his reinforcer. You could consider an activity reinforcer such as the chance to do a maths puzzle, but may reject this in case it is too weak a reinforcer to have the desired effect, or in case it adds maths to Adam's already long list of disliked academic activities.

Instead, you might institute a program that allowed Adam to gain points each time his behaviour met the criterion. Once sufficient points were earned, he could receive a social reinforcer such as collecting the class's lunch orders or being team leader in a sporting activity, or earn an activity reinforcer such as having time on the school computer, which Adam enjoys. As already mentioned, you would select these reinforcers in consultation with Adam and, to avoid satiation, would use each for one week only.

Step 7: Evaluation. You will need to maintain continuous records to evaluate the effectiveness of the program.

Step 8: Reduce undesirable behaviour. If Adam's on-task behaviour did not improve significantly with the reinforcement regime, even when a range of reinforcers was tried and the criteria for success refined, then you might need to institute a reductive procedure. The least intrusive of these has already been used—namely, differential reinforcement of incompatible behaviours; extinction is unsuitable because you cannot prevent Adam's peers from responding to him when he distracts them; response cost procedures (such as loss of points) are too elaborate for you to manage, and so you might select time out. Because there is no separate time-out room in the school where exclusionary time out could be supervised, you will elect to use nonseclusionary time out.

Step 9: Repeat the steps for other behaviours. Finally, you would turn your attention to the remaining behaviours and design successive interventions for each of these. As the second target behaviour, you might focus on Adam's social skills so that improved peer relationships provide the natural reinforcement for maintaining the improvements in his on-task behaviour. Following his success with the first target behaviour, he may be more motivated to undertake and adhere to a contract about his social and play skills.

Discussion questions

1   Does ABA take a wide enough view of antecedents? Are there any potential triggers that it ignores?
2   List some guidelines for the administration of effective reinforcers.
3   Discuss why extinction and punishment should not be among the first procedures used for modifying behaviour under the theory of applied behaviour analysis.
4   In your opinion, what ethical issues are raised by behaviourist approaches, and how could they be resolved?
5   Re-apply the case study that you generated in Chapter 2, this time using ABA principles and practices. What are the differences in recommended practices? What effect would these difference have on the individual student? On the whole class? On you?

Suggested further reading

Alberto, P.A. and Troutman, A.C. 1999 *Applied behavior analysis for teachers* 5th edn, Merrill, Upper Saddle River, NJ

Kerr, M.M. and Nelson, C.M. 1998 *Strategies for managing behavior problems in the classroom* 3rd edn, Merrill, Upper Saddle River, NJ

Martin, G. and Pear, J. 1999 *Behavior modification: what it is and how to do it* 6th edn, Prentice Hall, Upper Saddle River, NJ

Walker, J.E. and Shea, T.M. 1999 *Behavior management: a practical approach for educators* 7th edn, Merrill, Upper Saddle River, NJ

Wolery, M., Bailey, D.B. and Sugai, G.M. 1988 *Effective teaching: principles and procedures of applied behavior analysis with exceptional students* Allyn & Bacon, Boston, MA

Zirpoli, T.J. and Melloy, K.J. 1997 *Behavior management: applications for teachers and parents* 2nd edn, Merrill, Upper Saddle River, NJ

4　Cognitive-behaviourism

The cognitive-behavioral approaches [are] a purposeful attempt to preserve the demonstrated positive effects of behavioral therapy within a less doctrinaire context and to incorporate the cognitive activities of the client into the efforts to produce therapeutic change.

Kendall (1991: 4–5)

Key points

- Cognitive approaches aim to teach students effective ways of dealing with problems independently of you. They promote self-control.
- Success at any task depends on the environment, students' beliefs about themselves, their problem-solving skills, ability to do the task and ability to organise themselves to complete it.
- Cognitive restructuring can help both teachers and students remain in control of their own behaviour and emotions, reducing stress and increasing their personal effectiveness.

Introduction

Applied behaviour analysis (ABA) concentrates on content—that is, what students *do*—and emphasises that external forces control their behaviour; cognitive-behaviourism focuses more on students' thinking *processes* and aims to teach them to manage themselves so that they do not become dependent on adult supervision (Zirpoli & Melloy 1997). Cognitive-behaviourism is not a unified theory, but instead a set of models and strategies loosely tied together by a concern for the thinking processes of students (Hall & Hughes 1989; Zirpoli & Melloy 1997).

The double-barrelled title, cognitive-behaviourism, represents a continuum which starts with the purely behaviourist approach that believes that the environment controls actions but that you can teach students to alter their environment by changing their own behaviour (Agran & Martin 1987). The more cognitive end of the spectrum represents a coming together of behaviourist theory, social-learning theory and cognitive psychology (Zirpoli & Melloy 1997). It more specifically targets students' thinking processes in the belief that these affect their behaviour and academic performance.

This chapter will focus on these more cognitive approaches, and specifically those that are designed to reduce disruptive behaviour, although those that focus directly on academic skills—such as attention and memory training—will also indirectly improve behaviour.

Philosophical assumptions

The major distinction between cognitive behaviourism and pure behaviourism (ABA) is that cognitivists emphasise internal causes of behaviour. However, they recognise that the relationship is reciprocal: thinking and emotions influence behaviour, while behaviour affects thinking and emotions (Zirpoli & Melloy 1997).

Nature of childhood

Bernard (1986) argues that people are neither good nor bad: they are just alive, and do some good and some bad things. This implies that the cognitivists see individuals as possessing the capacity for both good and bad, and as people who make choices about their behaviour.

Conditions necessary for learning to occur

Cognitivists contend that children need to experience the world in order to learn. Cognitive teaching recognises students' responsibility for the learning process rather than focusing exclusively on the efforts of an outside trainer.

Purpose of discipline

Discipline has both a managerial function of creating order so that learning can occur, and two educational functions of promoting student self-discipline in the form of internalised compliance, and encouraging emotional regulation.

Reasons for disruptive behaviour

Cognitivists believe that people's actions are shaped both by the environment and by their understanding of it. While cognitivists acknowledge the effects of consequences on behaviour, they believe that the following elements also contribute to individuals' behaviour (Kendall 1991; Meyers et al. 1989):

- their *expectations* about anticipated consequences;
- their *attributions* about the causes of those consequences;
- their information-processing and *problem-solving skills*;
- their *emotional state* (such as self-esteem);
- in the case of children, their *developmental status*;
- the social *context*.

Cognitivists believe that when behaviour is maladaptive, this is often because of individuals' misinterpretations of events (Zirpoli & Melloy 1997), and so cognitivists would retrain students' thinking and emotions. In contrast, the purer behaviourists believe the reverse—namely, that individuals' behaviour affects how they think and feel; therefore, ABA practitioners would teach students to control their behaviours which, in turn, would improve their patterns of thinking and feeling (Agran & Martin 1987).

Teacher–student status

Under cognitive-behaviourism, the teacher–student relationship is still likely to have authoritarian overtones, although along with students you might jointly decide the goals for their behaviour and the steps to achieve them, rather than imposing these externally on students as in ABA. Therefore, cognitive-behaviourism is placed between the authoritarian and authoritative positions on the continuum of theories (see Figure 1.1 in Chapter 1).

Disciplinary role of the teacher

If you worked according to cognitive principles, your aim would be to encourage students to decide *for themselves* that it is in their interests to satisfy your expectations about their behaviour. You would seek to change how students make sense of experiences by focusing on their *knowledge* (about suitable behaviour), their *problem-solving skills*, and their awareness of the *effects* of their actions, so that in future they change how they choose to behave.

Components of task completion

Take a couple of minutes to identify the number of triangles in Figure 4.1.

When individuals have had previous negative experiences with this type of exercise, they attempt the task half-heartedly, which contributes to a lack of success (Napier & Gershenfeld 1993). Some people do not persist at the task because they do not expect to be able to get it right; some see it as a trick and decide that there is no point trying; some are trained to be competitive and so will persist with the task for an unduly long time to make sure that they get their answer right; while others wait to see how other people in the group will answer, and agree with people who they assess are likely to be correct. (You will find the correct answer at the end of this chapter.)

This exercise demonstrates that there is more to achievement than simple ability at a task. The various factors are depicted in Figure 4.2, which shows that, when faced with a task, students first need the cognitive skills to interpret it and its demands (phase I). Next, their beliefs about themselves and their chances of success affect their motivation to carry out the activity (phase II). In phase III, they engage in problem-solving to generate a range of behavioural options and to select one

Figure 4.1   Exercise in the perception of task demands

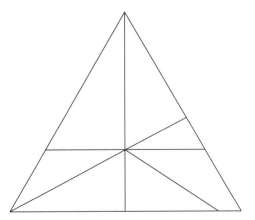

Source: Napier and Gershenfeld (1993: 4)

Figure 4.2   Components of task completion

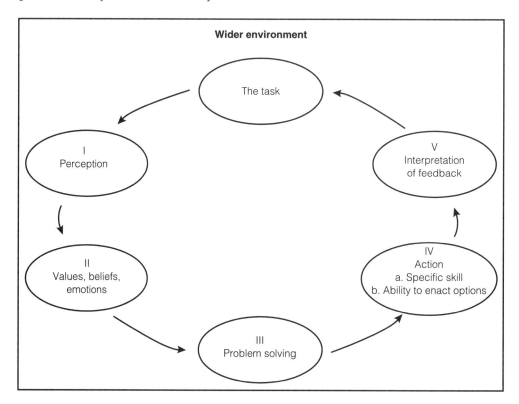

they judge most likely to work. In phase IV, they act on this assessment. This last phase requires that they possess the specific skill needed, and that they are able to organise themselves to complete the task in logical steps. Finally, at phase V they interpret feedback about their actions which, in turn, may provoke another task. All this goes on within the context of the wider environment, which both affects and is affected by the students' behaviours.

Wider environment

Instead of focusing only on individual students' deficiencies, the cognitivists acknowledge that the social context is a powerful influence on their behaviour (Burdon & Fraser 1993) and that, in turn, their actions will shape the environment (Meyers et al. 1989). The environment includes successful teaching practices and school organisation. These will affect the way students view the academic and behavioural tasks they are being asked to complete and will determine what resources are available to support their use of their personal skills. Bandura (1986) contends that a very negative context will have an overriding influence on student achievement, while in a more neutral or positive context the students' own cognitive processing skills will be more crucial to success.

Phase I: Perception

At phase I, students will encode or interpret what they are being asked to do. They will call on information from the past about how they have approached other similar tasks and about the general principles that guide these types of activities. To process this information, they need to know something about the type of task being undertaken. For a behavioural task, they need to know the general principles that govern behaviour, such as consideration of others and acceding to reasonable requests. This information is essential in order for the problem-solving process to begin.

Phase II: Attitudinal variables

A range of beliefs about themselves and their abilities gives rise to the students' willingness to complete the task (phase II of the model in Figure 4.2). Their beliefs will feed and be fed by their self-esteem, and will affect their motivation. These attitudes make the greatest contribution to success because, even if students have the ability to do the task, they will have limited success if they lack the motivation to perform it. This may be especially so for young children, who rely more than older children on their emotional interpretations of events (Meyers et al. 1989).

Learning set

A learning set is an individual's ability to use previous experience to learn. Not drawing on previous experience leads to reduced success and a lack of generalisation of learning. Because of a history of failure, some students—especially those with learning difficulties—may far rather avoid failure than achieve success and so will not apply themselves to a task. These students' apparent lack of concentration or other self-organisation skills result from their negative learning set rather than any inability to concentrate as such. Therefore, emotional—not academic—remediation is required.

To develop a positive learning set, students will need to be active in the learning process. Also, you will need to explain the links between past learning and the present activity, and help students to identify skills they already have for solving the present problem.

Self-efficacy

This is individuals' judgment about their ability to organise and execute a chosen action competently (Ashman & Conway 1997; Bandura 1986). Individuals believe that what happens in their lives is either due to their own behaviour or to outside forces. The former is termed an *internal locus of control*; the latter is an *external locus of control* and in its extreme form has been called *learned helplessness* (Seligman 1975). Students with an external locus of control might not attempt to manage their own behaviour independently, because they believe that doing so would make no difference to what happens to them.

Students must be accurate in their appraisal of their abilities: if they are unduly pessimistic, they will not be willing to undertake and persist at activities. This will cause them to fail and, in turn, they will believe still more strongly that they are incapable. On the other hand, if they have an inflated assessment of their skills, they may attempt tasks that are too difficult and so could fail unnecessarily (Bandura 1986).

Self-efficacy is vulnerable to repeated failures and to criticism (Bandura 1986). Unfortunately, it is not responsive to positive persuasion. This implies the following measures for helping students to be aware of their ability to be successful.

- Students will need to *experience* success, rather than simply be *told* that they are successful. Therefore, feedback needs to be specific and genuine. That is, you should not tell students that they have been successful when they have not, and should give feedback that is specific enough for them to be able to act on the information and correct their errors.
- The work you assign must be sufficiently challenging, as easy work will not raise students' opinion of their abilities (Bandura 1986).
- Give students experience of both success *and* failure, so that they can form a link between their actions and the outcome (Seligman 1975). If students are always successful, no matter what they do, they will feel just as helpless as if they were always a failure, no matter what they do. In either case, they will show low tolerance of frustration, poor persistence at tasks, and avoidance of challenge.

- Acknowledge independent thought more than correct answers, which would benefit students who have perfectionist standards about getting their work right. While fostering independent thinking, however, you should avoid competition, streaming and teaching the same material to all students, as this invites comparisons of their abilities (Bandura 1986).

- Because success depends more on hard work than on ability (Bandura 1986), you will need to teach students to describe why their approach succeeded or failed—that is, to attribute the outcome to the strategy they used (Cole & Chan 1990). This is called *attribution training*. Students who feel out of control of their learning often attribute their successes to good luck and their failures to their own inability (Zirpoli & Melloy 1997). Thus you will need to teach them to focus on their specific *actions*, not *themselves*, and let them know that a change in strategy will produce better results. For instance, rather than saying, 'That didn't work, because I'm hopeless at it', a student could comment, 'That didn't work because I didn't plan each step'.

- You can set work that gradually increases in difficulty and, once students begin to fail, instruct them in how to turn failure into success by changing their approach to solving the problem (Westwood 1997).

- You can negotiate individual contracts that specify what tasks students have to complete, but give them discretion for deciding in what order to do these (Westwood 1997). This gives students experience of being in control of their own learning, although their choice is restricted to *how* to learn, not *whether* to learn.

Self-esteem

Individuals' beliefs about their capacity to learn (their self-efficacy) and their sense of autonomy are integral to their self-esteem. While self-efficacy is a judgment about our capabilities, self-esteem is a judgment about the *value* of those capabilities (Bandura 1986). In order to increase students' self-esteem, the cognitivists advise you to praise them for positive behaviour, so that you highlight their successes and enhance the value of these to the students. (Note, however, that this advice is contrary to the cognitivists' use of self-reinforcement.)

Motivation

Students' self-efficacy, learning set, beliefs about their ability to control success and failure, and overall self-esteem will all affect their motivation to perform a particular task or behaviour. Cognitive methods for increasing students' motivation include the following.

- Make sure that the task is relevant to students (Fontana 1985). They must see that work is helping them in obvious ways to make a success of their lives. That is, you need to investigate what sense your class is making of the curriculum and change its content when it is meaningless to them, rather than obliging the students to change. An alternative is simply to explain to students how the work that you are asking them to do will benefit them.
- This guideline can be adapted to class rules: you will need to explain why the rules are in place so that students see them as relevant and fair, rather than being arbitrary (Conway & Gow 1990). This would increase their motivation to comply voluntarily.
- Also, if students play a part in formulating class rules, they will be more motivated to comply with these.
- To reinforce appropriate behaviour, where possible you should ensure that rewards are intrinsic to the task, and use a minimum of extrinsic rewards (Conway & Gow 1990).
- Self-regulation is thought to be intrinsically more rewarding than externally imposed controls (Corno 1989), because individuals seek to be in control of themselves. If students' motivation to use self-regulating approaches is suspect, then you can build in rewards for self-regulation as well as providing rewards for improvement in the target behaviour itself.

Phase III: Problem solving

The third phase of the model in Figure 4.2 comprises problem solving. This requires developing a plan to bring about a desired result (Ashman & Conway 1993). In order to achieve this, students need to examine what has to be done, scan a range of behavioural options, and select one that they think will be most successful. At this stage they need to be capable of paying attention, pacing themselves, persisting, and noting feedback, among other skills. Problem solving has the following aspects (Ashman & Conway 1989; Kaplan & Carter 1995; Zirpoli & Melloy 1997), the first two of which have already begun in phases I and II.

1 *Recognition that a problem exists.* Students need to identify that an issue exists and that it can be dealt with appropriately. This requires *interpersonal sensitivity*.

2   *Definition of the problem.* This involves accurate interpretation of the task or social demands and isolation of its relevant elements. Students will need *causal thinking*, which is the ability to explain why an event has happened or will happen, and knowledge of what they can do to make a difference to the problem. Many students have an external focus, which means that they leave themselves out of the definition of the problem and do not identify what they can do to solve it: they expect the other person to change (Kaplan & Carter 1995).

3   *Identification of goals.* So that the other person's goals are taken into account as well as their own, students will need skills in *perspective taking*, which is the ability to understand another person's experience, motives and actions.

4   *Awareness of the relevance of previous experience* and drawing on it.

5   *Generation of alternative solutions.* Students need to generate as many solutions as possible so that they do not become frustrated if their first one does not work out.

6   *Decision making.* Students will need to select one of the alternative solutions, on the basis of whether it is feasible and will meet their goal without making new problems for them. Next, they need to devise a plan for implementing their chosen solution. This step requires *consequential thinking*, which is the ability to consider the potential outcomes or consequences of a proposed behaviour, and *means–end thinking*. This refers to the ability to plan the steps needed to achieve a goal.

7   *Verification* that the plan is working and the problem is solved.

Bransford and colleagues (1986, in Ashman & Conway 1989) abbreviated these steps into the mnemonic, IDEAL—standing for Identify, Define, Explore, Act and Look.

Problem-solving training centres on teaching students how to deal with the structure of problems and provides practice in the skills involved. Once students are displaying appropriate behaviour, you may have to strengthen it by delivering behavioural reinforcement rather than relying on a purely cognitive approach alone.

Phase IVa: Action—applying task-specific skills

Phase IV of the model for task success (see Figure 4.2) comprises the ability to enact a chosen behaviour. The first enactment skill involves applying task-specific knowledge. For instance, to complete a maths problem, students need number concepts; to behave non-aggressively, they need prosocial skills for solving social disputes.

Phase IVb: Action—self-organisation skills

Once students have this specific information, they then need to be able to organise themselves to act on it. Students need several skills to be effective and independent managers of their own behaviour (Whitman et al. 1991):

- the ability to monitor their own actions;
- the verbal skills necessary for self-instruction;
- to be able to set appropriate standards or criteria by which to judge their performance;
- to be able to recognise accomplishments to add to their pool of information that can be drawn on during future tasks;
- to self-administer appropriate consequences for their actions.

Self-regulation is a complex cognitive skill that requires focused attention, continuous decision making, and an ability to delay both responding and gratification (Kanfer & Gaelick 1986, cited by Whitman et al. 1991). In order for them to be able to use these skills, you will need to teach students how to set goals, evaluate their own performances, understand the consequence that their behaviour earns, and select reinforcers (Alberto & Troutman 1999). The main methods for helping students to organise themselves are self-recording, self-instruction, self-evaluation and self-reinforcement (or self-punishment).

Self-recording

If individuals want to control their behaviour, they have to be aware of what they are doing (Bandura 1986). This means that the two of you will need to discuss the behaviour that concerns you, so that students become clear about what aspect of the behaviour is a problem, and why (Kaplan & Carter 1995). They will need to set goals for improvement in the target behaviour. This will help their motivation to change, as long as the goal is specific, challenging but achievable, and fairly immediate (in contrast to a long-term goal) (Alberto & Troutman 1999).

You will need to train students in how to record their own behaviour until they become fluent at it. During this training you might need to use prompts to remind them to self-record. They can record the *outcomes* of their behaviour (in terms of quantity, quality or rate of a behaviour) or their thinking *processes* (Bandura 1986; Maag et al. 1993; Reid & Harris 1993). It may be that students will be most successful when they are able to choose which aspect of their behaviour to monitor. Also, each aspect may be more or less relevant at given ages and for different tasks (Maag et al. 1993; Reid & Harris 1993).

Self-recording methods include simple tally sheets (perhaps with pictures for younger students) or counting devices. When using self-recording devices, these need to be portable, easy to use, inexpensive and obtrusive enough to remind students to record their behaviour while being undetectable by someone else (Shapiro 1984). The simplest form of recording is counting the number of times a behaviour occurs (Kaplan & Carter 1995). Students can do this by having their class time broken up into intervals on the recording sheet, and then noting on the sheet whether they did or did not perform the target behaviour during each interval. Less structured self-monitoring approaches may involve simply asking students whether they are complying with class rules at the time a violation begins.

The act of self-recording itself can produce a change in the behaviour (Alberto & Troutman 1999; Shapiro 1984). Its benefits tend to wear off, however, unless it is paired with reinforcement (Alberto & Troutman 1999) and it works best when students are observing successes rather than failures (Bandura 1986). Self-recording can motivate students to change (Schunk 1989), although it appears to be more effective at maintaining a change that was begun by teacher-controlled methods than it is at initiating change (Alberto & Troutman 1999).

Perhaps surprisingly, self-recording still works even if it is not accurate (Alberto & Troutman 1999; Kaplan & Carter 1995; Whitman et al. 1991). However, if you want to ensure that students are accurate when they self-record, at the outset of a behaviour management program you could make your own observations and then match your record with the students', delivering a reinforcement for accuracy as well as for appropriate behaviour. You could fade this procedure as individual students become clear about what is required.

Self-instruction

This is the use of 'personal verbal prompts' (Zirpoli & Melloy 1997: 187) to guide our behaviour. When a task is new or challenging to us, we talk about it out loud to ourselves; then our self-talk becomes covert; and, finally, we no longer need to self-instruct as the task has become automatic for us.

Because this inner talk can be adaptive or maladaptive, it will accordingly lead to functional or dysfunctional behaviour (Rogers 1994; Wragg 1989). Positive self-talk allows students to identify and guide themselves through the steps required to complete a task successfully or to behave appropriately. Thus your task is to teach students to guide their own behaviour using the following steps, which may be written or drawn on cue cards that they can refer to as a reminder.

1   Pause.
2   Ask: 'What is the problem?'
3   Ask: 'What do I want?'
4   Ask: 'Is what I'm doing helpful to me?'
5   If not, plan solutions: 'What else could I do?'
6   Choose what to do and do it.
7   Evaluate the results. (Go back to step 4.)
8   Self-reinforce.

You can build on the planning strategies that students are already using (Cole & Chan 1990; Conway & Gow 1990) or perform a task-analysis to determine the necessary steps inherent in the task. Next you can teach these skills explicitly, accompanying your actions or the students' attempts with a commentary on what is happening, thus teaching students to talk to themselves in this way, until eventually they can self-instruct quietly in their heads. Finally, you will need to teach strategies for dealing with failures, and ensure that once they have become competent at a task, students have enough time to practise and consolidate their skills.

As well as focusing on these self-management skills for solving problems, you will need to teach certain students some practical skills that Rogers (1994) calls *academic survival skills*. These include skills such as staying in one's seat, following classroom procedures, coping with frustration, and so on. As well as explicitly teaching these skills, you will need to give students many chances to rehearse them.

Phase V: Feedback (self-evaluation or self-assessment)

In this phase of self-regulation, students receive feedback and compare their performance against a preset standard to determine whether it meets this criterion. Setting appropriate self-imposed performance standards may be the most crucial phase of the self-management process (Whitman et al. 1991). Some students may set themselves very lenient standards, while others either do not give themselves enough reinforcement or are too demanding in their self-assessments (Alberto & Troutman 1999; Kaplan & Carter 1995). Therefore, you will need to give them some guidance about setting appropriate criteria for success and for judging whether they have attained them.

Self-reinforcement or self-punishment

Once external reinforcers are working, you can fade them out and instead give students the opportunity to assess their own behaviour and administer their own reinforcers (Shapiro & Klein 1980, cited by Whitman et al. 1991). The rationale for doing so is that self-reinforcement is likely to produce better results than external reinforcers (Alberto & Troutman 1999). Self-reinforcement is thought to improve the effectiveness of self-recording, although for some individuals it may not be any more effective than self-recording alone (Whitman et al. 1991).

The other aspect of self-delivery of consequences is self-punishment—commonly response-cost procedures and loss of tokens in a token economy system. It may be more difficult for students to do the arithmetic involved in subtracting tokens in a self-punishment procedure than to add tokens in a self-reinforcement process, and punishment procedures may activate a fear and increased awareness of failure and consequently reduce the students' motivation (Alberto & Troutman 1999). Therefore, self-reinforcement is preferable to self-punishment.

Guidelines for self-management

The following guidelines will increase the success of cognitive approaches (Zirpoli & Melloy 1997).

- The target behaviour should be under successful external control before you expect students to manage it independently.
- The use of behavioural contracts can provide some structure for self-management programs.
- In order to increase students' motivation to participate, you must involve them from the outset in developing the goals, defining the criteria for success, and planning the contingencies involved in the training. If you include a self-reinforcement element in the program, students need to be involved in selecting the reinforcer.
- You will need to monitor both the students' behaviour and their use of the self-management strategies.

Generalisation

Generalisation refers to students' ability to transfer skills from one task or setting to similar ones. Cognitive-behaviourism offers some specific strategies to promote generalisation, which has been a vexed issue for applied behaviour analysis. Although the effects of the cognitive approaches do not automatically generalise, you can encourage this by specifically teaching for generalisation. This could involve:

- motivating students so that their negative attitudes do not impair the transfer of learning;
- highlighting similarities between tasks by asking students to reflect on how the present task is similar to others;
- teaching students to analyse what they already know about solving the problem at hand (Whitman et al. 1991);
- giving them numerous opportunities to practise using the strategies (Zirpoli & Melloy 1997);
- teaching them to assess whether their approach is working;
- reinforcing students for using a suitable strategy (Zirpoli & Melloy 1997);
- when they need help, teaching both the strategy and how it can be used so that ultimately they can solve all similar problems independently. This is the essence of generalisation.

Clinical applications of cognitive-behavioural approaches

Kendall (1991) describes behavioural difficulties in three categories:

1 *distorted* thinking (characteristic of depression and anorexia) versus *deficient* thinking (as found in hyperactivity and autism);
2 *under-control* (for instance, in hyperactivity) versus *over-control* (demonstrated in anorexia);
3 *internal* versus *external* disorders (for example, depression and aggression respectively).

In accordance with the model in Figure 4.2, three aspects are targeted when dealing with behavioural problems: knowledge, motivation and organisation skills (Ashman & Conway 1993). However, the presenting difficulty will determine which of this triumvirate receives most emphasis. For instance, young people who are depressed might need information that they have more positive options than they realise: theirs might be a *knowledge* issue; aggression works for students and so they might not be *motivated* to change their behaviour unless supported by peers to do so; and with inattentive children who have received either of the attention-deficit disorder labels (ADD or ADHD), self-*organisation* will be the major issue. This is because, to overcome their learning difficulties, these children are already self-instructing more than the norm (Berk & Landau 1993; Berk & Potts 1991; Diaz & Berk 1995) and so they do not need to self-instruct more but instead to self-monitor more.

Even so, it is likely that cognitive approaches alone will only ever improve on, not supplant, behavioural and other treatments (such as medication) with young people who exhibit the difficult behaviour that accompanies aggression, ADHD or depression (Hinshaw & Erhardt 1991).

Unlearning dysfunctional thinking

Whereas the pure behaviourist approach asks students to handle situations better (*behave* differently) or avoid the circumstances (*antecedents*) that give rise to behavioural outbursts (Kaplan & Carter 1995), the cognitivists teach students to change what they *believe* about the events which, in turn, is intended to produce a change in their behaviour.

The first structured program for teaching people to think in more constructive ways appeared in the late 1950s in the form of Albert Ellis's rational-emotive therapy (RET). This is based on the concept that it is not events themselves that bother us, but what we believe particular events mean for us (Ellis 1962). What we tell ourselves about the events determines what feeling we experience, and the strength of that feeling. Ellis postulated an ABC sequence of reactions to events:

A   **A**ctivating event
B   **B**elief
C   Emotional **C**onsequence

Ellis contends that the individual's belief (B) about event A can be 'rational' or 'irrational'. If the belief is irrational, the emotional consequence at C is likely to be excessive or 'catastrophising'. These emotional over-reactions are common—for example, our occasional despair at 'having nothing to wear' to a party—but if they are persistently excessive, we can become unduly distressed and problems will be inevitable.

Cognitive restructuring for students

As well as teaching students to plan their approach to tasks, you can teach them to change self-defeating talk into helpful self-statements (Rogers 1994). For instance, 'This is too hard: I can't do it' can be changed to, 'This is tricky, but if I use my plan, it will be easier'.

Kaplan and Carter (1995) list the following subskills that you will need to teach students for unlearning their inaccurate beliefs.

- *Extreme emotions.* Teach students that feelings make life interesting and signal when we need to take some action, but that extreme emotions cause us to act unproductively.
- *Role of thinking.* Teach them that their feelings and subsequently their behaviour are controlled by their thinking. Other people and outside events do not *make* us feel anything: how we think about them leads to our feelings and behaviour.
- *Cognitive restructuring.* Teach students how to change their thinking by challenging their inaccurate beliefs. This 'cognitive restructuring' involves the following steps (Kaplan & Carter 1995).

  1 Become aware of their extreme feelings.
  2 Notice which events tend to trigger an extreme emotional or behavioural response. (Self-recording can be useful in steps 1 and 2.)
  3 Recognise that this response is maladaptive.
  4 Help them identify the beliefs that contribute to their distress—see Table 4.1.
  5 Guide them to ask the following questions about those beliefs (Roush 1984, in Kaplan & Carter 1995: 407):
     − Does this thinking keep me *alive*?
     − Does this thinking make me *feel* better?
     − Is this thinking based on *reality*?
     − Does this thinking help me get along with *others*?
     − Does this thinking help me to reach my own *goals*?
     Roush (1984, in Kaplan & Carter 1995) uses the acronym AFROG to help

Table 4.1   Characteristic dysfunctional thinking of children

Inaccurate thinking	Common theme	Examples	Emotion
Robot thinking	It's not my fault	I can't help it	Feeling of failure
I'm awful	It's all my fault	People are mean to me because I'm no good	Avoidance of risks
You're awful	It's all your fault	If you get into trouble, you deserve it	Belligerence
Fairytale thinking	It's not fair	I wish they wouldn't be mean to me	Hurt, anger
Woosie thinking (Namby pamby)	I can't stand it	Performing in front of others is scary	Anxiety, shyness Over-reaction to threats
Doomsday thinking	It's never going to get better	I'll never have any friends	Depression

Source: adapted from Roush (1984, in Kaplan & Carter 1995: 396)

students remember these questions. If they give a negative answer to any of the questions, then their beliefs are irrational, inaccurate or unhelpful.

6   Teach them to generate an alternative, more helpful, set of beliefs.

7   Have them practise the new thinking. Vehemence is necessary as it takes effort and persistence to overcome repetitive inaccurate self-talk.

As well as focusing on individual students whose thinking is creating behavioural difficulties, these same steps can be proactive. When using cognitive restructuring proactively, you simply teach the same tools to the whole class instead of focusing on individual students (Kaplan & Carter 1995).

- *Feedback and encouragement.* You can motivate students to change their thinking by using encouragement during rehearsal time and in class, and by giving specific feedback about their progress (Rogers 1994).

Teacher self-management

You can apply cognitive approaches to yourself as well as to your students. Your own behaviours can prevent students from developing a negative perception of learning and of their own ability to learn (Fontana 1985). For this reason, you will need to regulate your own behaviour so that your manner and actions communicate to students that you are interested in them and their work and have faith in their abilities. You will need to present as someone the students would like to get to know. You will need a confident manner, clear and consistent expectations and a willingness to help and guide students. You will need to provide sufficient structure for students to be able to achieve—including being able to anticipate and prevent problems—and to be alert to difficulties when they arise. These behaviours all help students to make sense of you and your role and consequently to understand their own role in the classroom.

To achieve this, knowledge of young people and their perspective is essential, but self-knowledge is also crucial. Your ability to regulate your own actions—and, in turn, to manage the class—is influenced by your own thinking, which includes your beliefs about yourself, your role as a teacher and your students.

Cognitive restructuring for teachers

Cognitive restructuring for adults can be particularly useful for stress reactions. One characteristic of the extreme thinking that engenders high emotion is what Ellis calls 'Absolutist' thinking. This can involve *personalisation*, where we over-estimate the degree to which, say, a student's behaviour is directed at us personally. It may include *filtering*, which causes us to notice more negatives than positives, and *over-generalising*, whereby one instance tells us that all other occasions will be the same. When we feel badly, we may *blame* other people, and may castigate ourselves for not being perfect. *Perfectionist* thinking is often characterised by the word 'should'. The individual feels driven to live by these standards, regardless of whether they are functional. Some perfectionist drivers (or 'shoulds') are listed in the box on the next page.

We may apply these 'shoulds' or unrealistic standards to ourselves or to students—for instance: 'Students *should* be respectful . . . Students *should* want to learn this: it's important . . . Students *shouldn't* behave this way . . . Students *should* be more appreciative . . .' and so on. And these demands can be extended to parents: 'Parents *should* want to be involved in the school . . . They *should* discipline their children better . . . Some parents *should*n't have children . . .' etc.

The corollaries of these and similar 'shoulds' are that when individual students or parents do not comply, then: 'They *should* be punished' . . . 'My job is intolerable', or even: 'Why should I try, as my students (or their parents) clearly aren't trying?' (by not complying with my view of how they 'should' behave).

These 'shoulds' are characteristic of the thinking patterns that I have already described for students and which can be translated into the following thinking patterns for teachers (Kaplan & Carter 1995):

- Robot thinkers feel helpless when it comes to behaviour management and so may instead refer disruptive students to specialists.
- 'I'm useless' thinkers seek their students' approval and so are not assertive enough in the classroom.
- 'You're useless' thinkers do not trust their students to behave considerately and so use controlling methods to force them to comply. These teachers are likely to think that there is something wrong with students who do not conform, rather than considering their own contribution to the students' difficulties.
- Fairytale thinkers complain of the injustices in their classrooms and in the education system but take little action to improve these.
- Woosie thinkers allow themselves to be scared of their students.
- Doomsday thinkers are too exhausted by worry to be very effective.

Teachers' dysfunctional beliefs

1 I must be a perfect teacher.
2 My students must always be interested and involved in class.
3 I should have the solution to every problem.
4 I should look after others, never myself.
5 I should never get tired, sick or inefficient.
6 If there is ever anything to be done, I must not relax until it is completed.
7 I must be liked and respected by all my colleagues. Therefore, I must always act to attract this regard.

8 I should worry a lot about bad things that have happened or which could go wrong for me or my students.
9 I have to have someone to rely on: I cannot survive alone.
10 I have problems now (as a person, or as a teacher) because of what has happened to me in the past and so I cannot change how I am now. Other people and events control my life.

Discarding the 'shoulds'

These beliefs, Ellis (1962) contends, make it difficult to conduct a settled and contented life, free of unnecessary stress. He acknowledges that the world would be a nicer place if everyone obeyed our high standards for them, but that this is not going to happen, and getting worked up about it is not going to make it so and will only add to our own stress. Therefore, we must dispute our dysfunctional beliefs.

When disputing your own beliefs, you can use the same steps as you use for your students: noticing your feelings; identifying common triggers or high-risk situations; recognising the thinking that contributes to the problem and acknowledging that it is illogical; disputing those beliefs; and practising more useful self-talk.

Part of this disputing process is to replace the demand 'should' with the desire 'want'. The *shoulds* compel us to live by standards that are not our own; their more accurate counterparts, the *wants*, are true values. We *want* to do a good job, and when we do not, we may feel badly about that—sometimes very badly—but failure does not make us a bad person with no redeeming qualities. Examples of teachers' functional thoughts are listed in the following box.

Teachers' functional beliefs

1 I would *like* to do a good job and I know I will feel disappointed if I do not. I can cope with that, however, and can take steps to improve my skills for the future.

2 My students are responsible for their own feelings. I can guide them but I cannot force them to learn or behave as I would like.

3 I do not have to know everything: I only have to be open to learning what I need to know.

4 Other people will feel disappointed if I do not do something they want me to do. I may be rejected and disapproved of, but I can cope with that and can accept myself and my decision.

5 I would like to do things well most of the time and will feel disappointed when I do not. However, I have the courage to be imperfect.

6 I am allowed to rest when I wish.

7 I would like to be respected by my colleagues and will feel lonely and isolated if I am not. I can cope with this, however, and can take steps to improve these relationships without submerging my own rights.

8 Worrying about things that could go wrong will not avoid their happening. I can live without guarantees and can focus on the good that is present now.

9 I like to have other people in my life although I can survive if I do not receive the support I would like.

10 I may have learned some ways of dealing with life's stressors that hinder rather than help me. I can continue to use these coping strategies or I can decide to learn new ways that may be more effective and rewarding for me.

Summary

Cognitive-behaviourism focuses on student self-management and also offers some advice to teachers on managing your own thinking and consequent approach to teaching. The theory addresses students' attitude to the learning task or to behavioural compliance, and their ability to organise themselves to achieve appropriate standards.

The aim is for students to become independent in managing their own behaviour, rather than to have this managed for them. The rationale for promoting self-management is to increase students' motivation to comply with expectations; ensure consistency (as students are always present to monitor their own behaviour, whereas teachers are not); to improve generalisation of new skills; to enhance the effectiveness of a behavioural program; and to free you from behaviour management (Alberto & Troutman 1999; Kaplan & Carter 1995; Zirpoli & Melloy 1997). When you teach students cognitive restructuring, you are also contributing to their mental health as well as their ability to observe the norms of the classroom (Kaplan & Carter 1995).

Case study

Adam is seven. He has difficulty with reading, spelling and writing, although he enjoys and is capable at maths. During non-maths lessons, you have noticed that he spends a considerable amount of time off-task, when he frequently disrupts the other students. This is worse in the afternoon than in the morning.

He is in a composite class of six- and seven-year-olds. He spends most of his play time with the younger children. Frequently a pair which includes Adam is apprehended during play times doing such things as harassing passers-by from an out-of-bounds area of the playground which is close to the street, rifling through rubbish bins for food or cans to swap for other items with students, or engaging in fights in and around the toilets.

He seems bemused by the trouble he gets into, usually saying when challenged that he doesn't know why he behaves in these inappropriate ways, that he couldn't remember a given behaviour was against the rules, or that the other child was at fault for suggesting the activity.

Until a recent assessment, it was believed that Adam behaved as he did because of low academic ability. However, a battery of tests has shown his overall ability (IQ) to be average, with his maths skills in the high–normal range and his reading and spelling skills, while delayed, still within the lower range of normal limits. Teaching staff are now at a loss to find a new explanation for his behaviour.

A cognitive-behavioural response

If you endorsed the cognitive-behavioural approach, you might respond to Adam's behaviour in the following steps.

Step 1: Define a target behaviour. Just as an ABA practitioner would decide which behaviour is of most concern and describe that in clear terms, so too you would begin a cognitive-behavioural intervention with this step (Carter 1993). You might start by targeting Adam's disruptive off-task behaviour.

Step 2: Assess the task. You would first examine how relevant the curriculum seems to Adam (and other students), including acknowledging that a curriculum is irrelevant if it is too easy or too difficult for students. As part of your reflection, you should examine possible differences in teaching style between subjects because, while Adam's better performance at maths may be due to his greater interest in and ability at maths (as indicated by his assessment results), it may also be due to a closer match between the teaching methods used in that subject and Adam's learning style. This step is similar to the behaviourists' attention to antecedents, although it takes a wider view of contextual features that could lead to troublesome behaviour.

Step 3: Assess your own contribution to the problem. Next, you would ask yourself whether any element of your reaction to Adam's behaviour is itself adding to your own stress, rather than the behaviour being the only trigger. You will need to ensure that your self-talk about Adam's behaviour is rational and does not inflame the difficulties between Adam and yourself.

Step 4: Emotional factors affecting success—self-esteem. Then you would address an anticipated low self-esteem resulting from Adam's repeated failure at school. Praising his achievements would be a key to enhancing Adam's self-esteem.

Step 5: Emotional factors affecting success—locus of control. The next step would be to challenge the external locus of control that is implied by Adam's denial of responsibility for his infractions of the school rules. You might do this by teaching Adam some self-statements about being in charge of his own behaviour and could systematise this teaching in the later phases of self-management.

Step 6: Emotional factors affecting success—motivation to observe rules. Next you would focus on enhancing Adam's motivation to observe rules. To make the rules more relevant for him and others, you would institute a class meeting in which the group nominated some rules and consequences for their infringement. Then you would teach students how to observe those rules.

Step 7: Cognitive restructuring. You will need to teach Adam how to give himself positive instructions. You will begin with increasing his awareness of his self-talk and then challenge his attributions about his failures and about other students. To assist in teaching Adam more positive attributions, you might tell him the results of his assessment, so that he hears that he has the ability to succeed.

Step 8: Self-management training. To help Adam to manage his own behaviour, you will write verbal prompts on cards (with cartoons to give extra cues). At first, you will prompt Adam to use these cards to guide his thinking, and then will gradually guide him to use them independently.

Step 9: Work contract. You will negotiate a contract with Adam, stating your expectations for his on-task behaviour, and specifying the activity reinforcer that he will earn if he satisfies this criterion. Wragg (1989) advises teachers to require a 25 per cent to 50 per cent reduction in the target behaviour, so this would be your initial criterion, adjusted later if necessary.

Step 10: Self-recording. At this stage, you will need to teach Adam how to record his behaviour. You might institute a tally chart, on which he has to write how often he completes a task within the allotted time. You will simultaneously record his behaviour and reinforce him for accurate record-keeping, until the two records are similar enough that recording can be done by Adam alone. The main focus is on teaching Adam to monitor his actions so that he is less impulsive.

Step 11: Self-reinforcement. Adam will give himself points for completing a task to the criterion level established in the contract, and then will trade in his points for the specified activity reinforcer. Accurate recording and reinforcement will earn Adam an occasional activity reinforcer of computer time or a social reinforcer of being class leader for an activity.

Step 12: Training for generalisation. Once Adam's behaviour has improved, you will need to teach him to self-record outside of the classroom, with other teachers, for different behaviours, and at different times of the day (Carter 1993). You will also need to substitute artificial reinforcers for natural ones so that these maintain his improved behaviour (Carter 1993).

Step 13: The wider environment. Because of Adam's social isolation, you will offer social skills training sessions for all students, focusing on solving social dilemmas and collaborating in play. You might also observe Adam's play and, where necessary and appropriate, teach Adam the skills needed for the games in which the other students engage at play time. For instance, if Adam has difficulty catching a ball and this activity takes up a good deal of student play time, then it will be difficult for him to become involved unless his ball skills improve.

Discussion questions

1 Cognitive-behaviourists say that internal factors (as well as external consequences) influence behaviour. Is this a significant change from applied behaviour analysis?
2 How could you motivate a reluctant student to participate in a self-management program?
3 Select a behaviour of interest—such as aggression, attention-deficit disorder or depression—and describe how you would address it using a cognitive-behavioural approach.
4 Reapply the case study you generated in Chapter 2, this time using cognitive-behavioural principles and practices. What new features are introduced into the

recommended practices? What effect would these differences have on the individual student? On the whole class? On you?

Suggested further reading

Kaplan, J.S. and Carter, J. 1995 *Beyond behavior modification: a cognitive-behavioral approach to behavior management in the school* 3rd edn, Pro-Ed, Austin, TX

Single chapters in the following texts are devoted to student self-management:

Alberto, P.A. and Troutman, A.C. 1999 *Applied behavior analysis for teachers* 5th edn, Merrill, Upper Saddle River, NJ

Zirpoli, T.J. and Melloy, K.J. 1997 *Behavior management: applications for teachers and parents* 2nd edn, Merrill, Upper Saddle River, NJ

Practical programs for cognitive restructuring are outlined by:

Rogers, W. 1994 *Behaviour recovery* ACER, Melbourne

Wragg, J. 1989 *Talk sense to yourself: a program for children and adolescents* ACER, Melbourne

A practical approach to cognitive-based instruction is outlined by:

Ashman, A.F. and Conway, R.N.F. 1993 *Using cognitive methods in the classroom* Routledge, London

Therapeutic interventions for aggressiveness, anger, depression, ADHD and other conditions are described by:

Kendall, P.C. ed. 1991 *Child and adolescent therapy: cognitive-behavioral procedures* Guilford, New York

Puzzle answer

The puzzle contains fifteen triangles: the large one, and six single triangles (which excludes the shape marked x as it has four sides) plus eight triangles formed from two or more singles: 1+2, 1+2+3, 2+3+4, 3+4, 3+4+5, 5+6, 5+6+x+1 and 6+x+1+2—see below.

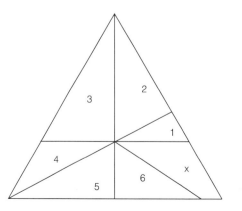

5   Neo-Adlerian theory

. . . each child needs encouragement like a plant needs water. Without it, his growth is stunted and his potential sapped.

Dinkmeyer & Dreikurs (1963: 3)

Key points

- The neo-Adlerians aim to increase students' sense of belonging and subsequent appropriate behaviour by establishing democratic relationships within the classroom that are based on mutual respect, cooperation and encouragement.
- Disruptive behaviour represents a faulty decision: disruptive students have selected an inappropriate way to meet their appropriate goal of seeking to belong in the group.
- You can identify the goals of students' disruptive behaviour by noting how you feel and respond to the behaviour, and how students respond to correction. Following this, your aim will be to guide students to satisfy the same goal through more appropriate behaviour.

Introduction

Neo-Adlerian theory is so named because some modern writers base their theory on the writings of Alfred Adler (1870–1937). The recent writers include Rudolf Dreikurs (1897–1972), Don and Don Dinkmeyer (senior and junior), who with Gary McKay wrote the *Systematic training for effective parenting* and *teaching* programs (STEP and STET), and Jane Nelsen and colleagues (1997, 1998). In Australia, this theory is taken up by Maurice Balson (1992, 1994) and Jeannette Harrison (1996).

Philosophical assumptions

Although crediting their philosophy and theory to Alfred Adler, the modern writers have also departed in some significant ways from his writings. Therefore, this section will at times compare Adler's foundation writings with the beliefs of his disciples.

Nature of childhood

The neo-Adlerians believe that children do more than merely respond to stimuli: they actively assign meaning to events. However, children are at risk of learning inadequate ways of responding to the many demands placed on them, because of their still-immature adjustment processes, and the countless pressures they endure (Adler 1957).

Conditions necessary for learning to occur

Children learn by overcoming feelings of inferiority (Adler 1957). These feelings are seen to be natural, given children's total dependence on adults for survival. Inferiority engenders ambition and is the driving force behind learning. However, it differs from discouragement which, in contrast, leads to despair.

Purpose of discipline

Neo-Adlerian discipline is intended to create the order that is necessary for learning to occur; to guide students to exercise self-discipline (in the form of internalised compliance); and to promote cooperation within the group.

Reasons for disruptive behaviour

These may include:

- *Low self-esteem.* Students' evaluations of themselves govern their actions. Adler (1957) lists many adult attitudes that contribute to children's feelings of inadequacy, including the excessive demands of the education system, not allowing children to take risks, ridiculing them, and not taking them seriously because they are children (which he said was especially true for girls). Later writers assert that discouragement arises from competition at home and in school (Dreikurs & Cassel 1990). This fosters in children the desire to be perfect, which stifles creativity, self-confidence and spontaneity.

- *Need to belong.* Whereas Adler believed that self-esteem was the primary force in children, his followers say that children's primary motivation is to belong. If children's legitimate behaviours are not acknowledged, they become discouraged and so seek to belong in any way they can, even if the resulting behaviour is antisocial.
- *Behaviour is purposeful and goal-directed.* The neo-Adlerians believe that all individual behaviour is goal-directed and purposive, aimed at satisfying individuals' goals. Because children actively interpret their surroundings, their actions are not determined by consequences, the past, heredity or even emotions. Instead, feelings are generated to achieve children's own goals, which relate to the future.
- *Faulty choices.* Thus children's antisocial behaviour is caused by their faulty choices about how to meet their need to belong, based on some mistaken assumptions about themselves, difficulties in the environment or other people.

Teacher–student status

The neo-Adlerian preventive approaches are based on democratic relationships in schools, which focus on individual responsibility. Adler (1957) contended that if we allow individuals to take responsibility for their own well-being—rather than placing them at the mercy of events outside their control—then there is hope even for those students whose home background or heredity may put them at risk of underachievement or behavioural difficulties at school.

Although its preventive approaches are democratic, I placed this theory between the authoritarian and authoritative-democratic positions on the teacher–student power continuum in Figure 1.1 (see Chapter 1), because its interventions are teacher-directed.

Disciplinary role of the teacher

Your role is to promote students' intellectual, social, emotional and physical development to their optimal levels (Balson 1992). At the same time, you must enable students to take responsibility for their own actions.

Prevention of classroom behaviour problems

The neo-Adlerians espouse three methods for preventing classroom behaviour problems: democratic student–teacher relationships; a reduction in competition among students and between the teacher and students; and the use of encouragement rather than praise, to offset any discouragement students may feel and which may give rise to mistaken behaviour.

Democratic student–teacher relationships

Democracy comprises a climate of mutual respect, encouragement of students, student participation in decision making, and promotion of student self-discipline (Dinkmeyer et al. 1980). Students and teachers enjoy the freedoms, but also exercise the responsibilities, of living in a democracy (Dreikurs & Cassel 1990). In contrast, autocratic teaching 'creates an atmosphere in which only a few good children become better, many bad children become worse and the majority are regulated by fear', according to Dreikurs and Cassel (1990: 16). The distinctions between autocracy and democracy are summarised in Table 5.1.

Democratic communication skills

The neo-Adlerians detail democratic techniques for interacting with students individually and in class discussion meetings. Like Gordon's communication roadblocks (to be discussed in Chapter 6), Dinkmeyer et al. (1980) describe some ineffective listening styles, which they list as: the commander-in-chief, the moralist, the judge,

Table 5.1   Contrast between autocratic and democratic teaching styles

Style	Autocratic	Democratic
Leadership	Boss	Leader
	Command	Invitation
	Power	Influence
	Demanding cooperation	Winning cooperation
	Domination	Guidance
	Punishing	Helping
	Sole responsibility of boss	Shared responsibility in team
Teaching	Pressure	Stimulation
	Imposing ideas	Selling ideas
	I tell you what you should do	I tell you what I will do
	I tell you	Discussion
	I decide, you obey	I suggest, and help you to decide
Interpersonal	Sharp voice	Friendly, courteous
	Criticism	Encouragement
	Fault-finding	Acknowledgment of achievement

Source: adapted from Dreikurs and Cassel (1990)

the critic, the amateur psychologist and the consoler. They detail alternatives to these counter-productive styles, including your non-verbal communication that you are comfortable with engaging interpersonally with students, and the verbal skills of reflective listening, assertiveness and collaborative problem-solving. These writers acknowledge Thomas Gordon (1970, 1974) as the source of many of these concepts; therefore the skills will be detailed in Chapter 6.

Class discussions

Like the democrats to be discussed in Chapters 6 and 7, Dreikurs and Cassel (1990: 78) advocate the use of weekly class discussion groups on the basis that:

> any problem child is a problem for the whole class, and the solution to the problem grows most naturally out of the helpful involvement of all class members.

Through class collaboration, discouraged students can begin to feel part of the group, thus reducing their discouragement. Meanwhile, all class members receive support to solve problems they are experiencing and learn to resolve issues in ways other than through fighting. Holding meetings regularly rather than only when problems arise avoids escalation and allows students to anticipate that difficulties will be solved.

Reduce competition

Neo-Adlerian principles suggest that schools abandon competition, as it does not motivate students for long, and even then motivates only those who can succeed. Competition cuts across cooperation (and in so doing, fosters self-centredness) and it leads to a lack of respect for the intrinsic worth of individuals. Dreikurs and Cassel (1990) contend that focusing on winning and losing detracts from mastery of the task at hand. Some methods for eliminating competition in classrooms include: focusing on what students have in common and fostering interaction and cooperation between them; asking students to listen to each other; and using encouragement rather than praise.

Encouragement

The neo-Adlerians prefer encouragement to praise because praise reflects an imbalance of power between teachers and students. In support of this argument, they discuss the costs of praise. These criticisms are supplemented by the humanists' view, as summarised below.

The costs of praise

Praise signals an inequality of power between you and students, and may even be used to put students in their place because, by offering judgment, you imply that you have some special competence (Ginott 1972). Praise aims to manipulate students into repeating a behaviour of which you approve, with you deciding what standards to enforce and when to give or withhold praise.

Effect on students' self-esteem

Praise tells students that you are judging them, and that your opinions are more important than their own. This stifles their self-reliance and threatens their sense of acceptance. Even a positive label (such as 'You're a good boy') can set up unrealistic standards for students' performance and, in turn, cause them to become discouraged about their inability to meet these.

Interference with learning

There are five ways in which praise may interfere with students' learning. The first impact on learning is that, when they rely on authority figures for approval, students try to 'read' you for signs that you approve. This 'adult watching' can take valuable energy away from the task they are doing. Second, praise causes students to focus on external rewards rather than on the rewards that come from the activity itself, so it reduces self-motivation and the joy of learning. Third, praise can be intrusive, interrupting students' absorption in their activity (Biederman et al. 1994). Fourth, praise and other rewards can also reduce generalisation, in that the desirable behaviour may cease when the reinforcement does (Wolery et al. 1988). Finally, praise can teach students to repeat a certain type of work which receives praise, rather than being adventurous and creative. In terms of academic accomplishments, if you reward students, say, for reading more books, they will choose easy ones that they can read quickly and effortlessly (Fields & Boesser 1998). They will stop taking intellectual risks. Thus the quest for a reward actually causes a deterioration in performance (Kohn 1993): rewards might get students to do *more* work, but it is usually of inferior *quality*.

Effects on behaviour

Discouraged students, afraid of failing to meet high expectations, may misbehave. Instead of judging their behaviour for them, teaching students to monitor their own successful behaviour improves their behaviour both directly, by enhancing their self-esteem, and indirectly, by giving them skills to regulate their own actions (appropriate and inappropriate). Also, children may copy their teachers' use of systematic rewards to manipulate their peers, which in their inexperienced hands may become coercive and manipulative, and so will amount to bribery (Wolery et al. 1988).

Ineffectiveness of praise

Praise can be automatic and therefore delivered in a meaningless way that lacks credibility (Hitz & Driscoll 1988). Credibility is also lost when you praise a painting for being, say, a beautiful house, only to have the student report that it is actually a rocket. More importantly, though, praise lacks credibility when students' evaluations do not match yours. If your praise seems invalid, students will doubt your integrity.

Praise is unfair

Considerable expertise is needed to know when and how much praise is fair. Some children become adept at 'pulling' praise from adults 'by smiling or beaming proudly, showing off work, or even communicating an expectation of praise' (Hitz & Driscoll 1988: 8). Other students who do not do this receive less praise than they deserve. So praise increases competition between students, who come to feel resentful or jealous if another student receives praise and they do not.

Finally, like other power-based methods, praise is manipulative, which students grow to resent. Also, their frequent experience of the unfairness of praise causes them to reject the adults who administer it.

Encouragement

Instead of using praise, neo-Adlerians advise you to acknowledge students' successes and, in so doing, show them how to recognise their achievements for themselves. This is termed *encouragement*, which differs from praise in the following ways:

1   Encouragement teaches students to *evaluate their own efforts*: 'What do you think of *that*? . . . Was that fun? . . . Are you pleased with yourself? . . . You seem

pleased that you do that so well.' In this way, encouragement helps students gain independence from you and raises their self-esteem, as they can aim for standards that are relevant to themselves, rather than imposed on them by others.

2 Unlike praise, encouragement *does not judge* students or their work. When you encourage, you might tell students how what they have done affects you, but this is only an opinion, not an evaluation. 'I like the colours you used' replaces the statement that a painting is 'beautiful'. This also avoids having to ask what a painting is, forcing children to draw 'things' rather than to experiment creatively.

3 Encouragement focuses on the *process* rather than the *outcome*. It highlights the value of learning (Edwards 1997). Students can be encouraged for what they are doing, rather than for the end product: 'I enjoy seeing you so intent on that', or 'It looks like you're having fun over there', or when the student has done well on a maths test: 'I see you're enjoying doing maths'.

4 Encouragement *avoids comparisons and competition*, such as 'That's better', or 'You're better at that than Richard'. Instead, you would describe the behaviour that you appreciated: 'Thanks for being quiet while I heard individual reading', or 'I appreciate that you put the equipment away'.

5 Encouragement is a *private* event that does not show students up in public or try to manipulate others into copying someone who is behaving to expectations.

Conclusion: Encouragement versus praise

Self-esteem is literally that: *self*-evaluation. To have a positive evaluation of themselves, students need to be allowed to evaluate their own successes, rather than have these judged by others. They may doubt other people's opinions of them, but will believe their own.

Attitudes that facilitate encouragement

In order to use encouragement, you will need to be willing to guarantee democratic rights and privileges to all members of the class. Other requirements include the following measures (Dinkmeyer & Dreikurs 1963; Dreikurs & Cassel 1990).

- *Accept students.* If you want to encourage students, you will need to accept them as they are (not as they could be), so that they can accept themselves (Harrison 1996). You will need to utilise the students' interests and focus on their strengths

Summary of the disadvantages of praise

Praise and other rewards imply that teachers know everything in all domains and so have a right and are able to judge whether students' achievements are adequate.

Effects on students' self-esteem include:

- Students will not feel accepted because they know that they are being judged.
- Students may expect themselves to be 'good' all the time, lowering their self-esteem when this is impossible.
- Praise teaches students that other people's opinions of them are more important than their own. This can stifle self-reliance.

Praise can impede learning

- Praised students may engage in 'adult watching' to assess whether you approve of them. This will distract them from their own tasks.
- Praise causes students to focus on external rather intrinsic rewards. It inhibits self-motivation.
- Praise and other rewards cause students' performance to deteriorate: they may do more work but it is of a lower quality.
- Praise can interrupt students' concentration.
- Praised students may strive to please and may fear making mistakes, and so might avoid being creative and adventurous.

Praise can provoke disruptive behaviour

- Discouragement about being unable to meet unrealistic expectations may cause some students to behave disruptively.
- Praise does not teach students to monitor their own behaviour and so does not give them the skills to regulate their inappropriate actions.
- Praise and other rewards might teach students how to manipulate their peers.

Praise can be ineffective

- Praise can be automatic for teachers, and therefore delivered in a meaningless way.
- Teachers and their praise will lose credibility if the students' evaluations of their work do not match that of their teacher.

Praise can be unfair

- Teachers need a high level of technical expertise to use praise well.
- While some students can 'pull' praise from teachers, other students cannot and receive less praise than they deserve.
- Praise increases competition between students.
- Their experience that praise is unfair causes some students to reject teachers who administer it.
- Many students come to resent being manipulated by praise.

and talents, rather than on their weaknesses. This will mean that, when commenting on their work, you will avoid pointing out their errors alone as this would discourage them from putting in effort in future (Balson 1992).

- *Have realistic expectations.* The neo-Adlerians advise that you must set standards that are achievable, for which knowledge of child development is crucial (Nelsen et al. 1998). You should communicate to students your faith that they can achieve, and that it is better to try (even if they make mistakes) than to do nothing and learn nothing. You should accept a good attempt and show confidence in students' ability to improve on it another time. Students need to know their worth does not depend on how successful they are (Harrison 1996).

- *Emphasise process.* You must recognise effort rather than the product. A second aspect of process is fostering social cooperation rather than competition and, when dealing with transgressions, a third involves separating the deed from the doer.

- *Be confident.* You will need to recognise that students' behaviour does not reflect on your worth as a teacher. Students are responsible for their own choices. Your self-esteem must be high for you to be willing to abandon the superior position afforded by authoritarian approaches, and to share your power through collaborative learning arrangements and classroom meetings so that students have a positive influence on each other.

Intervention with disruptive behaviour

Encouragement prevents students from misbehaving. On the understanding that disruptive behaviour results from discouragement, encouragement is also applied as an intervention. The following are additional interventive approaches suggested by the neo-Adlerian writers.

Goals of behaviour

Intervention with disruptive behaviour centres on identifying one of four goals that motivate students' behaviour and ensuring that their goal is satisfied by more appropriate actions. Students' beliefs about how to meet their goals give rise either to prosocial or antisocial behaviour. Prosocial beliefs and behaviour turn into antisocial acts if students become discouraged by unsuccessful attempts to win adult approval and attention. Antisocial behaviour has either an active, attacking mode

Table 5.2   Goals of behaviour and their expression

Goal	Positive belief	Prosocial behaviour	Discouraged belief	Antisocial behaviour
Attention Involvement	I belong by contributing	Helps Volunteers	I belong only when I am being noticed	Getting attention through disruptiveness, showing off, or being a nuisance
Power Autonomy	I am responsible for my own behaviour	Shows self-discipline	I belong only when I am in control (bossing others or not being bossed by them)	Uncooperative, comes into conflict with others, forgetful
Justice Fairness	I belong by cooperating	Returns kindness for hurt; ignores belittling comments	I belong only if I can get revenge	Destructive, cruel actions or sullen and morose
Withdrawal from conflict or challenge	I can belong without getting into conflict	Ignores provocation; withdraws from power contest to decide his or her own behaviour	I belong only by being inadequate	Under-achievement; absorbed in fantasy; solitary activity

or a passive, defensive way of pursuing one's goals (Balson 1992). The goals and associated behaviours are listed in Table 5.2.

Striving for attention

Adler said that children need affection and power (autonomy) to overcome their feelings of inferiority. The later writers restated this goal as a need for attention, and so the concept of *attention-seeking* behaviour was born. These writers explain such behaviour as a way of seeking status, but observe that students who are attention seeking require ever-increasing amounts of attention and so are constantly dissatisfied and constantly displaying inappropriate behaviour to get more attention.

As shown in Table 5.2, the positive expression of the need for attention is getting involved and making a contribution (Dinkmeyer & McKay 1989). Its active or attacking negative expression involves provoking you in ways that cannot be ignored—for example, by showing off, being the clown, making mischief, being a nuisance, and other distracting acts such as pencil twiddling or arriving late. Its passive or defending mode engages you unnecessarily by being untidy, cute, shy, fearful, tired, frivolous, in need of help and having speech difficulties (Balson 1992).

Power

Power is expressed in its prosocial form in autonomy and self-responsibility (Dinkmeyer & McKay 1989). Adler asserted that students who continually fail to satisfy their need for power because the environment is hostile, because they have disabilities, or because they are presented with insufficient challenges, may either display inadequacy or seek to express power over the environment and dominate others. Dreikurs and Cassel (1990) assert that power seeking becomes antisocial when attention seeking is dealt with inappropriately, and that, while the two forms of behaviour are similar, power-seeking behaviour is more intense.

Students who seek to dominate others have come to believe that the only thing they can control is the pleasure or displeasure of the adults in their lives. The active or attacking mode of power seeking is behaviour that sends the signal: 'You can't stop me' (Balson 1992). This includes carrying out forbidden acts, rebellion, defiance, truancy, tantrums and bullying. The passive or defending form of antisocial behaviour aimed at gaining power is based on the motto 'You can't make me' and includes stubbornness; uncooperative, non-compliant behaviour; forgetfulness; frequent illness; weakness; and apathy (Balson 1992).

Justice or revenge

As can be seen in Table 5.2, the prosocial expression of this goal is returning kindness for hurt and ignoring belittling remarks. Seeking revenge (with the justification that it is only fair) is provoked when students become so deeply discouraged because of being disliked and not belonging that they believe that they must hurt other people in return (Dreikurs & Cassel 1990). They blame others for their problems (Balson 1992) and so believe that justice is served by getting back at them.

In the behaviour's antisocial, attacking mode, students seem unlovable; seek out those who are vulnerable; and are vicious, destructive, and have a delinquent lifestyle involving stealing and vandalism (Balson 1992). Because of their behaviour, it is difficult for teachers to convince these students that others like them, as they do not like their *behaviour*. Dreikurs and Cassel (1990: 49) extend this point further:

> Unfortunately those who need encouragement most, get it the least because they behave in such a way that our reaction to them pushes them further into discouragement and rebellion.

In its defensive form, such behaviour may mean that these students become sullen and moody, and may refuse to participate.

Withdrawal

All individuals must feel inadequate to some extent, as this feeling provides the motivation for learning. The positive expression of withdrawal is the appropriate withdrawal from conflict (Dinkmeyer & McKay 1989). The antisocial expression is displaying inadequacy. There are three reasons for students to withdraw: they are over-ambitious, over-competitive, or too sensitive to pressure (Edwards 1997). These students see the environment as hostile or uncontrollable, and so they learn to doubt their chances of securing their goals.

For such students, the short-term goal of avoiding difficulties comes to override the long-term goal of seeking success. They will then demonstrate weakness which adults interpret as a need for help or as a signal to give up teaching them, as the students are not trying to succeed. This goal does not have an active mode. Its passive behaviours include being idle, 'acting stupid', refusing to mix with others, playing in solitary activities, playing in babyish ways, engaging in fantasy, and acting hopeless and helpless (Balson 1992).

Diagnosis of the behaviour's goals

Dreikurs and Cassel (1990) assert that, as there are only four goals for student misbehaviour, then diagnosis and subsequent treatment is actually fairly simple. Intervention centres on diagnosing the goal and then redirecting it. Diagnosis is based on observing your own emotional reactions and behavioural responses and noting the student's reaction to your attempts at correction.

Clue 1: Your own emotions

The first way you can determine which goals are motivating students is to note your own emotional reactions:

- If you feel annoyed, then students are *attention seeking*.
- If you feel threatened or defeated, then they are aiming for *power*.
- If you feel hurt, then students are motivated by *revenge*.
- If you feel helpless, then their goal is to *withdraw*.

Table 5.3   Three clues to diagnosing the goals of misbehaviour

If the teacher feels	If the teacher responds by	If the student's response to correction is	Then the student's goal is
Annoyed	Reminding, coaxing	Stops but then repeats the behaviour	Attention
Angry	Fighting or giving in	Confronts or ignores authority	Power
Hurt	Wanting to retaliate or get even	Becomes devious, violent or hostile	Revenge
Despairing or hopeless	Agreeing with the student that nothing can be done	Refuses to participate or cooperate	Withdrawal

Clue 2: Your response

A second clue to students' goals is to notice how you respond to the behaviour.

- If you coax and remind students, then the behaviour is *attention seeking.*
- If you tend either to give in or to fight power with power, then they are aiming to exercise *power.*
- If you try to retaliate, then they are motivated by *revenge.*
- If you believe that they are incompetent and you give up, then the goal is *withdrawal.*

Clue 3: The student's response to correction

A third clue to students' goals is to observe their responses to your attempts at correction (Balson 1992; Edwards 1997):

- If students stop the behaviour but then repeat it, their goal is *attention seeking.*
- If they confront or ignore authority, then their goal is *power.*
- If they become devious, violent or hostile, then they are seeking *revenge.*
- If they refuse to cooperate or participate, or remain uninterested, then the goal is *withdrawal.*

These three sets of clues are summarised in Table 5.3.

Confrontation

The neo-Adlerians contend that, while individuals are aware of their behaviour, they are not always conversant with their goals. These writers believe that becoming aware of the reasons for their behaviour (gaining insight) may allow students to change. Therefore, once you have identified their goal, you can confirm your diagnosis by discussing the possible goals with students. The Neo-Adlerians advise you to do this by confronting them and asking whether they know why they behave as they do and, if not, whether they would like to hear your ideas. Then you are to ask in a matter-of-fact way each of the following questions (Dreikurs & Cassel 1990: 42):

- Could it be that you want special attention?
- Could it be that you want your own way and hope to be boss?
- Could it be that you want to hurt others as much as you feel hurt by them?
- Could it be that you want to be left alone?

You are advised to ask all of these questions, in case students are motivated by more than one goal. Questioning is said to produce a 'recognition reflex' that indicates when your guess is correct. Young students may admit the goal once it has been explained to them; older students are more likely to try to hide their expression, but instead will give off non-verbal behaviour such as a shift in posture that discloses their goal (Edwards 1997).

Dreikurs and Cassel (1990) assert that this discussion alone might bring about a change in students' behaviour. If it proves to be insufficient, you may have to institute corrective measures such as encouragement (discussed earlier), goal re-direction, negotiating a learning contract or instituting consequences.

Goal redirection

Once you are aware of individual students' goals, then you should act to make sure the misbehaviour does not achieve its desired end, and that the students' needs are met through more appropriate behaviour.

This means ignoring *attention-seeking* behaviour whenever possible, and instead giving students attention in unexpected ways when they are not making a bid for it. A more positive first response is suggested by Nelsen et al. (1998), who recommend listening to attention-seeking students, reflecting what they might be feeling, and (if appropriate) giving a reassuring hug. Encouraging students when they are behaving appropriately teaches them that they have a place in the group without needing to resort to the antisocial behaviour. You are advised to refuse to remind, punish, reward or coax.

When students are seeking *power*, you should withdraw from the conflict in the knowledge that fighting or giving in will only increase their desire for power. Some time out might be beneficial here (Nelsen et al. 1998). You will need to give power-seeking students appropriate choices; solicit their help, cooperation or leadership in appropriate ways; and agree to solve the problem collaboratively (Nelsen et al. 1998). The aim is to teach these students to use power constructively.

When students want *revenge*, you must avoid feeling hurt and must not punish or retaliate, but once again listen to their feelings and recognise that a child who is hurtful is 'a hurting child' (Nelsen et al. 1998: 279). When someone else has been harmed, you will need to help the perpetrator to make amends (Nelsen et al. 1998). In the longer term, you will need to build a trusting relationship with students who want revenge, to convince them that they can be accepted without resorting to antisocial behaviour. Punishment is ineffective with revenge-seeking students, as it will only provoke further rebellion and will confirm their belief that they do not belong in school (Ansbacher & Ansbacher 1956). If they are so discouraged that they no longer care whether or not they are accepted at school, you may need to refer them for specialist help. Otherwise, you can institute class meetings for negotiating rules and confirming the place of these students in the group.

When discouraged students *withdraw* through displays of inadequacy, you need a sincere conviction that they are capable and can succeed. You must refuse to give up. You must recognise their deep discouragement and stop all criticism, acknowledge all positive effort, and not get hooked into pity or into agreeing that they are incompetent and that there is no hope. You will need to break tasks into small, achievable steps to encourage risk-taking, allow students to try—even if that involves failure—and teach them the skills they will need for success (Nelsen et al. 1998).

Learning contracts

You can negotiate with students a contract that specifies reasonable criteria by which their work will earn a particular grade or their behaviour meets your standards. You can renegotiate the agreement if it appears not to be working at any time.

Natural and logical consequences

Should the preventive and earlier interventive methods fail to bring about enough improvement in students' behaviour, then the neo-Adlerians recommend using natural or logical consequences. These are aimed at overcoming the disadvantages of punishments which were listed in Chapter 3.

A *natural consequence* is the natural outcome of an individual's actions, such as when a student trips over untied shoelaces. The consequence is not a punishment that is imposed by you, but is merely the natural outcome of students' choices.

Logical consequences are arranged by you but, unlike punishment, have a logical, cause-and-effect link with the student's actions. For example, if individual students will not cooperate in class (cause) then the effect is that you will ask them to go elsewhere until they have changed their mind. The neo-Adlerians believe that logical consequences are different from punishment, because with logical consequences you are objective about guiding students to take responsibility for their actions, with no disguised aim of forcing them to change their decision.

Experiencing the results of their choices teaches students that, while they can behave as they choose, they must still be responsible for their decisions. (The exception is physical danger.) Reality replaces the authority of the teacher (Dreikurs & Cassel 1990).

Table 5.4 summarises the neo-Adlerians' views of the differences between punishment and logical consequences (Dinkmeyer et al. 1980).

On the other hand, Nelsen et al. (1997, 1998) do not advocate consequences. Like the humanists and Glasser (see Chapters 6 and 7), Nelsen and colleagues say that finding solutions is more effective than administering punishments or consequences. This standpoint separates these writers from the majority of the other neo-Adlerians.

Table 5.4   Distinctions between punishment and logical consequences

Punishment	Logical consequences
Emphasis on the adult's power	Emphasis on the reality of the social order
Arbitrary and unrelated to the act	Logically related to the misbehaviour
Implies moral judgments	No moral judgment
Emphasis on past misbehaviour	Concerned with the present and future
Threatens disrespect	Communicates respect and goodwill Treats students with dignity
Demands compliance	Presents a choice

Source: Dinkmeyer et al. (1980)

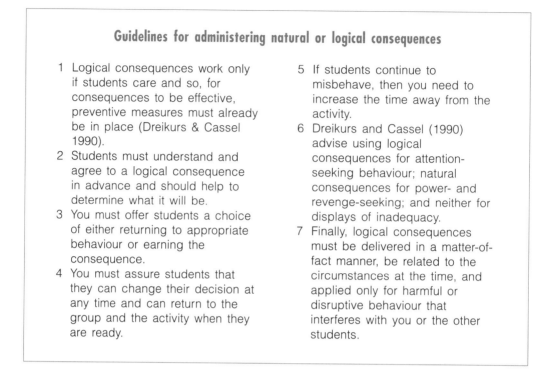

Guidelines for administering natural or logical consequences

1 Logical consequences work only if students care and so, for consequences to be effective, preventive measures must already be in place (Dreikurs & Cassel 1990).

2 Students must understand and agree to a logical consequence in advance and should help to determine what it will be.

3 You must offer students a choice of either returning to appropriate behaviour or earning the consequence.

4 You must assure students that they can change their decision at any time and can return to the group and the activity when they are ready.

5 If students continue to misbehave, then you need to increase the time away from the activity.

6 Dreikurs and Cassel (1990) advise using logical consequences for attention-seeking behaviour; natural consequences for power- and revenge-seeking; and neither for displays of inadequacy.

7 Finally, logical consequences must be delivered in a matter-of-fact manner, be related to the circumstances at the time, and applied only for harmful or disruptive behaviour that interferes with you or the other students.

Summary

The neo-Adlerian writers base their approach on the belief that children strive to belong, and that if they become discouraged about their ability to belong through prosocial behaviour, they will resort to antisocial behaviour to meet this fundamental need. Your role as teacher is to enact democratic classroom relationships that accept all students, reduce competition among them and between yourself and students, and encourage students. A key principle is to teach students to accept responsibility for their own behaviour through encouragement, contracts and the imposition of natural or logical consequences. You are to assess students' motivation for their behaviour and redirect their actions so that they become prosocial while still satisfying their goals.

Case study

Adam is seven. He has difficulty with reading, spelling and writing, although he enjoys and is capable at maths. During non-maths lessons, you have noticed that he spends a considerable amount of time off-task, when he frequently disrupts the other students. This is worse in the afternoon than in the morning.

He is in a composite class of six- and seven-year-olds. He spends most of his play time with the younger children. Frequently a pair which include Adam is apprehended during play times doing such things as harassing passers-by from an out-of-bounds area of the playground which is close to the street, rifling through rubbish bins for food or cans to swap for other items with students, or engaging in fights in and around the toilets.

He seems bemused by the trouble he gets into, usually saying when challenged that he doesn't know why he behaves in these inappropriate ways, that he couldn't remember a given behaviour was against the rules, or that the other child was at fault for suggesting the activity.

Until a recent assessment, it was believed that Adam behaved as he did because of low academic ability. However, a battery of tests has shown his overall ability (IQ) to be average, with his maths skills in the high–normal range and his reading and spelling skills, while delayed, still within the lower range of normal limits. Teaching staff are now at a loss to find a new explanation for his behaviour.

A neo-Adlerian application

As a neo-Adlerian teacher, you might use the following approach with Adam.

Step 1: Prevention. You would establish democratic relationships with Adam and other students, comprising mutual respect, student participation in decision making, and a reduction of competition between students and between the students and yourself.

Step 2: Problem solving. You would discuss Adam's behaviour both within a class meeting, and with Adam individually, beginning by listening to him and finding out how he sees the issues. You may then be able to collaborate with Adam in solving the problem, respecting Adam's perspective while also ensuring that your own needs are safeguarded. You would ensure that class meetings addressed how Adam (and any other excluded students) could become a more integral part of the group.

Step 3: Encouragement. You would cease praising Adam when his behaviour or work was appropriate, and instead would teach him to monitor his own successes through using encouragement.

Step 4: Work contract. In consultation with Adam, you would establish a contract for his learning so that he did both more work and work of a better quality.

Step 5: Diagnosis of goals. If the preventive approaches did not bring about sufficient improvement in Adam's behaviour, you would examine your own feelings and actions to determine which goal is motivating Adam's behaviour. You might notice that you frequently feel annoyed and constantly coax Adam to improve his work output and his behaviour. This information tells you that Adam is likely to be attention seeking.

Step 6: Confrontation. You would then confront Adam with the series of questions about the goals of misbehaviour, beginning with, 'Could it be that you want special attention?', but would ask all four questions, in case his behaviour has more than one goal. Adam would be expected to acknowledge non-verbally when your guess was correct.

Step 7: Goal redirection. Assuming that his goal does turn out to be attention seeking, you would ignore his inappropriate behaviour when you could, and instead make a special effort to give Adam your attention when his behaviour was neutral or appropriate. You would stop reminding, coaxing, rewarding and punishing.

Step 8: Consequences. If these measures were unsuccessful on occasion, Adam would need to experience the natural and logical consequences of his choice of behaviour. For instance, if he cannot confine himself to in-bounds areas of the playground, you will tell him that he cannot play, or you would keep him with the duty teacher at play times. If he insists on rifling through rubbish bins, you might give him playground litter duty for a specified period. His disruptive off-task behaviour would mean that he is not permitted to work in the classroom, given that he cannot work without interfering with others. You will determine these consequences in advance, in consultation with Adam.

Discussion questions

1   What do you think of the arguments against praising students? Does encouragement overcome these?

2   Can you identify reasons for students' misbehaviour besides the ones identified by Dreikurs?

3   What do you think of the three sets of clues which neo-Adlerian teachers use to diagnose students' goals?

4   What are your thoughts about the similarities and differences between punishments and logical consequences?

5   Reapply the case study that you generated in Chapter 2, this time using neo-Adlerian principles and practices. What new features are introduced into the recommended practices? What effect would these differences have on the individual student? On the whole class? On you?

Suggested further reading

The following texts detail the neo-Adlerian approach:

Dinkmeyer, D., McKay, G. and Dinkmeyer, D. 1980 *Systematic training for effective teaching* American Guidance Service, Circle Pines, MN

Dreikurs, R. and Cassel, P. 1990 *Discipline without tears* 2nd edn, Dutton, New York

Nelsen, J., Lott, L. and Glenn, H.S. 1997 *Positive discipline in the classroom*, rev. 2nd edn, Prima, Rocklin, CA

The Australian reader could refer to:

Balson, M. 1992 *Understanding classroom behaviour* 3rd edn, ACER, Melbourne

And, for younger children:

Harrison, J. 1996 *Understanding children* 2nd edn, ACER, Melbourne
Nelsen, J., Erwin, C. and Duffy, R. 1998 *Positive discipline for preschoolers: for their early years—raising children who are responsible, respectful, and resourceful* rev 2nd edn, Prima Publishing, Rocklin, CA

Parents may be referred to:

Balson, M. 1994 *Becoming better parents* 4th edn, ACER, Melbourne
Dinkmeyer, D. Snr, McKay, G.D., Dinkmeyer, J.S., Dinkmeyer, D. Jnr and McKay, J.L. 1997 *Parenting young children: systematic training for effective parenting (STEP) of children under six* American Guidance Service, Circle Pines, MN
Dinkmeyer, D. and McKay, G. 1989 *Systematic training for effective parenting* 3rd edn, American Guidance Service, Circle Pines, MN

6 Humanism

We need young adults who can think and act creatively, who value human life, are able to make discerning decisions, and know how to communicate and negotiate rather than fight. It is our responsibility as guardians of these values to establish learning environments that foster freedom and responsibility.

Rogers (in Rogers & Freiberg 1994: iv)

Key points

- You will promote students' achievement and considerate behaviour when you nurture their emotional needs and curiosity about learning.
- You can do this by establishing democratic relationships with students and by facilitating rather than directing their learning.
- Intervention with difficult behaviour is a problem-solving process rather than an attempt to punish a miscreant.
- To solve the problem, you will use the communication skills of listening to students who are in need, being assertive when your own needs are not being met, and collaborating to solve a problem that is interfering with both your own and your students' needs.

Introduction

The humanist approach to discipline arises from the progressive education movement whose founders include John Dewey, Maria Montessori and Friedrich Froebel, who originated kindergartens (Gartrell 1998). These early educators 'abhorred traditional didactic practices, with children planted behind desks and expected to recite lessons of little meaning in their lives' (Gartrell 1998: 7). Their philosophy about discipline is congruent with their beliefs about education: the two are inseparable.

Philosophical assumptions

The democratic approaches criticise authoritarian discipline methods for being out of keeping with schools' educational aims of preparing students to live by the democratic values of equality and social justice for all members of society (Goodman 1992; Knight 1991; Kohn 1996; McCaslin & Good 1992).

Nature of childhood

The fundamental belief of humanism is that age is no barrier to human rights. Humanists believe that children are unique beings with the right to respect and to the freedom to evaluate and make decisions about their own experience (Rogers & Freiberg 1994). Humanists trust all people's ability—and this includes children—to be self-directed if given the proper circumstances (Rogers, in Rogers & Freiberg 1994). They believe that children are as capable of considerate behaviour as they are of looking out for themselves (Kohn 1996), and that when adults do not threaten them with punishment or bribe them with incentives for behaviour of which we approve, young people are motivated, will make constructive choices, and are trustworthy (Rogers 1951; Rogers & Freiberg 1994).

Conditions necessary for learning to occur

Instead of asking, 'How can we make children conform to our expectations?', the humanist writers ask, 'How can we provide what children need so that they can learn?' (Kohn 1996). In order to answer that question, we need to consider what learning is. Rather than being a type of orderly cognitive, left-brain activity, the humanists regard any meaningful learning as involving both thinking and feeling (Rogers & Freiberg 1994).

This implies that you will promote learning when your curricula have emotional as well as cognitive content, and when you establish a non-threatening, accepting, person-oriented climate in which students can learn information and skills that will make a difference to their lives (Rogers 1951, 1978; Rogers & Freiberg 1994). Both the content and process of education must meet their needs for autonomy, related-ness and competence (Deci & Ryan 1990, in Kohn 1996).

To achieve the above educational goals, students require the social supports and freedom to grow emotionally, cognitively and creatively without limiting others (Knight 1991).

Purpose of discipline

Rather than mandating discipline, humanism aims to *develop* self-discipline in children. Self-discipline is 'knowledge about oneself and the actions needed to grow and develop as a person' (Rogers & Freiberg 1994: 221). Thus when humanists talk of self-discipline, they do not mean internalised compliance as with the authori-tarian theories; instead, they aim to create humane and compassionate students who can act in accord with their own high values. They want students to develop a system of *autonomous ethics*, to use their emotions to enliven rather than impoverish their lives, cooperate with others both in the immediate setting and in the wider community by balancing their own needs with the needs of the group, and have the confidence to act with integrity (Ginott 1972; Goodman 1992; Knight 1991; Kohn 1996; Porter 1999a). Disciplinary methods must teach the same skills that are promoted by the wider curriculum—skills such as self-management, consider-ateness, problem solving and communication.

Humanists are aware that learning these high-level skills takes all of childhood and that mistakes along the way are as inevitable as academic mistakes (Gartrell 1987b). Both, however, provide an opportunity to learn.

Reasons for behavioural disruptions

- *Secondary problems.* Gordon (1974) states that the problems of student apathy and other types of discontent, which teachers often regard as 'problem behav-iour', are only symptoms of a problem, not the problem itself. They believe that these behaviours result from methods teachers use to correct them and thus are secondary difficulties (see Chapter 1).
- *Exploration.* Students are exploring their social environment in just the same way as they explore their physical world and, not having the skills to predict the outcome in advance, at times they do not realise that their actions could negatively affect someone else (Gartrell 1987b, 1998).

- *Becoming emotionally overwhelmed.* Babies *must* communicate their every feeling so that they receive the care that they need to survive. Subsequently, however, growing children have to learn to regulate their emotions so that they remain emotionally safe; in the meantime, mistakes are inevitable as young people cannot always manage their feelings (Porter 1999a).
- *Socially influenced behaviour.* Students sometimes use a skill at the wrong time and place because it was appropriate elsewhere (Gartrell 1987b) or because they have copied someone else's inconsiderate behaviour, such as when children who are subjected to violent discipline become aggressive with other people (Gartrell 1998).
- *Unmet needs.* When students have trouble in their lives that is beyond their ability to understand and cope with, they display repeated dysfunctional behaviour that has strong emotional undertones (Gartrell 1987b, 1998). Their disruptiveness can take the form of doing whatever it takes to survive emotionally. Even when their deep unhappiness arises from their home circumstances, the school's job is to help students overcome disadvantages so that they can be successful intellectually and emotionally.

Teacher–student status

Tom Gordon's advice is that you gain your status from being skilled at what you do (authority based on *expertise*) rather than from having *power* over students (Gordon 1991). In contrast to Glasser's advocacy of a leadership role for teachers (see Chapter 7), humanist teachers *facilitate* student achievement: 'Leadership requires followers, but facilitating requires standing among others rather than standing apart' (Rogers & Freiberg 1994: 103).

At the same time as respecting students, humanist teachers also respect themselves and so will not allow their students to override their needs (Rogers 1978). This is the basis of authoritative dealings with young people.

Disciplinary role of the teacher

The disciplinary and teaching roles are integrated under humanist philosophy. Moreover, teaching is not a matter of instructing students in the skills and information that you and others have decided they need to know, but instead finding out what interests your students and using those topics as a vehicle for facilitating their learning. In contrast with an instructor's role, a facilitator's role is to supply those conditions that enable students to learn, which have already been described (Rogers & Freiberg 1994).

Just as learning facts does not teach students how to think, so too making students conform does not help them to become good people who can think about the effects of their actions on others (Kohn 1996). As a humanist teacher, you would not be concerned with teaching students 'consequences' in terms of what would happen *to them* if they behaved inconsiderately, but with teaching them what effect their behaviour may have on other people (Kohn 1996).

Preventive approaches

In terms of behavioural difficulties, the key focus of humanism is the prevention both of primary difficulties that result when students' needs are not being met, and secondary difficulties arising as a reaction against authoritarian management methods that demean students and rob them of their autonomy.

Develop a sense of community

The humanists aim to create a caring school community, in which students feel cared about and are encouraged to care about each other (Kohn 1996). Within such a setting, students will be more likely to take intellectual risks—and so will learn more—as they know that they will not be humiliated or punished for mistakes (Kohn 1996). A sense of cohesiveness allows students to accept each other and to trust other class members with their ideas and feelings.

Institute democratic relationships

A first step to creating a caring community is to relate to students with acceptance, respect, empathy, humanity and as a real person, rather than hiding behind your role or professional facade (Rogers & Freiberg 1994). More important than these qualities, however, is honesty—with yourself and your students. This involves *owning* your feelings—accepting personal responsibility for them—and being assertive about your needs (but not judgmental or aggressive) when your feelings conflict with those of your students.

Organise the physical setting

You can modify the classroom to facilitate learning and cooperation (Gordon 1974). Measures include *enriching* the environment—for example, by having a variety of activities and multimedia teaching—or, conversely, *impoverishing* or *restricting* it, to aid students' engagement. For example, you can restrict particular activities to certain areas in the classroom so that those who are working there can concentrate. To *simplify* the demands placed on students, you can break complex tasks into small steps that enable success. Keeping the area safe, and preparing students in advance for upcoming changes, such as a relief teacher, all prevent disruptions arising out of stress.

Offer a relevant curriculum

Respect for children implies that what we are asking them to learn should be worth knowing (Fields & Boesser 1998). Information is worth knowing when it helps students to understand their physical and social environment and themselves so that they can respect and care for the world and its people (Fields & Boesser 1998). To make the curriculum relevant, you can do the following:

- Consider your students' ages, and thus whether what you are teaching is relevant to them at this time in their lives (Fields & Boesser 1998).
- Make real problems the subject matter of your classes (Rogers & Freiberg 1994). You might begin with asking the students what issues confront them, or posing questions that they will need to deal with later in life. This fosters an attitude of inquiry.
- Teach students how to learn so that they become producers of ideas rather than mere consumers of information (Rogers & Freiberg 1994).
- Ensure that the curriculum has emotional as well as intellectual content (Rogers & Freiberg 1994).
- Use students' interests to provide a purpose for learning, such as when their interests excite them to research and read about their favourite topics (Fields & Boesser 1998).
- Explain what your planned activity aims to teach them so that students have a rationale for putting in the effort to learn it.
- Help students to become interested in compulsory topics by relating these to their own lives or to other topics that interest them—such as teaching nutrition

by having the students plan, shop for and cook a nutritious meal (Fields & Boesser 1998).

- Provide opportunities for experimentation and reflection, rather than transmitting information: students learn more when they can construct their own understandings than when they are taught directly (Fields & Boesser 1998).
- Match your teaching to each student's learning style. For instance, some students will prefer to be guided by you while others will flourish under self-direction (Rogers & Freiberg 1994). If they are to be free to learn, students will need to be free to choose *how* they learn (Rogers & Freiberg 1994). Therefore, you can divide students into groups of self-directed and outer-directed learners so that all have the opportunity to work within their preferred style.

Having determined the content of the curriculum, you will then organise resources—such as reading material, guest speakers and your own knowledge and experience—for students to consult when thinking about the issues raised. In this way, learning would be self-driven rather than taught.

You will need to monitor the class to ensure that all students are engaged in learning. When students are not responding to the curriculum, rather than placing the blame with them, you instead will assume that the curriculum is not meeting their needs and will adjust it accordingly (Gartrell 1998). Thus a relevant curriculum is both a preventive and interventive measure with disruptive behaviours.

Focus on the learning process

Keeping in mind the thinking and learning skills that you want your students to acquire and practise reminds you that the process of learning is more important than a perfect end-product. In the process of learning, you will want students to: learn to initiate their own actions and to take responsibility for their decisions; evaluate outcomes; know how to acquire useful knowledge; adapt flexibly to new situations; solve relevant problems; and work cooperatively with others (Rogers 1951).

We will prematurely limit students' exploration if we try to avoid mistakes (Fields & Boesser 1998); thus Ginott (1972) recommends that, instead of dwelling on mistakes, we need to acknowledge that correcting errors teaches skills.

Encourage student self-assessment

Furthering the neo-Adlerians' claims about the disadvantages of praise and other rewards, the humanists avoid judgmental or evaluative feedback to students about their achievements or behaviour. Instead, they rely on informative feedback, that describes to students—or asks them to reflect on—what they have achieved rather than evaluating it for them (Faber et al. 1995). Elsewhere, I have termed this 'acknowledgment' (Porter 1999a). While some students experience self-assessment as an opportunity for growth, those who are accustomed to authoritarian methods may at first need guidance in how to be self-accepting, rather than self-critical, when they are assessing their own work.

When testing and grades are imposed on you, this can become just one more problem for the students and you to solve jointly. For example, they might choose to submit questions that they think should be included in a test, or you could supplement their formal results with their own self-evaluations. This safeguards society's need for an accountable education system, while still promoting students' growth.

Establish class meetings

When students gather together regularly, they come to see themselves as a group and so develop a sense of community (Fields & Boesser 1998; Honig & Wittmer 1996). Class meetings are an excellent venue for airing issues that concern most members of the class (Kohn 1996). They can be a place for sharing news; deciding anything from how to arrange the classroom to how to raise funds for people in need; jointly planning field trips or other class activities; discussing the rationale for curriculum content and classroom procedures; and resolving issues (Kohn 1996). It is crucial that the class meeting does not become an exercise in control where you impose your views on the students, but support them in generating their own ideas and solutions, even to the point of running their own meetings (Kohn 1996). You will also need to ensure that the group does not scapegoat individual members: if one student's behaviour is upsetting others, then it would be wise to discuss the general principle—such as looking after each other—rather than the specific behaviour.

When resolving issues, you could ask students to discuss options from a list of possibilities; a more sophisticated task is for them to generate the possibilities themselves (Kohn 1996). They could vote on their options; a more sophisticated task is for them to discuss an issue until they can reach a consensus (Kohn 1996):

> The hard work of listening, considering others' points of view, and fashion-ing new solutions—in short, the guts of democracy—is all but absent when matters are just put to the vote. (Kohn 1996: 95)

Promote cooperative learning and peer tutoring

The humanists employ cooperative learning and peer tutoring to meet students' social needs and advance their cooperative skills. Given that humanist philosophy does not expand on these established practices, the actual methods are discussed in Chapter 13.

Negotiate reciprocal contracts

It should be apparent—but isn't—that the term 'reciprocal' when paired with the word 'contract' is a tautology: by their nature, contracts are reciprocal. I pay you for your house and, in exchange, you hand over the title to the property. But when it comes to contracts about students' behaviour, authoritarian contracts usually list what students must do and what will happen to them if they do not: there is no reciprocity. In contrast, humanist contracts would negotiate with students not only what they need to achieve, but also how you will help them to satisfy those expectations. Reciprocal contracts allow students to plan for meeting their learning and emotional needs, while also detailing the support that you will provide so that they can do so.

Exercise self-discipline

As a humanist teacher, you would demonstrate the same standards of courtesy and self-discipline that you want your students to observe (Ginott 1972). In your professional role, you need to maintain your professional ethics (Fields & Boesser 1998). You cannot allow students to determine your mood or your reactions. Moreover, because many students have been exposed to inappropriate ways of handling their emotions, your own efforts to regulate and communicate your own feelings can teach them skills for doing so themselves (Fields & Boesser 1998).

Further, as a humanist teacher, you would not use punishment or verbal violence to discipline students, even when provoked. You may act spontaneously but not impulsively, so that you encourage cooperation and problem solving (Ginott 1972).

Facilitate student participation

Students have both a right and an obligation to participate in the administration of their schools, as only by participation can they acquire a 'deliberative and democratic character' (Knight 1991: 127). However, participation alone is not enough: the issues addressed must be real and debate must produce socially useful results, according to Knight.

Participate in school administration

You equally have a right to participate in decisions about school policy and procedures (Ginott 1972; Rogers & Freiberg 1994). You have a right to limit intrusions of your work into your personal life and to demand respect and dignified treatment from school administrators (Ginott 1972).

Collaborate with parents

Just as humanist teachers aim to work *with* students, so too you would aim to collaborate with parents, recognising their skills and expertise and not imposing your own ideas on them. These partnerships need to be ongoing, not just activated in times of crisis. This collaborative approach is detailed in Chapter 14.

Intervention

Before detailing their specific interventions, it is important to specify what the humanists do *not* do. They reject punishments and rewards for the reasons already reported in Chapters 3 and 5 respectively. However, their disapproval of authoritarianism is even more fundamental than an objection to its particular methods.

Disadvantages of authoritarianism

Humanists believe that controlling others is both ineffective and unethical. In the vein of Calvin Coolidge's declaration that 'There is no right way to do the wrong thing' (Sapon-Shevin 1996: 196), the humanists reject the authoritarian goal of teaching obedience as this 'dilutes and obstructs' the educational goals of teaching democratic values, problem-solving skills and critical thinking (McCaslin & Good 1992: 12). Kohn (1996) also objects to the 'Do this and you'll get that' pragmatism which distracts children from considering what is right and focuses instead on what will happen *to them* if they behave inconsiderately.

Just as humanists refuse to punish, so too they refuse to reward. Loss of a hoped-for reward feels like a punishment (Fields & Boesser 1998), illustrating that the two are merely 'two sides of the same coin—and the coin doesn't buy very much' (Kohn 1996: 33). Rewards might buy temporary compliance, but even this runs counter to all of the humanists' long-term educational aims.

Finally, Kohn (1996) argues that control is not the way of the 'real world', as is sometimes claimed (see, e.g. Alberto & Troutman 1999). Many adults choose to work in lower-paying jobs for their high job satisfaction; many volunteer their time for no pay for the satisfaction of knowing that they are contributing to their community. In short, when free to do so, adults *choose* intrinsic reinforcers.

Ineffectiveness

Gordon (1991) argues that external controls are ineffective because they work only while students are dependent on teachers, but that by the time students reach adolescence, teachers run out of the power to coerce compliance. Gordon (1991: 94) states this argument: 'It's a paradox: Use power, lose influence.' At the same time that students have no power and do no work to control their own behaviour, teachers work increasingly hard to control them by coercion. Kohn (1996) expands on this point, asking if controlling approaches work, then why is it that they need to remain in place throughout the school years?

Effects on students' self-esteem

Authoritarian methods have two negative effects on students' self-esteem: they are likely to teach students that they are accepted only if they conform, and they rob students of control over themselves, which is a key component of self-esteem.

Provocation of secondary problems

Humanists believe that authoritarian methods (whether they are rewards or punishment) leave students feeling vengeful and hostile (Faber et al. 1995) and are likely to provoke *resistance, rebellion, retaliation, escape* or *submission* (Gordon 1970, 1991). These are the very behaviours which teachers are trying to control and which they most dislike in students. The first three reactions give rise to further punishment; escape and withdrawal lead to alienation from school; while submission leads to problems with peers because other youngsters do not like compliant, dutiful children.

Damage to relationships

Power-based approaches destroy trust between teachers and students and so students withdraw from learning (including leaving school) as soon as they can. Controlling methods also heighten rivalry and competitiveness within groups, as the students compete with each other for the limited amount of teacher approval and favours.

Lost influence

The power of authoritarian teachers is tenuous and is threatened if they are seen to change their mind about a ruling, to be flexible or open to negotiation. Yet, in contrast, teachers' ability to make wise decisions, taking into account the circumstances at the time, is what engenders students' respect.

Effects on society

Finally, Gordon (1991) asks whether societies actually want obedient youngsters, as more crimes against humanity have been committed in the name of obedience than in the name of rebellion. Furthermore, teaching obedience can encourage miscreants to escape responsibility for their actions by blaming someone else for their misdeeds.

Negotiate guidelines, not rules

Although humanism grants freedom to students, it does not give them licence (Rogers & Freiberg 1994). It is not permissive; indeed, it has high-level goals for children's personal development. To assist students in understanding these expectations, some guidelines are necessary, but these should specify 'what productive behavior is . . . not just admonish against mistaken behavior' (Gartrell 1998: 192). You can establish guidelines jointly with your students, as long as you are honest when some are non-negotiable (Gartrell 1998). The resulting guidelines then become reference points that help make your expectations predictable across situations. However, unlike rules, they allow you to choose your response and so

---

Humanists' assertions about the disadvantages of authoritarianism

Ineffectiveness
- Authoritarian methods teach obedience, in direct opposition to the educational purpose of teaching considerateness.
- Authoritarian methods become ineffective as students get older.
- Teachers overwork; students can be irresponsible.

Effects on students' self-esteem
- Punitive methods teach students that they are valued only if they conform.
- Students are not independent in controlling themselves, which is a key source of self-esteem.

Provocation of secondary effects
- Power-based methods provoke resistance, rebellion, retaliation, escape and submission.

- These reactions are maladaptive and excite further punishment or rejection.

Damage to relationships
- Controlling methods teach students to distrust teachers.
- The methods heighten rivalry and competitiveness between students.
- Coercive relationships are based on fear and will inevitably disintegrate.

Effects on teachers and society
- The power of authoritarian teachers is constantly under threat. This means that they cannot be flexible and as a result they lose students' respect.
- Obedience is used to excuse antisocial behaviour.

---

empower you to act professionally rather than as a technician who simply invokes a predetermined consequence (Gartrell 1998).

Solve problems through communication

Gordon's key interventive approach has two steps (1970, 1974). In the first step, you decide whether you find a student's behaviour acceptable. This decision is based on whether the behaviour violates someone's rights. Gordon advocates for a fair distinction between acceptable and unacceptable behaviours: if you find almost all student behaviours unacceptable, then you need to examine your expectations and standards.

The second step is identifying who *owns* the problem. The person whose rights are violated and who is being inconvenienced by the behaviour is said to own the problem—not the person performing the behaviour. The person being inconvenienced takes responsibility for asserting his or her needs and seeking a solution.

Gordon (1974) outlines four occasions when you will need to deal with interpersonal issues in the classroom:

1 when students' unmet needs are impeding their own learning or violating their own social or emotional needs: this is the individual student's problem;
2 when your own needs are not being met: you own the problem. When other students' needs are being violated, this too will become your problem, as you must protect all students from harm;
3 when neither student nor teacher is satisfied: both have unmet needs. There is a conflict, so you both own the problem;
4 when a problem seems apparent, but the individual affected can put it aside and focus on teaching or learning, then there is no problem.

The student has a need: Listening

Listening is more than mere hearing: it is an active process whose skills require practice. Ginott (1972: 77) says that the chronological and psychological distance between students and teachers can be bridged only by listening with genuine empathy, which he describes as 'the capacity to respond accurately to a child's needs, without being infected by them'. Ginott believes that your messages to students must be 'sane' so that students learn to trust their own feelings and perceptions, without being judged for what they feel. This helps distraught students to deal with their own feelings, and also avoids unwarranted emotional outbursts. While listening, your role is to withhold your own opinions and merely act as a sounding board.

Listening will involve paying attention to students' body language or being open when they approach you with a concern. You do not have to respond immediately if you are unable, but can agree on a suitable time to discuss their concerns later.

You might invite students to talk with you by waiting while they construct what they want to say, maintaining good eye contact and pausing in your other duties so that you can listen. Verbally, you might begin by describing their body language—'You look excited'—and asking if they want to talk. Once they start to tell you what is on their mind, you need only give a few minimal encouragers such as: 'Mm', 'Go on', or nodding. It will be wise to avoid asking a lot of questions, especially those that require only yes/no answers, as a series of questions can make students feel that they are being subjected to an inquisition and can direct the conversation away from their agenda.

Finally, it can help to reflect back non-judgmentally what they have said, not only reflecting on the content level, but also on their feelings and relationships (Ginott 1969). You can do this using paraphrasing, which Bolton (1987: 51) describes as:

- a *concise* response
- stating the *essence*
- of the *content*
- in the listener's *own words*.

Roadblocks to communication

How you talk to your students makes a big difference to how they listen to you (Fields & Boesser 1998). Sometimes we think we are listening effectively when unwittingly we are using 'roadblocks' that actively discourage conversation (Gordon 1970). These roadblocks fall into three categories: judging, sending solutions and avoiding the other person's feelings.

Judging. Responses that convey that you are judging students include *criticising*, *blaming* or *name calling*. It is likely that students will see these responses as unfair, become resentful, reject you and what you are saying, or believe your negative judgment (Ginott 1972; Gordon 1974). Another type of judgment is *praising* which, as we saw in Chapter 5, has many negative effects. The final form of judgment is *diagnosing* or *interpreting*. This is an attempt to tell students that their stated problem is not the 'real' issue, which ignores their perceptions and judges them negatively for their feelings.

Sending solutions. If you try to *direct* students to stop their present behaviour and instead do as you say, this tells them that their needs are not important: what you want is paramount. Giving orders disrespects students' ideas and abilities and restrains their development of autonomy (Fields & Boesser 1998). A solution may also be sent as a *threat*, which can make students fearful, resentful and liable to test you to see if you will carry out the threat. *Preaching* treats students as if they do not already know what you are saying. It is patronising. Students will not want to listen, as no one likes to hear unpleasant things (Fields & Boesser 1998). And the timing is wrong: even if the student needs, say, to think ahead before acting, and you want to explain this, now is not the time. When a person is drowning, that is not the time to give swimming lessons (Faber et al. 1995). *Interrogating* is a form of probing which suggests that you are about to find a solution for students instead of allowing them to find their own. Finally, *advising* treats students as if they cannot solve their own problems.

Of the many responses to students' problems, advising is the most common, because we want to help students to feel better. Advising has many disadvantages, however:

- When you offer your own solution, without having heard why students feel as they do, you are telling them that you will not listen to them.
- Giving a solution tells students that they are incompetent, that they cannot solve problems themselves.
- It reduces the chances that students will follow your suggestion, as they took no part in deciding what was to be done.
- Therefore, you will have to monitor and enforce the solution.
- Advising reduces opportunities for students to develop autonomy which is the ultimate goal of teaching. In the meantime, you will be working too hard to control their behaviour.
- Advising ignores the fact that if a solution were that obvious, others would have thought of it already. In recognition of this, Bolton (1987: 22) quotes Hammarskjold:

> Not knowing the question
> It was easy for him
> To give the answer

- Providing solutions makes you responsible for students' problems, which puts an unnecessary stress on you, as students also have useful skills for solving problems.

Avoiding students' feelings. This third group of communication roadblocks can arise because we so desperately want children to be happy that we avoid their feelings (Fields & Boesser 1998). Denial can also come about because some adults mistakenly think that 'little people have little feelings' (Fields & Boesser 1998: 119). Yet facing and responding to their unpleasant emotions can teach students some important skills (Fields & Boesser 1998).

The first form of avoidance is *distracting*, when you try to take students' minds off their worries. But instead they will simply learn that you do not listen to them and will be left stranded without supports. A second form of avoidance, *logical argument,* tells students: 'Don't feel: think'. And, finally, another avoidance method that looks harmless on the surface but which ignores the depth of students' feelings, is *reassuring.* Like the other avoidance responses, reassuring tells students that they are not allowed to feel as they do because you are uncomfortable when they are upset. When you tell students that they have nothing to fear, the original problem is compounded as they become scared of being afraid, anxious that they have to hide their fear but are unable to do so, and anxious about having to cope without support (Edwards 1997).

The thirteenth roadblock. Bolton (1987) adds a final roadblock to Gordon's 'dirty dozen', namely *accusing* other people of using the roadblocks when they communicate with us. We may also blame ourselves for using the roadblocks, which leads to *guilt.* Many people feel discouraged and disappointed in themselves when they realise that their communication habits harm their relationships. However, if you employ any of these habits, it will be because you are copying them from the way adults spoke to you when you were young. You learned them and so can unlearn them too. Your motivation for making the effort to unlearn old communication habits will be enhanced by the realisation that it will be easier for the next generation if they do not have to unlearn these habits as a result of how you speak with them now (Faber et al. 1995).

Prerequisites for effective listening

To be able to listen rather than resort in panic and habit to Gordon's communication stoppers, you will first need to accept students and have confidence in their abilities to solve their own problems. You will need genuinely to accept their feelings, even when they are different from your own or when you do not understand why they feel that way. You will need to *want* to help by listening, rather than trying a 'quick fix' solution of your own, and to wait while they decide whether to discuss their concerns, rather than invading their privacy by probing (Ginott 1972). Most fundamentally, you will need to respect them as people and speak to them as you would an adult (Fields & Boesser 1998).

The teacher has a need: Assertiveness

Respecting students' rights does *not* mean that you have no rights. The basis of democracy is that no one has to exert power over another person (neither person has to win and neither has to lose). You have limits on student behaviour to protect your rights and the rights of others in the class. You will therefore need to act when these rights are being infringed, being assertive about what you need. This is done with the formula:

> When you (*do such and such*)
> I feel (*x*)
> Because (*my rights are being interfered with in this way*).

Assertiveness compared with aggression

If you accuse or criticise students when expressing your needs, you will lower their self-esteem, damage your relationship with them and communicate inaccurately, as it is not really what you want to say. These 'you' messages are what people are referring to when they call someone aggressive. Ginott (1972) describes aggressive messages as insane, and states that labelling students with 'you' messages is disabling because it embarrasses them and may cause them to live down to your negative prediction of them.

The alternative is for you to tell students about yourself and your own needs. This type of message begins with the word 'I': 'I am disappointed that you forgot our agreement to share that equipment' or 'I need some quiet now while I concentrate on explaining this clearly'.

Thus, instead of using the communication blockers of criticising and accusing students, you can describe the problem, give some information about why it is a problem, offer students a choice of how they can fix it, describe how you feel, or use a playful instruction to engage students in fixing the problem (Faber et al. 1995).

Guidelines for framing assertive messages

The 'I' message is non-blaming. It accepts that the students' behaviour does not 'make' you feel as you do: you are responsible for your own feelings. This implies the following guidelines for assertive messages.

- *Take responsibility for yourself.* The most fundamental guideline is that you must take responsibility for your own feelings, rather than blaming these on your students.
- *State your feelings accurately.* Be accurate about how strongly you feel something—that is, do not understate your case (Gordon 1970). On the other hand, you should not overstate how you feel either, because students will learn to

ignore exaggeration and in future will not recognise when you are in fact deeply upset.

- *Avoid starting with 'I feel'.* 'I feel' messages run the risk of blaming students for your feelings. Instead, say how their behaviour actually affects you: 'I would like this corner tidied so that you can work here later' to replace a statement such as 'I feel annoyed when I see all this mess'.

- *Express your first feeling, not anger.* Ginott (1972) expresses the view that, when teaching, anger is inevitable, in which case he advises you to express what you see, feel and expect. At the same time, it can be useful not to express anger alone, because that is not the first or most important thing anyone feels. It is usually caused by earlier feelings of hurt, fright or worry for students' safety. If you let students know that you were scared or hurt, they will receive the correct message rather than some inaccurate message ('He's so angry with me. I'm no good'). Expressing anger alone is also likely to provoke an angry response (Fields & Boesser 1998).

- *Be brief.* Be brief when expressing your anger or other confronting feelings because both the target student and the observing class will close off if you are too talkative (Ginott 1972). Tirades detract from the excitement of learning.

- *Do not suggest solutions.* Use an 'I' message to tell students how you feel, but stop there: do not tell them what to do about that. Ask for help, but do not order students or otherwise impose your solution on them (Fields & Boesser 1998; Ginott n.d.; Gordon 1974).

- *Listen to the students' reaction.* Students may feel hurt, surprised, embarrassed, defensive, argumentative or even tearful after you have delivered your assertive message (Gordon 1974). In that case, revert to listening, because now *they* have the problem.

Advantages of assertion

Students are more likely to consider your needs if they learn what they are. By hearing what effect their behaviour is having, they can understand their world, and so will feel competent and confident within it. Assertiveness demonstrates to students that we all have a right to respect ourselves and uphold our needs.

Assertiveness avoids exasperation building up to anger, which may teach students that feelings are frightening, awful or out of control. In short, it avoids the disadvantages of non-assertion, which include a lack of respect from others, loss of self-respect, inability to control emotional outbursts that arise when we have pushed ourselves too far, and feeling walked over. On the other hand, it avoids the costs of aggression which are avoidance by others, loneliness, retaliation, fear, ill-health and being overwhelmed by being responsible for so much. Being assertive is honest: it builds relationships.

One limitation is that assertive messages assume that your students care about how you feel (Fields & Boesser 1998). This makes building a relationship with students a crucial foundation for solving problems that affect you.

Mutual problems: Collaboration

Gordon's third category of classroom difficulties is when both you and a student have unmet needs. Of the three occasions for problem solving, these shared problems are the most common. Humanists believe that students' behaviour is rational, which is to say that it is aimed at meeting their needs; disruptions, therefore, are similarly aimed at meeting their needs and imply that those needs are not being met in other ways. At the same time, a disruption is likely to interfere with your rights or the rights of other students, which it is your duty to protect. Therefore, both you and the student have a problem.

Conflict is a natural part of human relationships, but nevertheless many of us fear it—especially, says Gordon (1974), if we define good teachers as people who never experience conflict in their classrooms or if we feel that we have only two solutions from which to choose: *either* students win *or* teachers win. Instead, we can regard conflict as inevitable and healthy, and use its energy to generate workable solutions that protect all participants (Knight 1991).

Ginott (1972) advises you to side-step confrontations by allowing students to save face, as humiliation of students is to be avoided at all costs. Also, by listening when students express strong feelings, and by avoiding demands and commands, you will not unnecessarily provoke a confrontation. When it becomes clear, however, that neither your own nor a student's needs are being satisfied, then the two of you can collaborate to find a solution using collaborative problem solving. This involves the following six steps.

- *Step 1: Agree to talk it over together* so that the two of you can *define the problem*. Begin by finding out what the student needs, and then state your own needs, in order to establish where the conflict lies. This is the most crucial step, and requires willing involvement by the student, enough time to become clear about the issues, and a focus on problem definition without any concentration on solutions (Gordon 1974).

- *Step 2: Generate possible solutions.* Generate ideas that you *could* do, so that you would both get your needs met. At this stage, do not evaluate how practical the suggestions are, just brainstorm all possibilities—even silly ones—and write them down.
- *Step 3: Evaluate the solutions.* Next, evaluate the options and discard ones that would not be workable.
- *Step 4: Select a solution* that is likely to meet both people's needs. Do not choose a compromise, in which neither of you is satisfied, but instead persist until you find a solution that meets both your needs. Everyone must be able to agree to try the solution, even if not yet convinced that it will work.
- *Step 5: Determine implementation.* Plan when and how to carry out your chosen solution.
- *Step 6: Check that it is working.* Once it is in place, check whether the solution is working. Be on the lookout for commitments that were made with initial enthusiasm but which later turn out to be unrealistic or unworkable. Be prepared to discard or amend solutions that are not working.

Throughout this process, use active listening to clarify what the student needs and assertiveness skills to state your own needs and what solutions you can accept.

Outcomes of negotiation

Negotiation tells your students that you think their needs are important and worthy of consideration. It eliminates the need to use power, which always leads to a struggle of wills. Instead, teachers and students work with—rather than struggling against—each other, which reduces hostility and enhances the student–teacher relationship. This means that you do not have to work as hard, have all the answers or second-guess what students need or want.

As well as leading to higher quality solutions (because two heads are always better than one), helping to decide what should be done develops students' thinking skills. Students will be more motivated to carry out a joint decision because they have participated in making it, and therefore you do not have to enforce the solution.

The method can be equally well applied to conflicts among students and to establishing class rules within a class meeting. Collaboration works best when you can deal with each source of irritation at the time it surfaces, rather than leaving grievances to mount up and hurt feelings to turn to anger. The approach will not work when students are in danger, or when there is true time pressure to get something done. In these cases, you will need to take charge, but perhaps later you could explain your reasons.

Alternatives to punishment

As already stated, humanists reject the use of punishment. In its place, you could try one of the following options (Faber et al. 1995).

- Point out a way students could be helpful: 'It would be helpful if you could learn your lines while you are waiting for your turn on stage' (instead of mucking around and disrupting others).
- Express your strong disapproval without attacking students' characters—that is, by being assertive rather than aggressive.
- State your expectations in positive terms—that is, point out what needs to be done, not what students are doing wrong.
- If it would be helpful, suggest ways that students could satisfy your expectations.
- Offer a choice—not *whether* to meet your expectations, but *how* students could do so.
- Let students experience the natural consequences of their actions.

This last recommendation to use natural consequences is not a perfect solution, however. It ignores the fact that, in some cases, natural consequences have already occurred by the time a problem has become evident and so there is no need to prolong the experience (Miller 1984). In other cases, a natural effect of students' actions is too dangerous or unfair: you would not let students suffer peer rejection for aggressive behaviour, but instead would help them develop more caring peer relationships.

To overcome the limitations of natural consequences, some humanists recommend logical or related consequences *as a last resort*. While some say that these are just a euphemism for punishment (Gordon 1970; Kohn 1996), their advocates attempt to draw a distinction between logical consequences and punishment, suggesting that (Fields & Boesser 1998; Gartrell 1987b, 1998):

- your attitude of strictness versus firmness will determine whether a logical consequence feels like retaliation rather than a natural effect of a student's action;

- using consequences as a threat turns them into a punishment;
- preaching that 'I told you so' (or variations on that theme) makes consequences punitive as your message becomes moralistic instead of educational;
- logical consequences require you to withdraw from power; punishments require you to apply power;
- the connection between the behaviour and the outcome must be logical *to the child* so that learning results;
- the consequence should not be specified beforehand, otherwise it is a punishment;
- if you cannot identify a logical or related consequence, perhaps that should signal that there is no good reason why your limit should be observed.

Despite these distinctions, Kohn (1996) maintains that the difference between logical consequences and punishment is only a matter of degree (a quantitative difference) rather than of kind (a qualitative difference). Nevertheless, he does leave the door open for you to use logical consequences as a rare and last resort, but cautions that, in these instances, you should not fool yourself that you are doing anything other than punish. And you must realise that choosing to punish runs the risk that subsequently you might not be able to restore a caring relationship with a punished student.

No problem exists

Gordon's fourth category of interpersonal dilemmas is when either you or a student has a need but it can be set aside while you each get on with your work. In short, there is no problem to be solved. The main type of non-problem is when there is a conflict of values. Collaborative problem solving will not work for values conflicts for two reasons: first, the student's belief is likely to be strong; and, second, a conflict of values seldom harms the other person. The clue to a conflict of values is when your assertive message cannot fit the 'When you . . . I feel . . . because' formula, because the student's behaviour actually has no tangible effect on you. However, you can still ask students to consider your values—Gordon uses the example of asking students not to swear in front of you—without having any negative effect on your relationship with them. Students may consider your feelings and change their behaviour even though you can claim no ill-effects if they do not.

Resistance to abandoning authoritarianism

The humanists speculate on why the education system is so resistant to changing its traditional authoritarian stance. Rogers and Freiberg (1994) say that perhaps it is because we do not ask students for their opinions of school; we distrust democracy as clumsy and inefficient; we distrust that children can make wise decisions; we falsely believe that the workforce needs compliant workers when instead it needs creative thinkers to solve the problems associated with industrialisation; and because those in power seek to maintain their stronghold.

Gordon (1991) says that some of our reluctance to embrace democracy arises from the traditional Judaeo-Christian belief that children are bad by nature. Most teachers do not consciously endorse this idea but, in using controlling discipline methods, they *act as if they do* (Porter 1999a). Some even believe that children will 'go wild' if they are not subjected to external controls, which leads to 'either–or' thinking that *either* teachers must punish students *or* students will violate teachers' rights (Fields & Boesser 1998; Kohn 1996). This reflects a lack of understanding of alternative methods of teaching consideration.

Summary

The humanists recommend some fundamental changes in the philosophy that governs how schools and classrooms are organised. As a teacher, you are advised to change from being an expert who holds all knowledge to a facilitator who encourages critical inquiry in your students. When your curriculum content and learning processes meet students' needs, you would rarely need to intervene with disruptive behaviour. On the rare occasions when your intervention was necessary, your task would be to guide your students to solve the problem using a range of communication skills, as outlined in the box on the next page.

The humanists describe many benefits of listening to students, including students' enhanced emotional well-being and improved motivation to learn (Rogers 1951; Rogers & Freiberg 1994). Assertiveness provides a way to ensure that your rights are equally safeguarded, and collaborative problem solving is aimed at finding better solutions without violating the rights of either students or yourself. Nevertheless, the humanist teacher is not perfect: it takes a long time to become proficient at the problem-solving approach (Gartrell 1998). Humanist teachers, like anybody, will make mistakes; like their students, the aim is that they learn from them (Gartrell 1998).

Humanist interventions with behavioural disruptions

- Establish guidelines, not rules.
- Solve problems.
    - *Listen* when students' problems interfere with their participation or with meeting their own needs.
    - Be *assertive* when their behaviour violates your own needs or the needs of other students.
    - Use *collaborative problem-solving* steps when both students and you have unmet needs.
- If essential, and as a last resort, use natural or logical consequences (in the awareness that this may damage irretrievably your relationship with a punished student).

Case study

Adam is seven. He has difficulty with reading, spelling and writing, although he enjoys and is capable at maths. During non-maths lessons, you have noticed that he spends a considerable amount of time off-task, when he frequently disrupts the other students. This is worse in the afternoon than in the morning.

He is in a composite class of six- and seven-year-olds. He spends most of his play time with the younger children. Frequently a pair including Adam is apprehended during play times doing such things as harassing passers-by from an out-of-bounds area of the playground which is close to the street, rifling through rubbish bins for food or cans to swap for other items with students, or engaging in fights in and around the toilets.

He seems bemused by the trouble he gets into, usually saying when challenged that he doesn't know why he behaves in these inappropriate ways, that he couldn't remember a given behaviour was against the rules, or that the other child was at fault for suggesting the activity.

Until a recent assessment, it was believed that Adam behaved as he did because of low academic ability. However, a battery of tests has shown his overall ability (IQ) to be average, with his maths skills in the high–normal range and his reading and spelling skills, while delayed, still within the lower range of normal limits. Teaching staff are now at a loss to find a new explanation for his behaviour.

A humanist response

As a humanist teacher, you could take the following steps to help Adam overcome his difficulties (adapted from Kohn 1996).

Step 1: Build a relationship with Adam and all students so that they are willing to work with you to solve any problems.

Step 2: Teach problem-solving skills such as listening to others, generating suggestions and keeping calm. The best way to begin this type of instruction is by using the skills yourself when you are talking with Adam and all students.

Step 3: Examine your own practices with an eye to what you may be doing that provokes Adam's disruptive behaviours or to things you could do differently to make it easier for him and others to behave considerately.

Step 4: Collaborate with parents. Adam's constellation of behaviours, and the fact that they have persisted for some time, suggest that he is in survival mode. This will in part be due to school but could also relate to difficulties at home. To enlist his parents' help, you will need to meet with them and find out if they can suggest any solutions, and then act on these.

Step 5: Facilitate learning—content. You would take Adam's behaviour to be a signal that school work is not meeting his needs. Therefore, you would ask him and the other students about their interests and incorporate these into your program.

Learning process. At the same time, you would change from being the expert who presents information in the form of direct *instruction* to *facilitating* students' learning. You would assist them to research their topics of interest by arranging for resources to be available for them.

Step 6: Negotiate expectations. Involve students as a group and individually in determining standards for their behaviour and in finding solutions to disruptions. During discussions, you will avoid preaching to Adam and the other students so that they do not simply volunteer solutions that they think you want to hear. Seek authentic solutions: these are the only ones that have any chance of working.

Step 7: Promote collaborative learning. Establish small work teams for various projects, allowing students to help and learn from each other and to develop cooperative skills. This would also be aimed at improving Adam's play difficulties, by helping him gain entry to the group during class time.

Step 8: Institute peer tutoring. You might give another student the task of tutoring Adam in his weaker subjects, and Adam may tutor one of his peers in maths.

Step 9: Negotiate a reciprocal contract. You would write a contract with Adam, detailing some goals for both his academic achievement and behaviour and specifying how he would assess when he had reached his goals. In exchange, your section of the contract would specify what you would do to help him to meet his goals and your expectations, and to recognise for himself that he had done so.

Step 10: Identify who owns the problem. If Adam's behaviour were disruptive or if he violated your contract, you might assess that this is your problem. In that case, you would deliver an assertive message stating how Adam's behaviour directly affects you. Once you have delivered your assertive message, you might need to revert to listening if Adam becomes upset or defensive about your statement.

Step 11: Engage in collaborative problem solving. On the other hand, in most instances you are likely to see Adam's disruptive behaviour as a signal that his needs are not being met, while still recognising that neither are yours. In that case, you would make a time to renegotiate the contract and to solve the problem collaboratively. When talking with Adam about his behaviour, make sure that you address his and the victim's hurt feelings as well as the content of a dispute, so that they do not get into trouble again later on as a result of unresolved feelings. Overall, your aim will be to minimise the negative impact of your intervention on Adam, and maintain your faith that the two of you can sort it out together.

Step 12: Encourage reconciliation. If Adam's behaviour has harmed someone else, you will need to give him an opportunity to make amends, as long as you do not blame or shame him in this process. Forcing an apology might only teach him how to tell lies or to resent the person who forces him to lose face. Instead, you could take the aggrieved student aside with Adam and then *talk to the victim* (in Adam's hearing) about how Adam's behaviour has hurt—physically and/or emotionally—so that Adam can realise the effect that his behaviour has on others without being confronted with his mistake. This lack of confrontation may avoid a secondary behaviour problem—see Chapter 1 (Porter 1999b).

Step 13: Self-responsibility for homework. When Adam does not do his homework, you can ask him to write you a note saying what work he did not complete and when he will do it (Ginott 1972). This note should not give reasons why he did not do it, as this would teach him to make up excuses and tell lies. Instead, you are to assume that he has his reasons for not completing the work, and that homework is his personal responsibility. When he has competed the homework, you would return his note to him. At the same time, you could discuss with Adam's parents how they could give him some indirect help so that he could manage the process of getting his homework done, without themselves taking responsibility for helping him with the content or for changing his feelings about homework.

On the other hand, humanists believe that students will do work when they find it relevant, and so you might reconsider the value of assigning homework at all, or might redesign homework activities so that they are more relevant for Adam.

Step 14: Check back to make sure that any agreed solutions are working.

Discussion questions

1 What does Gordon's distinction between the two types of authority (expertise versus power) imply for discipline methods?

2 What do the humanists' goals for discipline imply for day-to-day instructional practice? What do they imply for intervention with disruptive behaviours?

3   Contrast the humanists' practices with those of the neo-Adlerians. Do you see any significant differences in their underlying philosophy and practices? Is your answer different for their interventive versus preventive approaches?

4   Reapply the case study that you generated in Chapter 2, this time using humanist principles and practices. What new features are introduced into the recommended practices? What effect would these differences have on the individual student? On the whole class? On you?

Suggested further reading

Any of the following texts will provide a description of the humanist philosophy, with communication and teaching skills also outlined:

Faber, A., Mazlish, E., Nyberg, L. and Templeton, R.A. 1995 *How to talk so kids can learn at home and in school* Fireside, New York

Gartrell, D. 1998 *A guidance approach to discipline for the encouraging classroom* 2nd edn Delmar, Albany, NY

Ginott, H.G. 1972 *Teacher and child* Macmillan, New York

Gordon, T. 1974 *Teacher effectiveness training* Peter H. Wyden, New York

——1991 *Teaching children self-discipline at home and at school* Random House, Sydney

Kohn, A. 1993 *Punished by rewards: the trouble with gold stars, incentive plans, A's, praise, and other bribes* Houghton Mifflin, Boston, MA

——1996 *Beyond discipline: from compliance to community* Association for Supervision and Curriculum Development, Alexandria, VA

Rogers, C. and Freiberg, H.J. 1994 *Freedom to learn* 3rd edn, Merrill, New York

For early childhood:

Fields, M. and Boesser, C. 1998 *Constructive guidance and discipline* 2nd edn, Merrill, Upper Saddle River, NJ

Porter, L. 1999 *Young children's behaviour: practical approaches for caregivers and teachers* MacLennan & Petty, Sydney

7   Choice theory

It is the responsibility of each individual child to work to succeed in the world, to rise above the handicaps that surround him [or her]; equally it is the responsibility of the society to provide a school system in which success is not only possible, but probable.

Glasser (1969: 6)

Key points

- Students will be motivated to do high quality work and to behave responsibly if schools are democratic and curricula are relevant to—that is, meet the needs of—students.
- These needs are survival, love and belonging, power, freedom and fun.
- In order to meet these needs, the most fundamental change to schools will be a move from bossing students to leading them.

Introduction

Glasser's approach draws on the humanist tradition plus cognitive theory. He seeks more than an orderly school in which students achieve adequate grades on tests about inconsequential content (Glasser 1998a): instead, he wants students to be learning worthwhile content, to a high level of mastery, in a setting that meets their needs and those of their teachers.

Philosophical assumptions

Three differences distinguish Glasser's philosophy from humanism. The first is its implied emphasis on the need for order in schools, something that probably results

140

from his history of working with young people with seriously disturbed behaviour. Second, he adds a counselling intervention to the humanist communication skills. And, third, unlike the humanists, Glasser places great emphasis on converting a whole school to the systematic application of his methods.

Just like humanism, however, choice theory contends that we choose everything we do. This standpoint is in direct opposition to the premise of applied behaviour analysis which states that external events dictate our behaviour (Glasser 1998a, 1998b, 1998c, 1998d). According to Glasser (1998b), all that the outside world can give us is information; we choose what we do with that information.

Nature of childhood

Glasser does not specifically address the nature of childhood, except to say that children are capable of adopting self-responsibility. Because the only person we can control is ourselves, other people cannot know what is right for anyone else, even for children (Glasser 1998c).

Conditions necessary for learning to occur

The most important thing to all of us is the quality of our lives. Glasser (1998b) says that students will learn at school when they know that what they are being asked to learn and how they are doing it will add quality to their lives. Quality is achieved when our basic needs are met. These needs are the following (Glasser 1998a, 1998b, 1998c, 1998d).

- *Survival*. Students' physical or survival needs for food, shelter and security must be satisfied before any learning can take place. Glasser (1998d: 22) states: 'Teachers are well aware that hungry students think of food, lonely students look for friends and powerless students for attention far more than they look for knowledge.'
- *Love and belonging* which is measured not only by how much affection we receive, but also by how much we are willing to give. When they have a meaningful relationship with their teachers and each other, students will work well (Glasser 1998c).
- *Power* does not mean the manipulation of others, but the need to choose for ourselves and be self-determining. At all times, our behaviour is aimed at trying to gain effective control over our own lives so that we can meet our needs. Power lies in our perception that we are making a meaningful impact on the

world (Strohl 1989). This is analogous to steering a car, taking charge of its direction (Glasser 1998a).

- *Freedom* refers to the need for independence or freedom from control by others. We feel threatened and are less creative when others try to control what we do with our lives. Power and freedom are opposite sides of the same coin. If individuals have too much power, they restrict the freedom of others. The need for freedom or independence can also be at odds with the need to belong, as individuals cannot belong if they are too different from their peers.
- *Fun* is the 'intangible joy' that we experience with the spontaneous satisfaction of our other needs (Glasser 1998c: 30). Learning must be fun, especially for younger students, who have so much to learn and at the same time have a particular need for fun.

In his earlier writing, Glasser (1969) also spoke of an identity need, which could be equated with self-esteem, although this need is not mentioned in his later works.

Purpose of discipline

Discipline enables students to make rational rather than emotional decisions about meeting their needs, without at the same time interfering with the needs of others. Thus Glasser agrees with the humanists' goals of helping students establish their own ethics, regulate their emotions, cooperate with others and act with integrity. Unlike the humanists, however, he also adds the managerial purpose of establishing and maintaining order.

Reasons for behavioural disruptions

Glasser believes that disruptive student behaviour arises because school work does not meet students' needs. In particular, both what they are being asked to do and how teachers relate to them can violate students' need for power. This leads to failure and, in turn, students' view of themselves as failures leads to apathy, delinquency and withdrawal from school and home, all of which cause loneliness.

Teacher–student status

Glasser's belief that we all choose our own behaviour underpins both a philosophical and a pragmatic commitment to democracy in schools: he believes that coercion is destructive, and that it does not work. Students comply with coercion because they judge that, all things considered, it would be better for them not to resist, but they resent being coerced and will do only the absolute minimum of what they have been asked (Glasser 1998a).

Disciplinary role of the teacher

On the grounds that disruptions are difficult to handle but easy to prevent, your instructional role within a 'quality school' is to show students how doing high-quality work at school will add to their quality of life, either now or in the future (Glasser 1998a). This means that the work will meet their needs (Glasser 1998b). Your disciplinary role is to build caring relationships with students so that they gain the strength to take responsibility for themselves (Glasser 1998c, 1998d).

Meet students' need for power

Individuals need power, although this must be balanced by a respect for the freedom of others. The following measures are all designed to make school a place where students choose to be and where, therefore, they neither choose to disrupt nor give tacit approval to their disrupting peers.

Lead management

In breach of students' need for power—that is, for control over their lives—teachers traditionally use a form of management that places them in charge of students. Glasser calls this *boss* management, in contrast with *lead* management. His distinction equates with Gordon's (1991) distinction between authority based on power versus expertise.

Boss authority burdens you with a style of management that is bound to fail, no matter how competent you are as a teacher. It involves imposing academic work and standards of behaviour on students, without their input. It is detrimental because you cannot motivate students from the outside and so it limits work quantity and quality and produces the discipline problems that you are trying to prevent (Glasser 1998a). Furthermore, the contest between you and your students uses much of your energies, which creates inefficiency and self-defeating behaviour. And because schools have very few rewards available to them for coercing students positively, external control methods frequently become very negative (Glasser

1998a). Students regard you as an adversary, ridicule or ignore you, or see you as an obstacle to getting the job done (Glasser 1998a).

While boss management appears to work for many students, Glasser contends that, instead, these students' success is due to their home backgrounds and occurs despite, rather than because of, the school system. Instead of schools acting to overcome students' disadvantaging home backgrounds, homes are expected to offset the failure that children experience at school, which not even the most loving home can do (Glasser 1969, 1998a).

In contrast, if you adopted a lead management style, you would combine what students need with what you ask of them. They would become self-driven. They would participate fully in making decisions in their school so that they would experience—rather than only learn about—the democratic responsibilities that they will need to exercise as adult citizens. Students would not have power over you, but they would expect you to listen to them.

- A boss drives. A leader leads.
- A boss relies on authority. A leader relies on cooperation.
- A boss says 'I'. A leader says 'We'.
- A boss creates fear. A leader creates confidence.
- A boss knows how. A leader shows how.
- A boss creates resentment. A leader breeds enthusiasm.
- A boss fixes blame. A leader fixes mistakes.
- A boss makes work drudgery. A leader makes work interesting.

Glasser (1998a: ix)

Negotiate minimal rules

Glasser (1998a) contends that lead managed schools need very few rules and that, in contrast, boss managed schools have many rules that themselves provoke defiance. This in turn creates a need for coercion, which engenders more defiance. Thus you will need to negotiate a minimum number of rules with your students, basing these on what constitutes courteous behaviour (Glasser 1998a). Fundamental to the principles of a quality school is that no one should put another person down (Glasser 1998b).

The resulting rules should have a clear cause-and-effect relationship to the behaviour. For instance, walking in corridors (cause) leads to fewer collisions (effect) (Tauber 1990). If this cause–effect relationship is not apparent to students, they will not abide by the rule or believe that school is a good place to be. Furthermore, violation of rules will not attract penalties but will merely signal that there is a problem to solve.

Emphasise high-quality work

Glasser (1998a, 1998b) believes that to prevent students' misconduct and under-achievement at school, schools themselves must be reorganised and curricula reshaped to expect and support high-quality work that produces useful outcomes for students. Curricula must be useful because 'There is no power in doing something useless' (Glasser 1998b: 34) and there is no way to motivate students to do something that is futile: 'Boredom is the enemy of [high] quality' (Glasser 1998a: 70).

Academic curricula must cover less ground so that students have more time to learn worthwhile content in greater depth and thus become competent (Glasser 1998a). Glasser (1992b: 694) justifies this suggestion by saying: 'We should never forget that people, not curriculum, are the desired outcomes of schooling.'

As well as promoting a high standard of academic work, you would encourage students to produce high-quality work in non-academic subjects such as the arts and drama, as this is where they get their first experience of cooperative learning (Glasser 1998b).

Offer relevant curricula

Glasser (1998a: 44) says that 'No human being is unmotivated' but that students will be motivated to do high-quality school work only when it meets their needs. The obvious corollary of this assertion is that, if students are choosing not to work, this will be because the work is not satisfying them.

Many students find that the opinions, experience, interests and observations that they bring from home are not valued at school (Glasser 1969). While some students tolerate that school has nothing to do with home (and vice versa), many do not and lose motivation to work. Thus, to motivate students to learn what you teach, you will need to (Glasser 1998a, 1998b):

- have respect for their interests and teach them more about what they want to know;
- incorporate your own interests in your teaching;
- explain why you are teaching given content, helping students to realise why,

when, where and how the information could be used by them or someone else, now or in the future (Glasser 1992b, 1998b).

- break down what you teach into recognisable parts;
- link information to the skill of using it;
- reinstate the emotional content of topics, as otherwise learning is emotionally dull for many students;
- refuse to require memorisation of facts as this involves no thinking and generates 'throwaway information' that students forget almost as quickly as they learn (Glasser 1969, 1992b). Instead, help students to understand social issues, allow them to ask questions, teach them how to make and follow through on decisions (which will involve strength, responsibility, commitment and judgment), and how to tolerate ambiguity and uncertainty;
- teach practical life skills that will help students run their lives and be relevant for them vocationally;
- foster creativity and originality;
- ensure a two-way exchange between home and school;
- having improved the quality of your teaching, ask students if they agree that what you are teaching is worth learning;
- if so, ask them to commit to learning the skills *well*.

In short, you have to sell the curriculum so that students see that it is worth learning but, in convincing them, you cannot *force* them to learn it, as that would reduce their motivation (Glasser 1998b).

Glasser (1969, 1998b) lists relevant skills as: reading, speaking, writing, arithmetic (not higher mathematics as it is not necessary for life), and problem-solving skills. Of these, writing and speaking have the highest pay-off in the real world and so are good places to start in requiring high-quality output from students (Glasser 1998b). If people can organise their ideas in written form, they will be able to read and speak well also (Glasser 1992b, 1998b). Glasser therefore recommends using word processors for teaching students to communicate ideas in written form, as computers make it is easier for them to improve their writing.

Meanwhile, reading is crucial as it can be used to acquire any other information. Therefore, you need to give students with reading difficulties separate remedial reading classes, from which they can graduate back to the regular class as their reading skills improve. (Meanwhile, for other subjects, they would remain in their usual class grouping.)

With relevant curricula on offer, students will not begin to do high-quality work immediately, but your job is to encourage them to keep working long enough so that they can experience the joy of achieving work that is of a high standard (Glasser 1998a, 1998b).

Concurrent evaluation

Grades are intended to give students a sense of achievement and to motivate them to work harder. However, they do not have this effect on students who do not care about your evaluations of them or their work (Glasser 1998a). Grades are used to force students to learn irrelevant material, can seldom be fair, and so for these and other reasons (detailed in the box below), Glasser (1998a) advocates teaching students to judge their own individual and collaborative work. In so doing, you would not only teach them how to evaluate their own work, but also that doing so is the most important part of their education (Glasser 1998a, 1998b). Only their own judgment about their grasp of useful skills (that is, self-evaluation of a relevant curriculum) will motivate them to achieve high-quality work.

Let's say that you are teaching maths and have a useful textbook on which to base your teaching. Glasser (1998b) recommends asking students to start at the beginning of the textbook until they find a group of problems that they do not yet know how to do, and mark that place in the book. This is now their individual starting place. Then you would form students into working groups of heterogeneous ability and ask them to help each other to progress through the next unit of work, each at his or her own pace. (You would supply help for those who were still having difficulty, even with peer support.) When they feel confident that they know that next unit, they should show you how they can solve one of its problems and explain to you how they arrived at that solution. Thus assessed, they could move on to the next unit of work.

Glasser (1998b: 84) uses the acronym SESIR to represent his assessment system for students:

S Show someone what they have achieved.
E Explain how they achieved it.
S Self-evaluate.
I Improve what has been done.
R Repeat the assessment until the work is of high quality.

To assist in this assessment process, you may need to recruit some teaching assistants (Glasser 1998a, 1998b).

Negative effects of grades

Low quality work

- Grades tell students and their teachers that no learning is worthwhile unless it can be measured (that is, unless it is graded). This means that students will study only what is to be tested, and so academic standards are lowered. Grades become more important to students than getting an education.
- Academic standards are again lowered by the anxiety that grading engenders in students, reducing their ability to study.
- Closed-book examinations are based, says Glasser (1969: 72), on the fallacy that 'knowledge remembered is better than knowledge looked up' and yet rote learning is suitable for a relatively small range of material, whereas research skills are useful for a vast array of material and for learning how to solve problems.
- Coercion (through tests) to memorise irrelevant information discourages independent thinking and causes students to cheat, not because they lack ethics but because they realise that 'there is no virtue in learning nonsense' (Glasser 1992a: 217).
- Coercion (through tests) to memorise facts causes many students to hate the subject matter, which 'is worse than just not knowing it' (Glasser 1992a: 231).

Demarcations between students

- When the curriculum is irrelevant, grades will encourage only the academically successful students to learn.
- Grades increase competition between classmates.

Unfairness

- While grades are supposed to be an objective measure of students' progress, it is hard to make any finer distinction than pass–fail. Attempts to do so are inaccurate, unfair and phoney.
- Grades are not a good indicator of success at anything other than school work, and are poor indicators of students' ability at work or higher education.
- Students are aware that, although a C grade is considered a pass, the only decent grades to achieve are a B or an A. When grading is done according to normal distributions, most students will never achieve high grades, with the result that many will become despondent.
- There is no recognition of late maturing and no second chance to redeem a poor school record—school failure damns one to failure for life.

Poor interpersonal relationships

- Finally, grades reduce human involvement between teachers and students, which is central to student motivation.

Students who are doing high-quality work might decide to reward themselves (Glasser 1998a), but as a lead teacher, you would not do so as rewards represent an imbalance of power between teachers and students and remove students' responsibility for their own behaviour.

Temporary grades

At times you are officially obliged to administer tests, or you need to establish where students need extra help and where they need to do more work. Nevertheless, such tests would be open-book, would test skills rather than the memorisation of facts, and you would ask students to nominate when they were ready to take these (Glasser 1998a, 1998b).

Students who did well on the test would proceed to new material; those who did not would be given the opportunity to practise further to improve on their work until it was of high quality. Glasser (1998a: 68) defends this suggestion with the observation that: 'If we are not going to try to improve what we do, there is little sense in assessing it.'

Glasser also suggests that, by learning the answers to his who, why, when and how questions, students who are preparing for public examinations would find it easier to remember the otherwise irrelevant facts that these tests call for and so most students receiving high-quality teaching would be more successful at exams.

Finally, if students did not pass a particular course, that course would not be entered on their transcripts, as permanent fail grades are not part of a high-quality school (Glasser 1998a, 1998b).

Voluntary homework

Compulsory homework is a fundamental source of coercion and irrelevance in schools and thus, as a Glasserian teacher, you would not assign compulsory homework (the disadvantages of which are summarised in the following box). However, there are four instances where homework is justifiable:

1   if the work can only be done at home and is not just an extension of class work—such as when students need to watch a particular TV program or interview relatives;
2   when students want to improve on a test grade—in which case, for instance, you could ask them to explain the concept being tested to an adult at home

and record one question that person asked and how they answered it (Glasser 1992b);

3 if individual students could not achieve high-quality work within the time allotted in class, you could counsel them about what extra work they could do voluntarily at home;

4 if students *choose* to revise and practise at home (Glasser 1998a).

If you did not have to set homework for all your students, you would be free to concentrate on the five or so students with learning difficulties who are in every class. For these few students, you could determine where their difficulties lay and plan a series of remedial homework activities. Freed from marking the unnecessary homework of your other students, you could then give individual feedback to the few students who were struggling, thus advancing their skills.

Teach choice theory to students

Glasser (1998b: 97) says that:

> In a traditional school, when a child is in any kind of trouble, the first suggestion is that he [or she] needs counseling. But if we depend on counseling, we find that there are too many students who need it and not nearly enough counselors available.

Therefore, rather than counselling students in a reactive manner, you will need to teach them choice theory to give them a sense of control over their lives and the skills to solve problems (Glasser 1998b). You would begin this in the first years of school by explaining the five basic needs and then by teaching that all of our behaviour is an attempt to meet those needs: we choose what we do.

Finally, with older students, you would teach them about total behaviour. This is to say that all behaviour has four components: acting, thinking, feeling and a biological response (Glasser 1998a, 1998c). As in a front-wheel drive car, thinking and acting are the two 'front wheels' that pull the other two aspects along with them. Thus, if students want to feel better, they will need to act and think more effectively (Glasser 1998a).

Last, you will need to teach students that emotions signal to us whether or not our needs are being met. Frustration is the feeling that we have when these needs are obstructed. But we can control what we feel by changing what we want, by changing our behaviour, or both: we can make better choices (Glasser 1998c).

Disadvantages of compulsory homework

Reduces student motivation and achievement

- Compulsory homework reduces the quality of students' lives: it does not meet their needs.
- Homework is irrelevant, especially until the most senior years of high school.
- Students have no choice about doing homework, which makes them unmotivated to complete it.
- Homework allows students to make the same mistakes over and over when studying at home without teacher supervision, and therefore they learn wrong approaches.
- Most homework is more easily and better done at school.

Contributes to student drop-out and burnout (stress)

- Homework is excessive, tedious and as irrelevant as the general school curriculum.
- Compulsory homework causes students to hate school and learning.
- Homework eats into relaxation time, which would offset stress.
- Bright students who are conscientious about doing homework have no time left to pursue other recreational activities; less able students do not do the homework but, because this defines them as failures, they do little else either. Thus both groups of students are denied other learning and enjoyable activities. And, by adulthood, they have not developed ways to enjoy their leisure time.

Contributes to demarcations between students

- Students from middle-class homes have the facilities at home for quiet study whereas students from working-class homes have not,

leading to a widening of the differences between their academic achievement levels.
- Just as it contributes to class differences in achievement, homework highlights academic differences between students, as only academically able students complete their homework.

Contributes to antagonism between teachers and students

- Compulsory homework leads to conflict between students and teachers, which in turn leads to low-quality work that exacerbates the friction between students and teachers . . . and so the cycle repeats.

Prevents high-quality teaching

- Assigning compulsory homework prevents teachers from planning exciting instruction.
- Homework must be graded, with all the disadvantages of grading.
- Failure to do homework must be punished, which violates all the principles of a high-quality school.
- To avoid arguments, teachers accept low-quality homework, sending the message that low-quality work is acceptable.

Family tension

- Compulsory homework creates tension between parents and children, as parents frequently believe that it is their role to oversee the completion of homework and so they nag their children. Instead, if the school sets the work, it should supervise it.
- Voluntary homework that involved talking to adults could help bring parents and children together, whereas compulsory homework only creates antagonism.

Glasser (1969, 1998a)

Satisfy students' need to belong

The need to belong is a central motivation for human beings. Glasser (1998a: 50) reports that: 'Students are saying that it is very hard for them to satisfy their needs in academic classes because most work is done alone and there is little or no class discussion.'

Be involved with students

When you engage students in a warm relationship that accepts them and their right to have their needs satisfied, they will be motivated to learn and to accept responsibility for their actions; if you remain aloof, it tells them that you are in charge (Glasser 1998a). The more that students know and like you, the more they will be willing to work for you, as it will satisfy their need to belong (Glasser 1998b). Therefore, over the first few months of working with a group, you should find natural occasions to tell them who you are, what you stand for, what you will and will not ask them to do, and what you will and will not do for them (Glasser 1998b: 25).

Establish cooperative working teams

Most learning should take place within cooperative groups, as learning together within a small team satisfies students' need to belong and to be independent of their teacher. To that end, you should establish groups of mixed ability, so that more able students can receive satisfaction from helping other students, while the less able can still achieve. In this way, more in-depth understanding of the work can be achieved by all members, and working with other members can provide a comparison against which students can assess their own progress.

Facilitate peer tutoring

You would train strong students to act as peer tutors for anyone who needed one-to-one tutoring, so that no one would sit in class needing, but not receiving, help. In recognition of their effort and commitment, tutors could receive credit in a course called 'academic leadership', or receive added credit in the subject being taught (Glasser 1998a).

Institute class meetings

You need to meet daily with your primary school classes and twice weekly with high school classes to discuss and resolve problems (Glasser 1969, 1998a, 1998b). The humanists have detailed suggestions for holding meetings that I will not repeat here; suffice to say that during meetings you will give your opinions sparingly and, when you do so, they should carry equal weight with students' views. Glasser recommends three types of meetings.

1 *Social problem solving* attempts to solve class disturbances (behavioural difficulties) that are of concern to any student, teacher or parent. These meetings should focus on finding a solution rather than finding fault with individuals (Glasser 1969). As Glasser's other measures are enacted, these meetings will become rare.
2 *Open-ended* meetings allow the students to discuss any issue that is relevant to their lives, including any dissatisfaction with school.
3 *Educational-diagnostic* meetings are related to what the class is studying. These are aimed at establishing whether the teaching procedures are effective in producing in the students a living, working understanding of the concepts being taught, rather than pure theoretical or fact-based learning.

Immediate intervention: Solve problems

Offering a high-quality education in a humane environment will avoid most occurrences of disruptive behaviour. However, on those rare occasions when students behave disruptively, you will need to take steps to stop the disruption without using coercion (Glasser 1998a).

As a lead teacher, you would communicate that students' disruptions are their problem, not yours, and that you are confident about how to respond (Glasser 1998a). Your response will reflect your awareness that students' behaviour represents a decision about how to satisfy their needs, even though their chosen actions may be ineffective or disruptive.

You will need to listen to disruptive behaviour and solve the problem that it signals. You may begin by realising that, like your students, you are choosing your own behaviour. On this basis, you can ask yourself: 'What am I doing that contributes to the problem?' If something is provoking problems for students or making it difficult for them to feel motivated—if what you are doing is not working—you should stop it (Glasser 1976).

One key might be to take steps to build a more respectful relationship within which students will care about your needs and will value school as a good place to be. Fundamental to this is the avoidance of coercion. If you do not punish young people, it will be harder for them to be angry at you (Glasser 1998a). Punishment detracts from students' quality of life, reduces their motivation to learn and their willingness to take responsibility for their actions, and causes them to focus on trying to outwit their controller (Glasser 1998a).

You would deal with the behaviour matter-of-factly, without anger (Glasser 1998a). Your first response, therefore, is simply to say to the student: 'It looks like you have a problem. How could I help you solve it?' (Glasser 1998a: 140).

Provide time out

You cannot solve problems until students cool off, so they must withdraw if they cannot calm down immediately (within around 20 seconds) and work with you to sort out the problem.

Thus, while establishing itself as a 'quality school', your school will need a time out room where students can withdraw to calm down (Glasser 1998a). This should be a temporary feature of your school and should be used only for students who are behaving disruptively, not for those who are simply off-task, as that is an educational problem, not a behavioural one (Glasser 1976).

The time out room can be a pleasant place, although students must remain there until they are ready to 'work it out'. You should not hurry students to get ready to return to the class, but as soon as they start to make an effort to solve the problem, they can go back.

A teacher must staff the time out room throughout the day. If you were on duty in the time out room, you would not argue with students or negate their complaints about the work or their teacher, although you could mention that no teachers like disruptions and ask if they think the class is boring, whether this room is any better (Glasser 1998a). While in the room, students can carry on with their work, sometimes together if that helps them, or you might give them help with the work yourself so that they do not fall behind (Glasser 1998a).

If students are disruptive in the quiet area, then you must send them home, as they cannot be in school until, and unless, they are willing to learn. Because school is a good place to be, they will not take pleasure from being excluded. Once at home, if they remain unwilling to attend school and obey the rules, you do not have the resources to solve this. In such cases, you should advise the parents of community agencies they could consult.

Throughout this process, Glasser's (1998a) advice is not to involve students' parents except to pass on positive information or to collaborate with solving non-discipline problems, such as their son or daughter's difficulty with making friends. This sends two messages to students: first, that you believe that you both can solve the problem independently of their parents and, second, that you want to solve the problem, not punish students, and you do not want their parents to punish them either.

Resolve the problem

After students have become calm again, you will probably find that you do not need to deliver a lecture about what Glasser (1998a: 143) terms their 'temporary foolishness'. They will realise their mistake and agree that it won't happen again.

If a disruption arose out of a dispute between two students, you might need to speak with them both about the conflict and negotiate a way that they can get along with each other better (Glasser 1998a). In this discussion, you are not looking to find out who is at fault, but simply looking for a solution.

Offer counselling

You can counsel both non-achieving and disruptive students about whether their behaviour does in reality meet their own goals. This does not have to take a long time as you will already have an ongoing, positive relationship with students that will be a good basis for a therapeutic discussion. The aim of such a discussion is to enable students to change their behaviour so that it still meets their emotional needs but also does not violate the needs of other people.

Hammel (1989) describes the following counselling steps:

- *Step 1: Secure students' involvement*, both in school and in your relationship. You will have achieved this by enacting the measures mentioned previously that are aimed at meeting students' needs.
- *Step 2: Guide students to identify their problem*. In so doing, focus on present rather than past misdemeanours or past 'causes', as these become excuses.

Permitting excuses communicates a lack of caring and a lack of interest in students' success:

> It is no kindness to treat unhappy people as helpless, hopeless, or inadequate, no matter what has happened to them. Kindness is having faith in the truth and that people can handle it and use it for their benefit. (Glasser 1998c: 158).

You know that changing behaviour can be difficult, so while you accept students' feelings, empathise with their difficult home life or with past traumatic events, you cannot allow them to use these as excuses for continued failure and suffering.

Thus it does not pay to focus on students' feelings as they have no direct control over those. While you can be sensitive to their distress, you need to focus on what they can *do* or *think* differently: their feelings will improve when they change how they are thinking and behaving (Glasser 1998a).

- *Step 3: Identify needs.* Help students to identify what they want from school. Their knowledge of choice theory will help them to identify their needs.
- *Step 4: Assess behaviour.* Ask them to judge whether their behaviour is working for them—that is, whether it meets their needs. This is a cause–effect judgment, not a moral one, as moralising links behaviour to students' character and so judges them.
- *Step 5: Seek their commitment* to finding other ways of meeting their needs.
- *Step 6: Plan a new behaviour.* In so doing, students will take responsibility for their behaviour. You will not solve the problem for them, but you will work with them to solve it in a way that meets both your own and their needs.

  If students have legitimate complaints about a class, you can allow them to change to a different class after they have demonstrated that they are willing to work where they are. Slacking off is their choice, but it will not allow them to escape responsibility for their learning and behaviour. You could say that everyone is doing all they can to make school a good place for them to be, but that they have to do something as well if they want to make it better (Glasser 1998a).
- *Step 7: Commit to the plan.* Having formulated a plan, students must then commit to pursuing it. You will want to know how and when they plan to fulfil the agreement.

- *Step 8: Evaluate whether the plan is working.* Accept no excuses for failing to abide by the plan, as excuses are past-focused. But do not punish transgressions either. Instead, modify the plan if it is not working, or reconfirm students' commitment to it.

Students may take a long time to be willing to risk abandoning tried and true methods of gaining control, even when these attract a high price. They may not trust that other, unknown, methods would work better. Therefore, you must persevere, and must never revert to boss management while students experiment with change. 'How long is "never"?' asks Tauber (1990). In answer, Glasser (1977: 61) offers this guiding rule: 'Hang in there longer than the student thinks you will.'

Summary

Glasser's approach requires a fundamental revision of schools' teaching content and processes. It begins with ensuring that students regard school as a good place where their needs will be met. In order to promote their feelings of power, you must expect and support responsible behaviour and high-quality work through offering a relevant curriculum and leading rather than bossing students. To satisfy students' need to belong, you must develop warm relationships with your students, and foster caring peer relationships among them.

When students behave disruptively, Glasser recommends solving the problem collaboratively as soon as students are calm enough to contribute to this process.

Glasser's democratic principles extend beyond student–teacher relationships, to include the school hierarchy and how it affects all members of the school. Principals need to have faith in their staff and students' ability to make responsible decisions.

Case study

Adam is seven. He has difficulty with reading, spelling and writing, although he enjoys and is capable at maths. During non-maths lessons, you have noticed that he spends a considerable amount of time off-task, when he frequently disrupts the other students. This is worse in the afternoon than in the morning.

He is in a composite class of six- and seven-year-olds. He spends most of his play time with the younger children. Frequently a pair which includes Adam is apprehended during play times doing such things as harassing passers-by from an out-of-bounds area of the playground which is close to the street, rifling through rubbish bins for food or cans to swap for other items with students, or engaging in fights in and around the toilets.

He seems bemused by the trouble he gets into, usually saying when challenged that he doesn't know why he behaves in these inappropriate ways, that he couldn't remember a given behaviour was against the rules, or that the other child was at fault for suggesting the activity.

Until a recent assessment, it was believed that Adam behaved as he did because of low academic ability. However, a battery of tests has shown his overall ability (IQ) to be average, with his maths skills in the high–normal range and his reading and spelling skills, while delayed, still within the lower range of normal limits. Teaching staff are now at a loss to find a new explanation for his behaviour.

A choice theory application

If you adopted the Glasserian approach, you would respond to Adam's difficulties using the following steps.

Step 1: Build rapport. Build rapport with Adam by taking notice of him when his behaviour is neutral or acceptable, so that your relationship becomes warmer. Let him get to know you and what you stand for.

Step 2: Modify curricula. Look at which aspects of your teaching might be provoking Adam's behaviour. The first of these may be irrelevant curricula. Although you are aware that the curriculum is set down to a large extent, you can ask Adam about his interests, and ensure that you include these in your teaching, and you can explain how established curricula are useful and relevant to him.

Step 3: Satisfy students' emotional needs. You will realise that Adam's lack of motivation is due to the fact that the work does not meet his needs. This implies that you can increase his motivation by:

- grouping students into teams to allow them to meet their social needs through collaborative work. You may also need to institute a social skills program to ensure that they have the skills to negotiate team work in socially acceptable ways;
- giving Adam remedial reading, as this skill is a high priority for education. Build in a way for Adam to assess his own progress;
- ceasing to assign compulsory homework. At the same time, you could counsel Adam about extra work that he could do so that he could be more successful and thus enjoy his school work more. You might delay doing this, however, until he is starting to gain some enjoyment from succeeding in class.

Step 4: Class meetings. Conduct daily class meetings. Ensure that you have a balance between social problem-solving, open-ended and educational-diagnostic meetings. In the early meetings, establish class rules and discuss how you will help students solve problems that arise when individuals cannot observe the rules. In social problem-solving meetings, you might ask students to suggest other ways that Adam could be involved in their play besides his present antisocial play activities.

Step 5: Change your own behaviour. Next, consider what you are doing that is keeping Adam's behaviour in place, and stop doing that. An instance may be your constant berating and interrogation of Adam following an infraction of the rules. Stop punishing him.

Step 6: Problem-solving. Help Adam to make a plan to meet his needs at school. Ask him what he wants from school, and how he thinks he could get that. Is his present behaviour helping?

Step 7: Solve immediate disruptions. At the time of a disruption, ask Adam if you can help to solve the problem. If he is not ready yet to find a solution, allow him to withdraw to a quiet corner in the classroom; if he cannot calm down there, send him to the time-out room until he is calm enough to be ready to solve the problem.

Step 8: Write a plan. Now that Adam is calm, write a plan with him that requires him to produce high-quality work and to abide by the rules established by the class.

Step 9: Evaluate the plan. Review your agreement throughout the coming days and ask Adam if he thinks it is meeting his needs.

Step 10: Parental collaboration. Until now, you will have avoided bringing in Adam's parents so that his school behaviour does not create a problem for him at home. However, if your school-based intervention does not work, you could ask his parents for their suggestions, as long as you are clear with them that you expect to solve the problem yourself and are not expecting them to do this for you.

Step 11: Referral. If neither the parents nor you can suggest a solution, then you might advise the parents of counselling agencies that they could consult.

Step 12: Suspension. Suspension from school is the final potential consequence but would not be used for a child of Adam's age or for behaviour that is so minor.

Discussion questions

1   In what ways do Glasser's recommended practices differ from humanism? Are these differences significant, in your opinion?

2   What aspects of classroom management does Glasser believe will contribute to students' belief that school is a good place to be?

3   How could you or your school enact the counselling approach to long-term disciplinary problems? Do you foresee any difficulties in the implementation of this approach?

4   Apply Glasser's recommendation to the case study that you generated in Chapter 2. What key features does Glasser introduce that have not been used by earlier theorists? What effect would these differences have on the individual student? On the whole class? On you?

Suggested further reading

Any of Glasser's texts, referenced fully in the bibliography, give an outline of his philosophy. His titles include: *Schools without failure* (1969), *Choice theory in the classroom* (1998), *The quality school: managing students without coercion* (1998) and *The quality school teacher* (1998).

8 Systems theory

You cannot solve the problem with the same kind of thinking that has created the problem.

Albert Einstein (in de Shazer 1993: 84)

Key points

- Systems theory provides a framework for thinking about recurring problems in new ways.
- There are four main branches of systems theory; the one highlighted in this chapter—solution-focused therapy—believes that behaviour problems arise when behaviour is accidentally mishandled and so an attempted solution has not worked.
- Change, then, is brought about by changing how the behaviour is handled. To do this, you need to identify previous solution attempts and do something different from those.

Introduction

Individual theories see a person as a whole, made up of parts; systems theory sees the individual as part of a whole system or group. A system is any ongoing group—such as a family, school, class or work group—that has characteristic communication patterns, roles and rules. Thus the word *system* implies that the group interacts in systematic ways that obey implicit rules and expectations.

Systems theory focuses on these patterns of interactions, observing that the system's rules can become so inflexible that the problem—in our case, difficult behaviour—is not being solved successfully.

At the risk of over-simplifying this theory, this chapter will mainly concentrate on just one of its branches: solution-focused therapy. This is by no means the only school of systems theory, but is likely to be the most accessible to new initiates to systemic thinking and also is likely to be the most relevant for your role as a teacher. This branch of systems theory is especially useful for school practitioners who need quick solutions to severe problems (Dicocco et al. 1987). (If you are interested in pursuing the differences between the various branches of systems theory, you could refer to Hayes 1991; Nichols & Schwartz 1995; Smyrnios & Kirkby 1992; or Walsh & McGraw 1996.)

When applied to school-based behavioural difficulties, systems theory is silent on the issue of curriculum. This could give the impression that it is purely an interventive approach; however, as you will read in this chapter, it is more a way of thinking than a particular form of intervention as such (Kral 1992). It is a way of looking at problems by examining their effects on the *relationships* between people. Subsequently, it may use any of the methods of the other theories, but with a new rationale for their use.

Philosophical assumptions

Systems theory—and family therapy, which is the counselling model that sprang from it—has been applied to the full range of human behaviour and so does not specifically discuss the six philosophical dimensions used to introduce the earlier theories. Nevertheless, it is possible to infer systems theory's assumptions about these.

Nature of childhood

Like everyone, children do the best they can with the information that is available to them. Even if at times their behaviour is dysfunctional, nevertheless, they already have the skills to solve their own problems (Bonnington 1993; Murphy 1994).

Conditions necessary for learning to occur

Not being a specifically educational theory, systems theory does not detail the conditions that are necessary to motivate students to learn academic content.

However, it believes that learning new behaviours does not require insight—that is, self-awareness of the reasons for our actions. Instead, we require three things to be willing to change: first, some discomfort with the results of our present behaviour; second, information about alternative ways to act; and third, because change is difficult, we need strong motivation to adopt a new behaviour.

Purpose of discipline

Systems theory would not regard itself as an instrument of discipline and so makes no statements about the purpose of discipline. Its role is to maintain the healthy functioning of individuals and the systems or groups of which they are a part. Because it believes that this in part relies on a healthy hierarchy, we can infer that it would promote *order* in classrooms and *cooperation* with others. With its emphasis on individuals' healthy functioning, we can assume that it aims for *emotional self-regulation*. Finally, this theory often considers the marginalising effects on individuals of oppressive social systems (e.g. Stacey & Loptson 1995), in which case we can infer an ethical theory base that emphasises *integrity*.

Reasons for disruptive behaviour

The various branches of systems theory have different explanations for how dysfunctional behaviour develops, some simple and some more complex (Cooper & Upton 1990):

- *Inadvertently, the wrong solution is applied.* The simple explanation is that problematic behaviour arises when everyday developmental challenges or crises are accidentally mishandled. The methods that were aimed at solving the problem unintentionally maintain or intensify it (Amatea 1988; Amatea & Sherrard 1991; Fisch et al. 1982). Despite the failure of their methods, participants persist with their solution, not because they are mad, foolish or illogical, but because they conscientiously follow the wrong advice—namely, that 'If at first you don't succeed, try, try again' (Fisch et al. 1982).
- *Behaviour safeguards relationships.* The more complex explanation is that individuals behave as they do because their behaviour *works*. But, unlike with ABA, the behaviour works not so much by earning individuals something they want, but by perpetuating the rules of their interactions with others. Those relationships affected might be immediate ones—such as the relationship between

disruptive students and the teacher who is attempting to end the disruption—or more distant relationships, such as when students' behaviour at school engages their parents in solving the problem (Cooper & Upton 1990).

- *Causes do not matter.* A third point of view is offered by solution-focused therapy. This branch of systems theory takes little interest in how problems arise but focuses instead on how solutions can be developed (Nichols & Schwartz 1995). It has a future orientation, rather than an interest in the past (Molnar & de Shazer 1987; Murphy 1994), which focuses on what is happening rather than why (Watzlawick et al. 1974).

- *Internal problems.* Systems theory does not deny that students can have neurological impairments or learning difficulties that interfere with their performance at school (Murphy 1994). However, it recognises that a medical or educational intervention alone might not be enough to solve such problems. Systemic interventions can complement these other interventions by changing the interactions that surround students' difficulties—perhaps, for instance, by helping them comply with a necessary medical regime.

Thus, whereas individual theories start and stop with the individual, systems theory states that, if the individual level of understanding of the problem does not produce a solution, then you can expand your inquiry to students' other relationships in ever-widening circles: their interactions with teachers, with peers, with the school as an institution, the relationships between the family and school, relationships of the family with other community agencies. This expanding focus of inquiry is depicted in Figure 8.1.

Teacher–student status

Childhood is a time of restricted responsibility in which young people need adults to be in executive control of the system, while at the same time children are accountable for what they do (Combrinck-Graham 1991). Despite unequal responsibilities, however, children and adults nevertheless have equal rights.

Disciplinary role of the teacher

In terms of helping students to change dysfunctional behaviour, systems theory states that you will need to understand students' perspectives on their problems, empower them to solve these themselves rather than telling them what to do, and respect their ability to make decisions (Murphy 1994; Rhodes 1993). This theory

Figure 8.1   Systems in which to locate solutions

believes that the more you try to coerce change, the more others will resist (Cooper & Upton 1991). It also asks you to consider your own role in the life of disruptive behaviour. These philosophies fit within a humanist approach to discipline.

Systems theory sees that the problem is not the disruptive behaviour itself, but the fact that you are having to respond to it so often, producing a recurring cycle of (student) action and (teacher) reaction. The problem is not the dancers, but the dance in which they are engaging. Given that you cannot change others—in this case, your students—your job is to respond in new ways to their repetitive behaviour and thus break the cycle surrounding it.

Key systemic concepts

Despite their different intervention methods, all branches of systems theory share some fundamental philosophies. These are contrasted with the philosophy of individual theories in Table 8.1.

Multiple views of reality

Think about the various maps of a country: there are road maps, geophysical maps that indicate mineral deposits, and elevation maps which show heights above sea level, to name but a few. If I were to ask you which one of these maps is the best, you would surely answer that it depends on your purpose. If you want to pan for gold, a geophysical map would be useful; if you wanted to hike in the mountains, a map which showed elevations would be helpful in locating the hills; and if you wanted to plan a road tour from Adelaide to Darwin, then neither of these maps would be ideal: instead, the road map would be best.

So it is with our verbal 'maps' or explanations of the behaviours of other people. Systems theory accepts that 'different people see the same thing differently' (Cooper

Table 8.1   Assumptions of individual versus solution-focused theories

Individual theories	Solution-focused theory
School problems are someone's fault: students, parents or teachers.	School problems are not due to anyone's deficiencies: problems just *happen*.
The problem is the student's behaviour.	The problem is the interaction between the student and the adults who are responding to the behaviour.
The student's behaviour has to change.	The interaction pattern has to change, because it inadvertently maintains the problem, despite being aimed at resolving it.
Once we know the cause of a problem, we are better able to solve it.	Understanding the 'cause' of a problem does not necessarily imply how to solve it. What maintains it may be different from what started it.
If the present solution is not working, do more of it. (Be more consistent.)	If the present solution is not working, stop it and try something different. (Change a losing game.)

Source: adapted from Durrant (1995)

& Upton 1991: 26). Furthermore, any view might be 'the truth', although not all views are equally *useful*. When we are trying to help other people to change, the views that are least helpful are those that describe how they *cannot* change, such as explanations that blame the behaviour on the past or students' personality, both of which are difficult to alter. So, even though these explanations might be 'true', systems theorists do not use them because they are not useful *for the purposes of helping someone change*.

In short, systems theory maintains that there are many ways of looking at the same events and that, when choosing one interpretation to guide our actions, we might as well choose one that is helpful. We, therefore, do not have to find out the 'facts' of the situation. While this is highly subjective, it is not necessary to assess 'reality' because participants act *as if* their explanations *are* reality, and so it is enough to understand how they perceive events (Fine 1992).

Cooperation

When students and teachers are caught up over long periods of time in repetitive cycles of action and reaction, it is a safe bet that they both feel victimised by the other's behaviour. The student complains of being picked on and that it is 'unfair'. Teachers do likewise (although perhaps using more mature terms). This realisation allows us to begin to see the situation from the student's point of view (as well as our own)—without excusing the behaviour, of course.

This is the principle of cooperation: we need to view the situation from the other person's perspective. The first step for doing so, as I have just said, is being aware that everyone within the system is feeling victimised. The second step is recognising that people stop a behaviour when it does not work for them. The fact that the behaviour is continuing is a sure sign that it is working in some way for the student, albeit at considerable (and often escalating) personal cost.

In the language of other therapies, cooperation is called *empathy*. However, rather than being directed only at the individual, the systemic practitioner's understanding focuses on individuals' predicament as individuals *and* as a group, both now and in their history (Perry 1993).

An extension of the concept of cooperation is that, when students seem to be resisting our attempts to help or teach them, this is simply because our attempts are misdirected: we will need to change our approach, instead of asking the students to change (Molnar 1986). When they appear to be 'resisting' us, they are actually cooperating with rules in other relationships, such as when a student is under-achieving out of loyalty to his parents' beliefs that school is 'a waste of time'.

Cooperating with students' perspective and refusing to continue to struggle with them about their behaviour often has two effects: first, they may feel understood for the first time; and, second, they may begin cooperating with you in return (Molnar & Lindquist 1989).

Circular causality

Individual theories believe that the problem resides within individuals. On this basis, they set about assessing what the problem is, and almost inevitably find that there is something 'wrong' academically or emotionally with students whose behaviour is disruptive or dysfunctional. Sometimes, students are said to behave as they do because they 'are aggressive', have been abused, have a learning difficulty, have a difficult home life . . . or whatever. The trouble with this sort of explanation is that it is static: it tells you how these young people *are* and so says that they can*not* change, instead of that they *can*.

Moreover, individual explanations are linear: they contend that cause A leads to event B (Fisch et al. 1982)—for instance, that students' learning difficulties cause them to become discouraged and behave disruptively. This linear explanation implies that, if only we could find out a cause, we could arrive at a solution. In contrast, systems theorists argue that, even when you can find a cause, you still may not find a solution. The cause may be virtually untreatable, such as a central auditory processing difficulty; or what started the problem may not necessarily be what is maintaining it now. Or the search for the cause may take up so much time and resources that there is no time left over for intervention (J.E. Brown 1986).

In contrast, systems theory believes the problem is that, over and over again, you are having to respond to a student's disruptive behaviour and, over and over again, your correction has little or no effect. There is a recurring cycle in which the student disrupts, you attempt to correct the behaviour, the student responds to correction, you respond to that reaction . . . and so on. Both parties to this interaction believe that their behaviour is justified in light of the behaviour of the other person, but this self-righteousness does not help to resolve the problem (Cooper & Upton 1991).

When the issue is circular in this way, the search for the initial cause is both fruitless and unnecessary, because there *is* no beginning or end in a circle. What an observer regards as a cause, and what as an effect, is purely arbitrary. Instead, systems theorists look at what is *maintaining* the problem. They believe that the attempts at correction, despite being intended to repair the situation, are in fact maintaining the problem. This is no one's fault: it just *happens*.

So systems theory looks sideways, outwards from students to their interactions with other people, at what is going on *around* them, first in the immediate interactions and, if that is unsuccessful, in the next most immediate relationships, and so on until a solution can be found (see Figure 8.1 on p. 165).

Neutrality

Systems need both stability and the ability to change. Our survival—as individuals and as groups—demands that we achieve a balance between having to cope with too much change, and being so inflexible that we cannot adapt to new circumstances. This tension means that, if an outside force demands that we change, we will attempt to regain balance by favouring staying as we are.

The *principle of neutrality* states that, to avoid activating this rebalancing manoeuvre, you must not argue that students should change their behaviour. This, however, is not the same as having no bias. You can point out to troublesome students that change is difficult and risky: it may not be successful; whereas their present behaviour works to some extent, even though it has its penalties. If they continue as they are, they will maintain the benefits that the behaviour presently achieves—say, high status with a delinquent peer group—but at a personal cost to themselves.

On the other hand, in the fervent belief that they are making a mistake, you can point out how you are gravely concerned about their ultimate decision. But, at the same time, you can add that you are aware that there is nothing you can do to force their decision one way or the other. The choice between their two options is theirs alone.

This may seem dishonest. It *feels* as if you would have more success if you tried to talk them into changing their ways, but democratic theories believe that no one can coerce another to change, while systems theory extends this principle to say that the harder you try to coerce, the more students will resist in an attempt to stay stable. All you would do is set up a vicious cycle that solves nothing.

A cautionary note: neutrality is *not* the same as reverse psychology. With reverse psychology, you do not believe the suggestion and are trying to arrange for the other person to behave in a certain way; the principle of neutrality requires that you believe what you are suggesting.

Avoid more of the same

Although a range of solutions—such as chastising students, using detention or time out, sending them to the principal's office and sending notes home to the parents—may already have been tried, these usually all have the same theme: they are trying to discourage the disruptive behaviour. This type of change is called first-order change, whereby your solutions are actually more of the same class. In contrast, second-order change refers to a change of type. When driving uphill, you can depress the accelerator pedal harder (first-order change), or you can change down a gear (second-order change).

Most previous solution attempts will have been directed at getting the student to stop the behaviour. Given that the behaviour is continuing, this approach has clearly failed and, therefore, you will avoid using the same class of interventions again.

'From little things, big things grow'

These words of singer Paul Kelly introduce the final crucial concept of systems theory—namely, that even when a problem has assumed massive proportions, it nevertheless does not need a big solution (Kral 1988). Your intervention does not have to be elaborate: it only needs to be different from the old, repetitive, unsuccessful attempts at a solution (de Shazer et al. 1986). A new way of relating to disruptive students can change your relationship with them and, in turn, will change the problem.

Just as a skeleton key will open many locks, a particular intervention may be suitable for many different problems. This is the principle of *equifinality* or, in colloquial terms, the principle that 'there is more than one way to skin a cat'.

Solution-oriented interventions

Solution-oriented practitioners have a simple explanation of repeated behavioural difficulties: they believe that problems endure because they have not yet been solved. The attempts at a solution have not worked, so something else needs to be done.

Decide whom to involve

Because there is no beginning or end in the repeated cycle of interaction that surrounds chronic disruptive behaviour, and because no one can make anyone else change, and because a teacher is always more powerful in the school hierarchy than students, the point where you will choose to intervene in this repetitive cycle is with *yourself*. In most instances, you are the one who is most concerned about the difficulty. In solution-focused terms, you are the 'customer'.

Often parents or other school staff are distressed but feel powerless to act. Their role is that of reporters or 'informants' who can give you information but will not be directly involved in the solution (Rhodes 1993).

With regard to the involved students, it is unlikely that you would attempt to change them, for three reasons. First, they may not be motivated to change, in which case they are called the 'visitor'. You cannot change visitors, only customers. Second, most previous interventions would have tried to change students and these have failed, so you should not do more of the same. Third, within the context of chronic problems, students are the least powerful members of their home and school systems and so should not be the direct focus of intervention unless no other focus is possible (Amatea 1989).

Define the problem

As already mentioned, in your description of the problem, you will include both the student's behaviour and your response. You have been caught up in doing 'the same damn thing over and over' (de Shazer et al. 1986: 210) and *that* is the problem. The problem is defined as being interpersonal rather than being due to any individual's personal deficiency.

Define the goal

It is easier to get somewhere if you know where you want to go (de Shazer et al. 1986). Your job will be to help students and yourself define how you will know when the behaviour has improved, and in what ways the improvement will be different from the presenting pattern. The goals must be small, realistically achievable and stated in specific, concrete, behavioural and measurable terms (Berg & de Shazer 1989). Goals need to specify what you want to see continue, rather than what behaviour you want stopped, because the absence of something is difficult to notice. Some questions that can help students or yourself to clarify your goals are:

- 'Think about the best student you could be—the ideal you. Make sure that it is possible, and give that person 100 points. Now tell me, how many points would you give yourself at the moment?' (Kral 1989a: 62).
- 'On a scale of 1 to 10, rate how happy you are with how many points you have just given yourself' (Kral 1989a: 62). (This will tell you how motivated a student is to change his or her behaviour.)
- 'When you move from (your present rating) to (a higher rating), what will be different? What will have changed? What will you be doing differently? Have you ever been (at the higher rating) before? If so, what was happening then? What is the highest you've ever been on the scale? What was happening then?' (Kral 1989a: 63).
- 'What are the chances that you could (behave as if you were at a higher rating) again (or now)?'.
- 'How will you know that you are making progress? What will the first signs be?' (Rhodes 1993: 30).
- 'When this problem is solved, what will be happening that is different from what is happening now?' (Rhodes 1993: 28).
- If you are questioning another teacher, you could ask: 'How do you think this problem could be solved? If you had all the resources you needed, what would these be and how would they help?' (Rhodes 1993: 30).

Such questions provide clues about what students could do to change what is happening, or about what they are already doing that they can do more of (Rhodes 1993). Using scales to report on progress helps them to recognise small improvements and avoids the either/or thinking that 'either I'm depressed or I'm not', when obviously there are shades in between (de Shazer & Molnar 1984). Finally, using 'when' rather than 'if' in your questioning sends a clear message that this problem is solvable (Rhodes 1993).

Examine exceptions

When a problem has been occurring for a long time, those involved mistakenly believe that it is 'always' happening (Bonnington 1993). But this is an illusion: change is inevitable (Chang & Phillips 1993; Kral 1988). There will always be times when the problem is not occurring or is happening less often (Rhodes 1993) and you can expect these times to continue (de Shazer & Molnar 1984).

You will need to ask about these instances, so that together you and the student can identify what features allow these exceptions to happen. This discussion will help to ascertain:

- times that students have overcome similar problems;
- whether students think that the exceptions are flukes or are within their control;
- whether students already knew the solution but have been forgetting to use it. Such solutions are easy to do again (Rhodes 1993).

The process from here has branched options: you might find it useful as you read on to refer to Figure 8.2 (p. 175) so that you can see the pathway that your decisions can take.

Practising (or continuing) success

If your questioning has been able to elucidate what makes exceptions possible, you simply need to encourage students to use these successful strategies more often. Once they are managing this, you can use a technique that is termed 'positive blame' that asks 'How did you get that to happen?' (Kral 1989b). In this way, you give students responsibility for improvements (Kral 1989b).

Observation tasks

A second possibility is that students are not able to identify what brings about the exceptions. If they believe that the exceptions are just flukes, you can give them the task of predicting whether the flukes are likely to occur more or less often (Molnar & de Shazer 1987).

If students feel that they could control exceptions but do not yet know how, you could give them the task of paying attention to what they do when they overcome the urge to engage in the dysfunctional behaviour (Molnar & de Shazer 1987).

Formulate potential exceptions

Sometimes students are determined that the problem *is* always happening: they cannot identify any exceptions. In that case, you will need to examine what *potential* exceptions would look like. You can do this by asking the miracle question: 'Suppose one night while you slept, a miracle happened, and the complaint was solved: what would you notice was different when you woke up?'

Conduct experiments

Now that students can conceive of potential exceptions, you can give them the following experimental tasks:

- Do something that *potentially* could help.
- In the morning, rate the possibility that you might avoid the urge to perform the problematic behaviour that day and, after school, check whether your prediction was correct. If it was, what did you do to bring that about? (Kral 1989b). This makes explicit those useful things that the student inadvertently does (Kral 1989b).
- Pretend that the problem has improved by acting 'as if' the miracle/solution/goal has been achieved. This, you can explain, is not a change as such: it is only trying change on, to see if it suits.

Durrant (1995: 94) gives the example of inviting a student to act *as if* he did not feel like throwing things at the other students, was having fun and was enjoying his work. In that case, the teacher's task was to attempt to guess when the student was pretending and when he was not. This allowed the teacher to observe those times when the student's behaviour had improved, instead of naturally focusing on the disruptions, and so to change how he related to the student. It also adds an element of fun, which is particularly engaging with young people.

Structured tasks

If students cannot even conceive that exceptions could ever occur, you could give them some structured tasks such as keeping a diary, perhaps using scaling techniques to help them recognise naturally occurring events that are positive and thus represent exceptions to the problem; or you could ask them to think about how come their problem is no worse than it is: what is keeping it from becoming even more serious? (Molnar & de Shazer 1987).

Conclusion: Solution-focused therapy

The above steps are summarised in Figure 8.2. This is not meant to be a prescription for your interventions, but merely a pictorial representation of some options. Clearly, it is a simplification of the processes of helping students with chronic problems: if it were always that straightforward, there would be few problems remaining. But it can offer a framework for new initiates to this theory, from which more sophisticated approaches can grow as you gain more knowledge of the methods.

Figure 8.2   Solution-focused steps for resolving students' behavioural difficulties

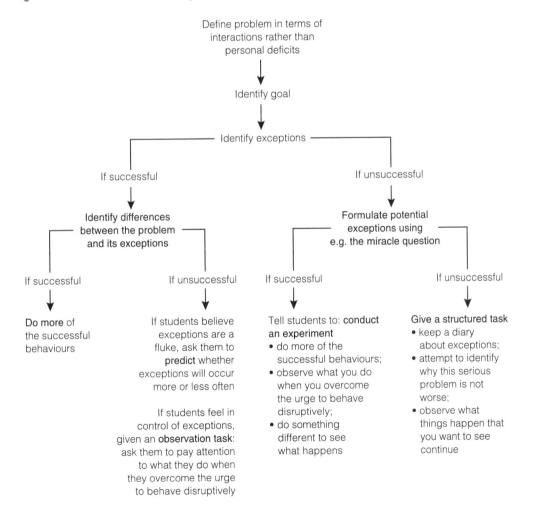

Source: Molnar and de Shazer (1987: 354)

Strategic interventions

A second branch of systems theory, brief strategic therapy, believes that school behavioural problems arise because somehow they safeguard a student's relationships. If the more simple solution-focused interventions have not worked, it could pay to consider this possibility and use some strategic interventions as well.

Reframing

You explain behaviour in terms that seem most logical to you, depending on your experience and training. You then respond to the behaviour in ways suggested by your explanation. However, when a problem has become chronic, this is a clue that your understanding of it is not helping (Molnar & Lindquist 1989). Your present solution attempts are failing because they are based on an explanation that has remained stable over time, producing in turn interventions that have remained the same over time. A new solution will require a new way of looking at the problem.

The technique for changing your description or explanation of a problem is termed *reframing*. Just as an old photo looks different in a new picture frame, so too an old pattern takes on new meanings when you explain (or 'frame') the problem differently. Building on the concept of cooperation, reframing embodies the belief that problem behaviour can be legitimately interpreted in a variety of ways (Molnar & Lindquist 1989).

The new understanding of the behaviour must be plausible to the participants, fit the interactions that surround the behaviour, and help to design an intervention (Watzlawick et al. 1974). If it does not, then you need to generate yet another view that is more useful. The new interpretations are usually positive because, if we are critical of others, they are less likely to change. At the same time, however, the reframe must not downplay the significance of the complaint, because to call it something nice without implying a solution would only allow the disruptive behaviour to continue unabated, which is against the interests of all participants.

The following are the steps involved in reframing (Molnar & Lindquist 1989).

Step 1: Define what is occurring. Detail in specific behavioural terms what the student does, when and in what circumstances. Identify who is involved in attempts to correct the behaviour, what the complaint entails, how that is a problem and to whom it is a problem (Fisch et al. 1982). In so doing, the aim is not to find diagnostic explanations, but simply to understand how the problem is manifested.

Step 2: Describe your corrective measures. Next, describe what your attempt at correction usually involves and what effect that has. Think of this effect in interactional terms, not in individual terms, however: look at what the corrective measures do to the student's *relationships*.

Step 3: Identify your present explanation for the student's behaviour. You will respond differently to the same behaviours, depending on what you think they *mean*. Your beliefs about the behaviour will account for why you have attempted some solutions and not others, and will explain why the problem has persisted (Amatea 1989). By observing your interactions with the student, you are likely to identify either of the following beliefs (Amatea 1989).

- The student is 'doing it deliberately'. This explanation is usually used when young people are aggressive and appear not to care about the effects of their actions (Morgenson 1989). Teachers usually find such an attitude intolerable and feel victimised, angry and frustrated by the behaviour (Amatea & Sherrard 1989).

  When you believe that students are disrupting deliberately, you usually try to make them stop. You might use a whole range of ways to achieve this—such as rewards for more appropriate behaviour, loss of privileges for disruptive behaviour, punishments such as playground litter duty, detention (sometimes called 'time out') or reprimands from the principal—but the thrust of all these responses is to make students stop the behaviour. They are all 'more of the same' approach. And they lead to more of the same responses from students, most of which can be characterised as Gordon's (1991) three Rs of 'resistance, rebellion or retaliation'.

- The behaviour is involuntary. The belief that the student concerned cannot help the behaviour is likeliest with passive behaviours such as mood disturbances, phobic reactions or learning disabilities (Amatea & Sherrard 1989) and when students seem to have a problem with how they are behaving (Morgenson 1989).

  If students believe that they cannot help themselves, they avoid taking charge of the problem. When *you* believe that they cannot help how they behave, you will be too solicitous and will avoid making demands on them in the belief that they could not cope with higher expectations (Amatea & Sherrard 1989). You may blame their parents, setting up a struggle between you and them whereby they think you are not doing enough for their child and you become exasperated with them (Amatea & Sherrard 1989).

Guided by the belief that students cannot help themselves, you are likely to exercise inappropriate patience which excuses students from behaving more considerately, alternated with frustration and exasperation which demands that they 'pull their socks up'. The mixed message is seldom effective: students shift back and forward between feeling so comfortable that they are not motivated to change, alternated with feeling picked on, against which they rebel.

Step 4: Create a range of positive alternative explanations. This is the reframing step. You will be looking at the effect that the behaviour has on the students' relationships: the immediate and, if necessary, more distant ones (see Figure 8.1 on p. 165). In so doing, you will be replacing explanations that have been critical of students with positive alternatives. This is termed 'positive connotation'. You can positively connote:

- students' *personalities*: students who have been labelled as lazy could instead be described as being expert at getting others to do things for them; a 'crazy' person could instead be described as eccentric (Haley 1980) or as an expert at failing;
- students' *motives*: students who are clowning around in class could be termed 'defiant' or 'attention seeking' but you could equally well interpret this behaviour positively by observing that they are sacrificing themselves by being willing to entertain the class, even when it gets them into trouble. The reframe does not imply their *intent*, but simply describes an *outcome* of the behaviour;
- *effects of the behaviour*: few acts are completely negative; it is just a matter of finding the positive effects. For example, students who do not complete their homework create little marking for you. Therefore, you can simply thank them for contributing to your lighter workload (as long as you can do so sincerely). Again, this is a focus on outcomes rather than intentions.

This reframing step can be difficult because you will not want to appear to be lowering your standards by cooperating with a negative behaviour, or may find it hard to see anything other than the negative aspects of the problem. However, fixed views of the problem have brought about fixed solutions, so a change in approach can only be achieved by a change in thinking.

Step 5: Select a positive explanation that will seem plausible and honest to those involved with the problem.

Step 6: Describe this new explanation in a sentence or two. You may or may not communicate your new understanding to the student concerned, because insight is not necessary for change to take place.

Step 7: Act in a way suggested by the new explanation. Because the problematic behaviour has unwittingly been maintained by the attempted solutions, the aim of a new view of the problem is to enable you to let go of an ineffective solution so that you can try another one instead (Fisch et al. 1982). You have now given the problem a new meaning and so can no longer respond to it in the old way.

An example of reframing

A boy in his last year of primary school frequently became violent at school, to the point where his mother would be asked to come to school and settle him down. This had been occurring around twice a week for the past three years.

To solve this problem, I followed the steps just outlined, beginning by defining the problem as the child's aggression *and* the teachers' unsuccessful corrective measures. The next step was to examine why these measures were not working, for which we needed to identify the school's explanation for the child's behaviour. This was that the boy had been sexually abused by his father and was emotionally disturbed as a result. This sympathetic understanding of his predicament might have been an accurate explanation of events but *it wasn't helping*. Therefore, we needed an alternative explanation (a reframe).

The mother reported that, when she had found out that her husband was abusing his sons (then aged six and four years), she expelled him from the household. Subsequently, the mother experienced what she characterised as a nervous breakdown. The boy's problems began at this time. His mother was now well in command of her life, yet the problems with her son continued, verifying to the individually focused adults that he was emotionally scarred by his early experiences.

In generating a reframe, I was aware that there is always one well-meaning but misguided relative who, when a child's father leaves, tries to alleviate his distress with the notion that he is 'the man of the house' now. Instead of comforting a child, however, this platitude results in the theft of his childhood. When his father left, this young lad was aged six, at which time he began taking care of his mother.

Recall that the sequence in this case was that the boy acted up at school and his mother was called in to sort him out. So, with this sequence in mind, the reframe went like this: When your job is to look after your mother, you and she must be together. When you are a school student, you are not allowed to leave the school grounds. So what is your only alternative? The answer is obvious: ensure that your mother visits the school so that you can check that she is okay. Once you have done that, she is free to leave again.

Thus the reframe was that he was maintaining the habit of being head of the household, even though it was no longer necessary. The child was a caring son who was looking after his mother.

The final step was to act in a new way suggested by the reframe. In this case, the mother thanked her son for being willing to sacrifice his childhood by looking after her. He was clearly an honourable and loyal child and would grow into a fine and gentle man. Next, she told him that she was able to look after herself again now and wanted to look after him too. And, as he did not have a father who could teach him how to grow up to be an honourable young man, he now needed to stop looking after his mother and devote himself to learning how to be a man.

Meanwhile, at school, the teachers developed a new respect for the boy and could understand his perspective better. Their increased care and respect for the boy was, in turn, communicated to him indirectly and supported him in his efforts to change.

Comments on the example

The reframe of events in this case is no more accurate than the first explanation that the child was emotionally disturbed. But we could not cure emotional disturbance. We could not change past events or how he felt about them, even with access to trained counsellors. And while counselling was taking place, the school would still be having to deal with his disruptions. In contrast, the second explanation implies that the earlier family difficulties still had a life in the mind of this young person: he still felt that he had to look after his mother. Thus our task was to change how he understood the events *now*, so that he could change how he presently acted.

Pattern interruption

Let's say that the simple 'reframe' of the child's situation in the above example did not produce a change. In that case, we could use another strategic intervention, perhaps selecting 'pattern interruption' (Durrant 1995). With this approach, you allow the disruptive behaviour to continue, on the understanding *that* it is helping the student in some way, even if you do not understand *how*. In line with the principle of cooperation, you cannot frustrate that legitimate goal, but you *can* insist that the resulting behaviour becomes less disruptive to others (Molnar & Lindquist 1989).

There is an old saying that a chain is only as strong as its weakest link. With this in mind, we can break up the chain of events, producing a new pattern—that is, a new interaction. The old rules will be broken and, in their place, a new interaction sequence will be born. We can disrupt the pattern when we (de Shazer et al. 1986; Durrant 1995):

- change its location;
- change who is involved;
- change the sequence of the steps involved;
- add a new element;
- introduce random starting and stopping;
- increase the frequency of the pattern.

To remind ourselves, the pattern in the above example was that the child disrupted in class, his teacher became exasperated, the parent was called in, calmed the child, and then left. Without detailing all the options, possibilities for pattern interruption include: allowing the child to go home at lunchtime to check on his mother (change the *location*); insisting that he go home at both recess and lunchtimes to check on her (increasing the *frequency*) until he realises that there is no need to continue to verify her safety; allowing him to call his mother into the school at times when his behaviour is fine (changing the *sequence* of the steps) so that he can remain at school without behaving disruptively, while still checking on his mother; or, with the same aim, asking his mother to visit the school whenever she has a free minute (introducing *random starting and stopping*).

Maybe only one of these options will work and there is no way of knowing ahead of time which one it will be. It will take some intuitive judgment and trial and error to choose an approach and to change it if it appears not to be working. But that is better than the single option that was being applied before—namely, trying to get the child to stop the disruptions.

A more everyday example is of the student who continually leaves her seat. Instead of resisting this behaviour, you can assume that the young person needs to do this, even though you do not know why. So you can give her permission to continue with it but with some modifications so that her movement around the room does not disrupt others. You might, for instance, invite her to move about before activities begin, instead of during them.

Reversals

Unlike reframing that is based on changing our thinking about the problem, reversals merely involve doing the opposite of previous responses, regardless of whether you understand why that might help. The use of reversals is based on the belief that, if present responses to students' difficulties were going to work, they would have by now. So, instead of trying to be more consistent in your response, you will need to do something different. In the words of Fisch and colleagues (1982: 88): 'Always change a losing game' or, more simply: 'If something isn't working, stop doing it.'

For students who you thought could not help their behaviour, an opposite response will involve looking for exceptions; for students who you thought were being deliberately disruptive, you would stop coercion and use pattern interruption. Your new solution will work as long as it can be readily incorporated into your daily routine and can happen often enough to have an impact on the behaviour.

Compress time

Instead of generating a different response for each of a constellation of behaviours, you can describe them all as belonging to one pattern, which you might call a 'career' or pathway in life. This technique is called 'compression of time' because, in the here-and-now, you describe how the student's behaviour was, is and will develop in the future.

For instance, rather than dealing with a full gamut of aggressive and disruptive acts, you could describe an aggressive student as having a career as a delinquent, as long as this is not done in a scolding way that tells the student to stop the behaviour. (Violation of the principle of neutrality will activate the student's reasons for not changing.)

Collaborating with parents

There are three types of school-related behavioural difficulties: problems in the family that disturb the school; problems at school that disturb the family; and problems at school that do not disturb the family (Lindquist et al. 1987). Nevertheless, you will concentrate only on school-based problems in the recognition that family counselling is not a teacher's role and realising that improvements at school will resound to the family anyway (Amatea 1989).

When communicating with parents, systems theory advises that you avoid all criticism of them, encourage their cooperation and confirm their status as family leaders who have the skills to solve their own difficulties. This is a significant reversal of the pattern of uncooperative and unproductive relationships between families and school that often becomes entrenched when students have a school-based behavioural problem (Lindquist et al. 1987; Lusterman 1985).

Collaborating with other professionals

If parents are involved with other agencies, you will need to cooperate with these professionals so that you do not undermine each other's attempts at a solution. The results of a lack of collaboration between professionals can be that the problem remains unchanged among the confusion, and that each agency applies the same unsuccessful solution. The family's chaos is mirrored by a chaotic helping system (Reder 1983) which perpetuates and even adds to the family's difficulties.

Steps for success

The following steps provide a guide to the use of systemic interventions.

- *Start small.* Because a small change can have a significant impact, you can start by aiming for a small improvement and by working on small problems rather than crises (Molnar & Lindquist 1989).
- *Be sincere.* In order to use systemic ideas sincerely, you will need to believe that there *are* many ways to view a problem, all equally hypothetical, and that any one view is as likely to be true as any other. To be able to persist with an intervention, you need to believe in the new view on which it is based, or else you might revert to the old management method, which would appear hypocritical.
- *Storm the back door.* Molnar and Lindquist (1989) use this term to refer to an indirect way to build more constructive relationships with students. Without focusing at all on the particular behaviour that is causing concern, you can

acknowledge something positive or neutral about the students' behaviour. Because all interactions are linked, changing any one interaction—even when it has nothing to do with the problem—changes the relationship and so changes the problem.

- *Go slowly.* Often, desperation leads to a sense of urgency about finding a solution. However, if a solution were that obvious, the participants would have found it long ago. Therefore, when using a systems approach, you will need to buy time and not let yourself be pressured into acting prematurely (Fisch et al. 1982).

- *Harness outsiders' skills.* Systemic interventions may appear illogical to outsiders and so you will need to lay the groundwork carefully with other staff (Amatea 1989). If they remain sceptical, they can unwittingly sabotage your intervention. To avoid this, you can ask a sceptic to be the impartial observer who is charged with identifying any changes in the student's behaviour. This person's scepticism is useful because he or she will not imagine that changes are occurring when they are not and this data can then inform subsequent steps of the intervention.

- *Use humour.* Chronic problems can make participants feel desperate and will generate inflexible solutions (Molnar & Lindquist 1989). Instead, finding humour in an intense situation may in itself solve the problem—or at least be a vehicle for doing so.

- *Notice change.* Once an intervention has begun, it is crucial to notice changes, even those that do not appear to be related to the problem or its solution. Because chronic problems represent a lack of change, students may revert to old patterns if no one notices their progress. On the other hand, you should not praise improvements because that argues for change (is not neutral), and might actually provoke a return to old patterns. When change has not occurred, you can compare bad days with worse days and ask about what creates the difference (McLeod 1989).

- *Borrow approaches from other theories.* Systems theory provides a new way of looking at a stale problem. Once you have generated a new view of the problem, you can use any treatment approach that fits within the new perspective. You might, for instance, set up a contract for restricted practice of the behaviour under a pattern interruption approach. You might use notes home to parents to highlight progress (as long as you remain neutral). Or you might formalise your instructions and feedback to the student if, when you observed exceptions, you identified that the student required more academic structure.

Whenever an intervention is borrowed from another theory but is applied for a different reason, its flavour will be different, and so can be expected to have very different effects.

- *Check the technique.* If the intervention is less than successful, check that you implemented it correctly and that you were sincere. After an initial attempt, did you revert to old ways of responding? If the intervention was accurate, you will have to persist with it, or you may need to generate yet another view of the problem.

- *Try another approach.* When an intervention is failing, ask if there is another part of the system that should be involved (see Figure 8.1 on p. 165). When a school problem stems from home, a school focus might fail because it does not involve the key participants. You will need to recognise the signs of this source of failure and, if suspected, invite the family to consult a family therapist.

- *Warn about relapses.* Occasionally, a problem fights back and relapses occur (Kowalski 1990), which can unnerve and discourage participants. To help students handle relapses, you can predict these in advance. Kral (1989b) calls this 'Flagging the minefield'. You can advise them that relapses are normal ways in which they test themselves to see if they can 'get back on track' (Kowalski 1990). Next, remind them of the strategies that they used to overcome the problem in the first place and encourage them to resume using those (Kowalski 1990).

Problems that are not suited to systemic interventions

You should use the simplest intervention that is likely to work, and employ more complex strategies only when others have failed (Amatea 1989; Walsh & McGraw 1996). Systems theory is not appropriate for certain problems, such as when students are in emotional turmoil from a recent trauma; where their families are so disorganised that students lack the stability needed to learn predictable behaviour—in which case, specialist family intervention is necessary; or when the students' difficulties are due to specific learning deficits that need educational remediation (Amatea 1989; Murphy 1994). However, young people sometimes behave more helplessly than their condition warrants (Frey 1984), and therefore a systemic intervention might help students to cooperate with other forms of intervention (Rhodes 1993).

Summary

The systems perspective is a circular view of the world. Whereas individual psychological theories see the individual as a whole made up of parts, systems theory sees the individual as being part of a larger whole. Robinson (1980: 187) confirms this, noting that the whole is more than the sum of its parts and saying that: 'Any attempt to understand the "whole" by breaking it down into its component "parts" will always miss the nature of the relationship between the "parts" and the quality of their interaction.'

Although many of the approaches of systems theory could be explained using the framework of other theorists covered in this text, Molnar and Lindquist (1989) advise against the transfer of ideas. They assert that using ideas from individually based theories could perpetuate your present description of problem behaviours, in turn maintain the present solution, and so maintain the problem. Instead, when these theories have not suggested a solution, you will need to try something different. In the words of de Shazer and colleagues (1986: 212):

> If something works, do more of it. (Look for exceptions.)
> If something isn't working, stop it. (Do less of the same.)
> If something isn't working, do something else. (Do something different.)

Case study

Adam is seven. He has difficulty with reading, spelling and writing, although he enjoys and is capable at maths. During non-maths lessons, you have noticed that he spends a considerable amount of time off-task, when he frequently disrupts the other students. This is worse in the afternoon than in the morning.

He is in a composite class of six- and seven-year-olds. He spends most of his play time with the younger children. Frequently a pair which includes Adam is apprehended during play times doing such things as harassing passers-by from an out-of-bounds area of the playground which is close to the street, rifling through rubbish bins for food or cans to swap for other items with students, or engaging in fights in and around the toilets.

He seems bemused by the trouble he gets into, usually saying when challenged that he doesn't know why he behaves in these inappropriate ways, that he couldn't remember a given behaviour was against the rules, or that the other child was at fault for suggesting the activity.

Until a recent assessment, it was believed that Adam behaved as he did because of low academic ability. However, a battery of tests has shown his overall ability (IQ) to be average, with his maths skills in the high–normal range and his reading and spelling skills, while delayed, still within the lower range of normal limits. Teaching staff are now at a loss to find a new explanation for his behaviour.

A systemic response

Step 1: Define the problem. The previous individually based explanation of Adam's behaviour suggested that he had some learning difficulties that made it difficult for him to take responsibility for his own behaviour. Now you will define the problem as including not only Adam's behaviour but the irritating need for you to respond to it. The problem is the repetitive interactions that occur when Adam behaves inappropriately.

Step 2: Identify who is involved (roles). Adam has least power in the school system and, with respect to his behaviour, could be said to be a visitor, as he is not concerned about it. Therefore, as the main person concerned about the behaviour, the one who most often responds to it and the one most able to make a difference to it, you will regard yourself as the customer.

You will engage Adam's parents as informants about how he behaves at home, what he tells them about the reasons for his school difficulties, what they find works with him, and so on. This information will help you to generate a solution.

Step 3: Define the goals. You would like Adam to achieve more and for his behaviour to disrupt other students less often. You would also like to be able to stop reminding Adam of school rules.

Step 4: Examine exceptions. Adam remembers his swimming gear (and Adam loves swimming)—and yet cannot remember school rules. This demonstrates that he does not have a learning or memory problem, but that he lacks motivation to remember certain things. He also remembers to play inside the designated play areas when there is an organised game such as soccer in which he can participate skilfully. As to his school work, he seldom distracts during maths, indicating once again that he is able to work conscientiously when motivated.

Step 5: Identify causes of the exceptions. Let's say that, during your discussion with Adam, he recognises the above exceptions but cannot explain why they occur. He thinks that they 'just happen'.

Step 6: Allocate a task. In that case, following the path in Figure 8.2, you would ask him to do an observation task to help him notice what is different at the times of an exception compared to the times when the problem occurs. You could ask Adam each morning to predict what sort of a day he will have at school that day (on a scale of 1 to 10) and then, if his prediction is on target, ask him to note that afternoon what he did to make the prediction come true.

Step 7: Reframing. Until the recent assessment, you had thought that Adam had significant learning difficulties that caused his off-task behaviour and made it difficult for him to remember rules. On the other hand, at times you have also believed that Adam was being wilfully disruptive.

This caused you, at times, to try to force Adam to behave appropriately by coaxing and reminding him, sending notes home to his parents, trying to make them oversee homework activities and, when he had not done these, having him complete his work at recess. Although you thought that these responses were all different, you now realise that they have all been of the same class (*first-order solutions*). All have attempted to coerce compliance.

Looking at this from Adam's perspective, Adam almost certainly believes that you are picking on him. With this as his justification, he reacts by reasserting his autonomy in any way he can, most readily through disruptive acts.

At other times you have been patient and solicitous. However, your patience with Adam might have given him the impression that you think that he cannot do any better and is incompetent. If this were so, then his behaviour is only an implicit agreement with this judgment. Adam is conforming to your view of him. This is a new and more *positive connotation* of Adam's personality, which in the past has been described as non-compliant.

Step 8: Respond differently. You now accept that Adam's behaviour is understandable from his perspective. As a result, you can now be more positive with him and inject some humour and fun into your relationship with him and his peers. You might build a more constructive relationship with him (*storming the back door*), which in itself will be beneficial and will also give Adam confidence to try a new solution. You could make an extra effort to acknowledge Adam's achievements and thoughtful behaviour—without, however, praising these, as praise is not neutral.

Step 9: Do something different. The new reframe that Adam is agreeing with your low expectations could imply that you need to give him explicit directions about his work and how to remain on task, in the expectation that he can be more successful. However, you realise that this solution may be so similar to the previous coercive attempts that Adam might not be able to tell the difference. Therefore, you decide to be clear with Adam that you now realise two things: (1) that he is a capable lad (as evidenced by his assessment results); and (2) that he is in charge of his own behaviour. You will tell Adam that, from now on, you will refuse to remind and coax him, as he is able to remember when he chooses to.

Step 10: Pattern interruption. You understand that change is difficult, and that Adam's behaviour works for him, at least partially. Therefore, you will not force him to change it. At the time of Adam's disruptions, you will approach him quietly and reaffirm that he needs a way to cope with school pressures and, as this is the only way he knows, he must use it. At the same time, however, his coping strategy stresses the other students, and so you will invite him to withdraw from the room until he feels that he can cope again. He can do whatever he likes in a nearby area, and come back when he feels better, at which time he will be welcomed. (Note that this may look like ABA's time-out procedure, but it is merely time away from stress and is not a punishment: if it conveys the flavour of a punishment, it will fail.)

Step 11: Evaluate. If the new approach does not work, you will need to generate a different reframe. The number of new solutions or reframes is limited only by your imagination and so, in theory, any number can be tried until one is successful.

Alternatively, you could consult again with Adam's parents to determine whether a home-based problem might be causing the school difficulties, which might account for the lack of success of your intervention. If so, you could attempt to solve both sets of problems jointly or you may invite his parents to consult a family therapist.

Discussion questions

1 What is the significance of locating problems within relationships instead of within individuals?

2 In what ways do the solution-focused steps differ from the usual individually focused interventions?

3 Think about a student's behaviour with which you have been involved. How could it be reframed? What difference would the new view of the problem make to the type of response it received?

4 How would systems theory recommend you respond to the student in the case study that you generated in Chapter 2? What effect would its unique recommendations have on the individual student? On the whole class? On you?

Suggested further reading

For a description of systems theory and practice applied to student behaviour problems:

Amatea, E.S. 1989 *Brief strategic intervention for school behavior problems* Jossey-Bass, San Francisco, CA

Durrant, M. 1995 *Creative strategies for school problems* Eastwood Family Therapy Centre, Epping, NSW. Simultaneously published by W.W. Norton, New York

Molnar, A. and Lindquist, B. 1989 *Changing problem behaviour in schools* Jossey-Bass, San Francisco, CA

For some case studies unrelated to school-based problems but which give an introduction to the breadth of interventions used in systems theory:

Haley, J. 1973 *Uncommon therapy: the psychiatric techniques of Milton H. Erickson, M.D.* W.W. Norton, New York

——1980 *Leaving home: the therapy of disturbed young people* McGraw-Hill, New York

——1984 *Ordeal therapy* Jossey-Bass, San Francisco, CA

Lang, T. and Lang, M. 1986 *Corrupting the young (and other stories of a family therapist)* Rene Gordon, Melbourne

For an overview of the various models of systems theory and family therapy:

Walsh, W. M. and McGraw, J. A. 1996 *Essentials of family therapy: a therapist's guide to eight approaches* Love Publishing, Denver, CO

And for more detail on the various approaches:

Nichols, M.P. and Schwartz, R.C. 1995 *Family therapy: concepts and methods* 3rd edn, Allyn & Bacon, Boston, MA

9 Critique of the theories

There is a time to admire the grace and persuasive power of an influential idea, and there is a time to fear its hold over us. The time to worry is when the idea is so widely shared that we no longer even notice it, when it is so deeply rooted that it feels to us like plain common sense. At the point when objections are not answered anymore because they are no longer even raised, we are not in control: we do not have the idea; it has us.

Kohn (1993: 3)

Key points

- All theories say that they are effective—that is, they meet their goals. The question to ask is: what are their goals?
- Discipline policies and practices in schools are not selected in a vacuum but within the context of a society that marginalises and silences powerless groups—in this case, young people.
- Thus, while all theories have their strengths, we need to consider also what negative side-effects they may provoke for the recipients of their measures.

Introduction

Now that you are familiar with the main theories of discipline in schools, you can compare and contrast them so that, ultimately, you are able to judge which best suits your own style and circumstances. The first step to resolving the dilemmas about discipline in schools is to recognise that theories and their practices are political and problematical, with inherent values, assumptions and contradictions (Johnson et al. 1994). It is clear that:

- discipline practices are value-laden;
- practices reflect imbalances of political power—in our case, between adults and children;
- these imbalances are frequently legitimised—in the case of school discipline, on the grounds of the developmental incompetence of children;
- some groups are served by the maintenance of this power imbalance; in schools, children are marginalised and disadvantaged by them (Johnson et al. 1994).

All the theories have two basic assumptions in common: first, that teachers are obligated to be concerned and interested in students; second, that when responding to disruptive behaviour, you should remain calm (Lewis 1997). The debates, however, are how you define 'concern and interest' and what you actually *do* while being calm.

Effectiveness

Researching the effects of various teaching styles is fraught with difficulties, given the number of aspects of curricular content, teaching processes and classroom interactions that must be considered, and the number of student outcomes that could be measured (Kyriacou & Newson 1982). Yet, despite the paucity of evidence, all of the theories described in this text say that they work, which is to say that they achieve what they set out to achieve. But the question that is seldom asked is: 'What do they set out to achieve?'

Goals of discipline

Kohn (1996) argues that almost all school discipline programs set out to achieve students' compliance with teachers' instructions. Yet there are many reasons why this may be a dangerous aim. First, individual children are made unsafe, as obedient children will collude with abusive practices if an adult directs them to. Second, surrounding children are unsafe as a ringleader can direct peers (who have been trained to do as they are told) to pick on a student whom they regard as weaker than themselves. This is a common form of school bullying. Third, whole societies are unsafe when people who have been trained to comply carry out a despotic leader's orders to harm others (Gordon 1991). I once read (and the source is now lost to me) that the Holocaust did not occur because there were too many Nazis, but because there were too few Oscar Schindlers.

Thus obedience is never a goal of humanist discipline approaches. To require this is both ineffective (even dangerous) and unethical (Curwin & Mendler 1988; Gartrell 1987a; Gordon 1991; Kohn 1996). Adults do not have a divine right to make children comply with their commands, although they do have the right to ask for considerate behaviour, which at times will include a level of orderliness in classrooms so that everyone can function. But there is no need, under a humanist approach, to aim for orderliness as a separate goal: it is already subsumed under the educational goals of discipline.

Limit-setting approaches

Despite practitioner support for the limit-setting approaches, there is little research evidence verifying its effectiveness (Charles 1999). One well-designed study showed that assertive discipline achieved a decline in off-task behaviour from 12.5 per cent to 7.5 per cent (Canter 1989), but findings from other studies were less positive, especially when schools did not originally have extremely serious behavioural problems, in which case almost any discipline would have improved matters (Render et al. 1989). After institution of assertive discipline programs, studies found either neutral effects or increased referral rates for behavioural difficulties, detentions and truancy (Emmer & Aussiker 1990), with some studies reporting increases in students' negative behaviours and attitudes to school, including lowered student morale.

Applied behaviour analysis

A considerable body of research has demonstrated the effectiveness of ABA's methods (Alberto & Troutman 1999; Kaplan & Carter 1995), although mainly with people with severe intellectual disabilities (Walker & Shea 1999). Furthermore, there is doubt that behavioural gains achieved during intervention are maintained, even when teachers specifically instruct students in skills for generalisation (Kaplan & Carter 1995; Walker & Shea 1999). A third limitation on our confidence in the effectiveness of ABA is that most studies take place in rigorous conditions that are not normally replicable in the average classroom or are impractical in group settings (Doyle 1986; Kaplan & Carter 1995).

In terms of unwanted side-effects, the controlling approach of ABA may reduce on-task behaviour (Doyle 1986). It can also be contagious: a program that is designed to target a single student or a priority behaviour can then spread to other behaviours of that student or to other students. Peers can perceive it as unfair that the student with the poorest behaviour receives the most attention and reinforcement, and might copy the target student's behaviour and, in turn, require a behavioural program themselves.

Cognitive-behaviourism

Advocates of cognitive-behaviourism say that it works, although its critics contend that cognitive theory has a less sound research basis than ABA for such claims (James 1993; Lee 1993), especially with children (Hall & Hughes 1989). Nevertheless, there is accumulating evidence of its effectiveness with a range of difficulties from learning disabilities to impulsivity and aggression; at a range of ages; and at various ability levels of students (Alberto & Troutman 1999; Ashman & Conway 1997; Kaplan & Carter 1995; Zirpoli & Melloy 1997). Cognitive techniques may be more suitable for older and more able students than behaviourism alone (Kaplan & Carter 1995). Nevertheless, they require some linguistic and intellectual sophistication, which may preclude students with severe intellectual or language disabilities (Hall & Hughes 1989).

Advocates claim that using students' resources for solving their own problems is likely to be more effective than imposing solutions on them (Bandura 1986). When they are in control of the intervention, students become more motivated to change their behaviour and more persistent at using skills that lead to school success (Fontana 1985).

In criticism, many behaviourists (e.g. Lee 1993) find the strategies of cognitive-behaviourism more vague than pure behaviourism. The fact that cognitivism is not a unified theory, but a disjointed collection of approaches, means that application can be incoherent and ill-advised (Benson & Presbury 1989). On the other hand, the complexity gives flexibility and also gives rise to interventions that are designed for individuals (Dobson & Pusch 1993; Dyck 1993).

A final point relates to the effectiveness of the cognitive methods in preventing difficulties. Although there were early criticisms that there were few cognitive approaches for preventing behavioural problems (Meyers et al. 1989), many more recent approaches have potential for preventing dysfunction. These include social skills training, suicide prevention, substance abuse prevention, protective behaviours and stress reduction for students and teachers (Conoley 1989).

Neo-Adlerian theory

Neo-Adlerian theory has little research evidence backing its claims of effectiveness. It relies mainly on practitioners' reports of success, although even these are not well documented. One exception is that studies comparing behavioural with neo-Adlerian parent training courses found that the neo-Adlerian model was more effective with both parents and children (Thompson & Rudolph 1996).

Humanism

In answer to Skinner's criticism (1989) that humanism lacks scientific rigour and efficacy data, McCaslin and Good (1992) argue that Baumrind's work (1967) differentiating authoritarian, authoritative and *laissez-faire* discipline styles does supply convincing data on the superiority of authoritative—that is, democratic—methods.

Further support comes from Emmer and Aussiker's (1990) meta-analytic study. In general, teacher effectiveness training achieved improved student attitudes to schooling, to themselves and to their teachers, plus achievement gains, with some studies also demonstrating positive benefits for teachers (Emmer & Aussiker 1990).

Choice theory

Emmer and Aussiker's (1990) meta-analytic study found that teachers who were trained in choice theory developed more positive attitudes to school and disciplinary issues. They made fewer referrals for behavioural difficulties after the implementation of choice theory. However, research limitations make it difficult to know whether this was because fewer problems were actually occurring, whether the teachers simply felt better equipped to cope themselves with any difficulties that arose, or because of the support they received from a whole-school approach (Emmer & Aussiker 1990).

Glasser's method reduced the recidivism rate at one school from 90 per cent to 20 per cent in a short period of time (Thompson & Rudolph 1996). These writers conclude that it is clear that choice theory works well when the whole school and parent population endorse its philosophy and provide practical support, such as a time-out room. Although individual teachers can use Glasser's approach to problem solving in isolation from the rest of their school (Charles 1999), it is likely to be less effective than when the entire approach is comprehensively applied.

In terms of its applicability to students with learning difficulties, Glasser (1986) contends that, because choice theory's interventions are verbal, they cannot be used by students who cannot talk, and therefore those with severe or profound intellectual disabilities may not be able to participate fully in the counselling and goal-setting methods. Glasser reports that his approach has been used with young people with moderate disabilities, however, with no major modifications.

The strongest findings for choice theory have been for individual students who were displaying chronic behavioural difficulties (Emmer & Aussiker 1990). Most studies found immediate positive results in terms of fewer peer disputes, reduced absenteeism and improved on-task rates (Emmer & Aussiker 1990).

Systems theory

Evaluation of the effectiveness of approaches based on systems theory is made difficult by the wide range of definitions of family therapy, and how the research defines and then measures therapeutic effectiveness (Nicholson 1989). Many early studies had methodological inadequacies and lacked statistical rigour (Kirkby & Smyrnios 1990; Smyrnios & Kirkby 1989; Smyrnios et al. 1988), although a growing body of more recent studies has demonstrated positive benefits of family therapy for a range of difficulties, when compared both with no treatment or alternative treatment modes (Nichols & Schwartz 1995; Sprenkle & Bischoff 1995). The problems addressed range from childhood stealing (Seymour & Epston 1989) to conduct disorders, juvenile delinquency and emotional disturbances (see Sprenkle & Bischoff 1995). Gains include cost savings (Thompson & Rudolph 1996), parents' improved marital satisfaction following resolution of children's behavioural difficulties (Sayger et al. 1993) and direct improvement in the presenting problem (Nicholson 1989).

Conclusion: Effectiveness

Three conclusions are possible from the above review. The first is that, with our present state of knowledge, it is not possible to disentangle which elements of each theory are responsible for generating the findings on the effectiveness of each approach (Emmer & Aussiker 1990). Without this information, as a practitioner, you cannot select components from the various theories in any confidence that you have chosen their most effective features.

The second conclusion is that you do need to be clear about what you are aiming for so that you can select a theory or combination of theories that has most potential for achieving your goals (Emmer & Aussiker 1990).

Third, although authoritarian and democratic teaching may produce similar levels of productivity in students, it is not enough that disciplinary practices simply *work* (Curwin & Mendler 1988). You must also select practices that minimise secondary reactions. Authoritarian interactions with students may have undesirable side-effects such as encouraging dependency, competition, powerlessness and alienation from learning (Schmuck & Schmuck 1997). When evaluating effectiveness, these unintended effects must be considered.

Efficiency of the theories

Efficiency means being able to find a solution that frees both you and your students to get on with the business of learning and teaching. Much of teachers' time is spent responding to behavioural disruptions. Thus all the theories of school-based discipline argue that, although it takes time for teachers to become proficient in the techniques each recommends, doing so is more efficient than unplanned or unsystematic responding.

Limit-setting approaches

Canter (1988) claims that assertive discipline produces quick results and that competing approaches (such as teaching students self-management) take longer. Its critics concede that this may be so, but reply that any worthwhile learning is slow and requires teachers to take more risks, but that this does not diminish our enthusiasm for teaching valuable academic skills and the same should be true of teaching self-discipline skills (Curwin & Mendler 1988).

Applied behaviour analysis

Applied behaviour analysis began as an answer to psychoanalysis, with its lengthy investigations into clients' subconscious and past life events. The early behaviourists believed that clients presenting for help about their present life circumstances needed help *now*, not after years of therapy. Behaviourism, therefore, aims to give more effective help more efficiently, as this is more humane than leaving people to suffer during prolonged interventions.

On the other hand, the observation and data gathering required for a behavioural program can be prohibitive for teachers (Wolery et al. 1988). Writing specific behavioural objectives also demands a great deal of time. These can be so precise that they may apply only to specific skills and not broader abilities such as creativity or problem solving. As a result, the behaviourist's focus can be on trivial behaviours, rather than on patterns of behaviour over time (Thompson & Rudolph 1996). This can reduce the focus to minor infractions, and can also swamp teachers with detailed interventions for each and every behaviour.

Also, having to teach parents and teachers a new set of jargon both uses up time that could be spent intervening with target behaviour, and lacks respect for their present skills. This can undermine their confidence, making them less open to suggested interventions.

Cognitive-behaviourism

It can be difficult to acquire the skills necessary for teaching cognitive strategies to students and difficult to incorporate them naturally into the regular curriculum (Ashman & Conway 1993).

On the other hand, students frequently present with a constellation of difficulties in three areas: low school achievement, disruptive behaviour and low self-esteem. The self-regulatory skills of self-instruction, self-monitoring and self-evaluation promote self-discipline and therefore can resolve problems in all three areas at once. The link between the three areas is represented in Figure 9.1 on the following page.

Ideas about the time it takes to teach students to manage their own behaviour are mixed: some authors say it requires less teacher time and improves generalisation of skills compared with ABA (Kaplan & Carter 1995), while others say it takes considerable teacher time to teach these skills and evidence of improved generalisation is promising but not conclusive (Ashman & Conway 1993; Grossman 1995; Hall & Hughes 1989), especially when treatment gains are to be generalised to the classroom (Meyers et al. 1989). The difference in opinion may reflect the target group: complex conduct difficulties such as aggression, social problems and depression are certainly time-consuming to treat. Perhaps also, the time demands reflect the fact that learning self-management is a life-long process for all individuals.

Figure 9.1   Cognitivists' view of the interrelatedness of achievement, behaviour and self-esteem

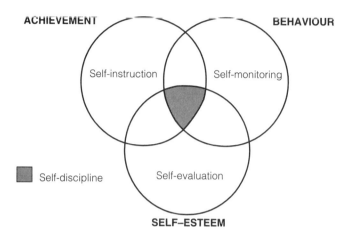

Neo-Adlerian theory

Dreikurs claims that, as there are only four goals of students' behaviour, it is relatively easy to learn and to apply the recommendations of this theory. However, as there is no evidence for his goals (Thompson & Rudolph 1996), resulting interventions may be ineffective and, if so, cannot possibly be efficient.

Humanism

Students may not respond immediately to the problem-solving approach of humanism but instead 'test' the negotiation process (Duke & Meckel 1984; Kohn 1996). However, Gordon (1970) says that they will come to accept the approach and believe in their teachers' integrity when teachers do not resort to coercion during this testing phase.

Choice theory

As choice theory requires a wholesale overhaul of the school curriculum and in-depth training of all teachers and school personnel, it takes some years to implement comprehensively. Once in place, however, choice theory would be highly efficient.

Systems theory

Schools need speedy change when a student's behaviour is seriously disturbing; systems theory (especially solution-focused therapy) is tailored to work quickly (Dicocco et al. 1987). Its proponents say that it promotes efficiency in many ways. First, success is promoted by the advice that only a small change is needed to effect a larger change that spreads throughout the system. Second, systems theory does not blame students' school difficulties on their home circumstances, which avoids the hopeless orientation that things at school cannot improve unless the home circumstances change. Instead, it expects changes at school to spread to home, and thereby to remove some of the assumed cause of the school-based problem.

Systems theory also achieves efficiency by not having to teach a new set of jargon to teachers or parents. Thus the theory can be used immediately by anyone willing to look at chronic problems in a new way. In accepting not only the language but also the beliefs of others, the practitioner is able to engage in a cooperative relationship with students and parents, which is likely to lead to less resistance to suggested solutions and therefore to their greater efficiency (Murphy 1992).

Fourth, systems theory engages children readily through its imaginative and active techniques (Combrinck-Graham 1991; Heins 1988). With their engagement comes a fund of information to which adults do not have access or which they may deny, and this information is useful in devising an intervention.

A final efficiency of systems theory is that techniques such as reframing and compression of time allow all the student's behaviours to be classified as belonging to a single pattern, and so to be dealt with by a single intervention.

On the other hand, systems theory poses some threats to efficiency. Under this approach, rather than applying interventions in a 'cookbook fashion', the practitioner selects an individual intervention in each case (Dicocco et al. 1987; Murphy 1992). While this makes the approach more powerful, it also makes family therapy a difficult theory to learn, as it has few specific guidelines for practice.

The way in which systems ideas are written about makes them especially difficult to grasp and thus inaccessible for the new practitioner. Furthermore, most school-based systemic literature is written from the standpoint of a consultant to schools. If, as a teacher, you want to apply these ideas, you are obliged to translate the literature for your own circumstances. Nevertheless, you do not need extensive training in the theory and can retain your own personal style (Amatea 1989; Molnar & Lindquist 1989), in which case learning the concepts can be efficient.

Philosophical assumptions

Each chapter so far has opened with a description of the philosophical assumptions of each theory. These are summarised in Table 9.1 below. In comparing these beliefs, it is useful to consider the deeper issues that give rise to them.

Table 9.1   Philosophical assumptions of each theory of student behaviour management

	Limit-setting approaches	Applied behaviour analysis	Cognitive-behaviourism
Nature of childhood	Children need clear limits	Children's behaviour follows the same laws as adults'	Children have the capacity for both good and ill
Nature of learning	Learning requires order	Learning is the acquisition of new behaviours	Children learn by experience
Goal of discipline	Order Obedience	Order Compliance	Order Internalised compliance Emotional regulation
Reasons for students' disruptive behaviour	Lack of parental guidance Non-assertive teachers	Consequences that reinforce desirable behaviour and reduce inappropriate behaviour have not been enforced	Consequences plus the child's expectations, beliefs, skills and context all influence behaviour
Teacher–student status	Teachers have a right and responsibility to be in charge (authoritarian)	Teachers have the right to control students (authoritarian)	Teachers are controlling, although consult with the student (partially democratic)
Role of teachers	Establish order	Arrange conditions to alter the rate of behaviour	Encourage student self-responsibility (in terms of internalised compliance)

Cause and freedom

A fundamental difference between the authoritarian and authoritative theories is their view about what causes human behaviour. Proponents of ABA believe that humans are not free to choose but are subjected to external manipulation from their environment. All behaviour is lawful and can be predicted from assessing external events. All that you have to do, then, is manipulate those events to induce the types of behaviours that you want your students to display.

The democratic theorists, however, argue that laws linking a behaviour to an antecedent or consequence only *describe* individuals' actions but do not *prescribe*

Table 9.1 continued

Neo-Adlerian theory	Humanism	Choice theory	Systems theory
Children actively assign meaning to their experiences	Children are rational and trustworthy	Children are capable of self-discipline	Children have restricted responsibilities
Children learn by overcoming feelings of inferiority	Children learn when curricula are relevant and teachers are personally involved	Children learn when curricula meet their emotional needs and teaching is of high quality	Learning requires discomfort, new ways to act and good reasons to change
Order Internalised compliance Cooperation	Autonomous ethics Emotional regulation Cooperation Integrity	Order Autonomous ethics Emotional regulation Cooperation Integrity	Order Emotional regulation Cooperation Integrity
Low self-esteem Need to belong is not met at school Discouragement Faulty choices	Authoritarian responses provoke disruptive student behaviour. Children naturally make mistakes. Sometimes they are overwhelmed emotionally	Low-quality education Student needs are not met at school	Behaviour has been maintained by unwitting mishandling Behaviour stabilises the system
Democratic preventive methods; authoritarian interventions	Students and teachers have equal rights to have their needs met but occupy different roles (democratic)	Students and teachers have equal rights to have their needs met but occupy different roles (democratic)	Students and teachers have equal rights to have their needs met but occupy different roles (democratic)
Promote student development and self-responsibility	Facilitate learning Relate warmly Nourish curiosity Promote personal growth of students	Promote student responsibility and personal growth	Change solutions to chronic problems

them. Even if their behaviour is 'lawful' in the sense of being predictable, individuals are not *compelled* to behave as they do (Schlick 1966).

Although seemingly esoteric, this debate is crucial for educators: if we maintain a mechanistic belief in external causes, we will control the environments of our students in an authoritarian manner; if we believe in individuals' freedom to decide their own attitudes and responses to events, we will facilitate students' autonomy.

The first view aligns with a victim mentality which says that people cannot overcome disadvantaging backgrounds unless their circumstances change. Although behaviourists argue that students can act to change their environment—and so they would deny the claim that they perpetuate victimisation—their view of relevant environmental conditions is restricted to the immediate events preceding and following a behaviour.

The second view presents hope that disadvantaged and failing students can change how they think and feel about their conditions and so do not have to remain as victims. Humanists and even the cognitivists take a much wider view of external causes than behaviourists and therefore provide a more comprehensive array of interventions to help students overcome their difficulties.

View of human nature

A second philosophical difference between the theories is their view of human nature. Alfie Kohn (1996) contends that the authoritarian theories are based on a negative view of children which says that children will not choose prosocial behaviour unless manipulated (through rewards and punishment) into doing so. Kohn (1996: 6–7) reports Marilyn Watson's observation that 'discipline plans typically seem to proceed from the assumption that Thomas Hobbes's famous characterization of life also applies to children: they are nasty, brutish, and short'. The use of punishment, Kohn (1996: 7) says, is predicated on the belief that 'children need to feel pain before they will stop behaving badly'. He rejects what he calls this sour view of children and assumes instead that they are equally capable of altruism as they are of being thoughtless. Like Gordon (1970), Kohn believes that the disruptive actions of students are actually *reactions* to being denied autonomy. In turn, these reactions verify authoritarian teachers' negative predictions of their students and perpetuate a power-based system in which there are no demands on anyone—other than students—to change (Curwin & Mendler 1989).

Focus of intervention

The seven theories described in this text differ in where they direct their intervention. Figure 9.2 below shows the predominant focus of *intervention* expounded by each theory. The diagram illustrates that, while a given theory may have many aspects, its priority for *intervention* is in the area indicated. This does not mean, however, that a theory ignores all other aspects of students or their behaviour, but that additional aspects may be only a secondary focus. Those theories to

Figure 9.2 Primary focus of intervention for each theory of student behaviour management

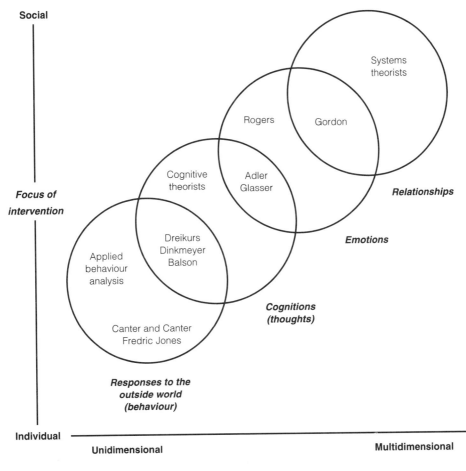

Source: Carey & Porter (pers. comm. 1992)

the right, however, are more likely than those to the left to include more than a single dimension in their explanation of and intervention with disruptive student behaviour.

Unique features of the theories

As well as their claims to effectiveness and efficiency, and differing underlying philosophical assumptions, each theory has its own unique strengths and weaknesses.

The authoritarian theories

Canter's assertive discipline, Jones' positive classroom discipline and applied behaviour analysis attract all of the criticisms that are directed at the authoritarian theories and which were reported in Chapter 6. To summarise these here, the three democratic theories argue that:

- No one *can* control someone else's behaviour. It simply does not work that way: individuals make their own choices.
- To attempt to do so is *counter-productive* as it teaches the opposite skills to those we are trying to instil, helps to create the disciplinary problems that teachers struggle with, and reduces students' motivation to learn and willingness to accept responsibility for the effects of their actions on others.
- It is *unethical* to attempt to control other people. Students' youth does not restrict their human rights and all humans require autonomy.
- Attending only to students' actions allows teachers to ignore the effects that their teaching content and methods may be having on students' behaviour (Jones & Jones 1998).

Limit-setting approaches

Canter's defence to criticisms of authoritarianism is that the assertive discipline program is harsh only when it is implemented improperly (Charles 1999). However, the humanists would argue that 'There is no right way to do the wrong thing' and that at best the program is open to misuse, while at worst it violates students' emotional and social needs. Although Canter believes that it offers students choices, critics claim that 'Realistically, the only choice Assertive Discipline offers is, "behave or else!"' (Curwin & Mendler 1989: 83).

The skills focus of the limit-setting approaches equips teachers with practical skills for establishing order in a classroom (Charles 1999). However, too much control can limit learning (Doyle 1986; Honig & Wittmer 1996; McCaslin & Good 1992). Just as your students can be restricted by assertive discipline, you too are constrained by its methods: you become a technocrat who dispenses predetermined consequences without the true professional's use of discretion (Curwin & Mendler 1988; Gartrell 1987a; Kohn 1996). Jones and Jones (1998) accuse assertive discipline of being over-simplified and impersonal, leading to mistrust and fear between students and teachers.

The limit-setting approaches have no educational theory to guide your use of their techniques: they do not connect discipline with theories about teaching, motivation or the emotional needs of students (Curwin & Mendler 1989). (The only student 'need' that Canter identifies is the 'need' for limits [Charles 1999].) This lack of a theory base neglects the role of inappropriate curricula and teaching methods in provoking behavioural difficulties (Corey 1996; Curwin & Mendler 1988; Gartrell 1987a; Glasser 1998b). By imposing solutions on students, it fails to teach them how to think about and solve problems (Carlsson-Paige & Levin 1992). Finally, it can lead to inappropriate disciplinary practices, such as Jones' recommendation (1987a) to penalise a whole class for individual non-compliance, which is contrary to research findings on the benefits of supportive peer relationships.

Applied behaviour analysis (ABA)

Applied behaviour analysis has set the standard for rigorous observation of behaviours, avoiding diagnosis and interpretations—which can be biased—and instead requiring you to specify exactly what behaviour took place, under what conditions and to what effect. With the exception of neo-Adlerian theory, all theories of student behaviour uphold this standard of impartial observation of behaviour. While this is beneficial when observing outward behaviours, however, it does overlook the importance of internal factors (Ashman & Conway 1997).

Although the methods of ABA are clear, applying its techniques is more complex than it looks: their effective and ethical application takes considerable competence (Alberto & Troutman 1999). Even those teachers who favour praise mainly deliver it non-contingently (especially to low achievers), rendering it an ineffective reinforcer (Brophy 1981).

Advocates recognise that ABA does deny students freedom of choice, but argue that if we do not restrict students' choice to fail, their options as adults will be restricted for them (Alberto & Troutman 1999; Bailey 1991; Kaplan & Carter 1995). They claim that ABA expands students' options and personal freedom and gives them the dignity of success while also avoiding other more intrusive interventions (such as drug or electro-convulsive therapies), meaning that it not only helps individuals to achieve their goals, but also does so efficiently and without unnecessary suffering. As to isolating and stigmatising targeted students, advocates say that these children's subsequently improved behaviour can help their social inclusion (Jones & Jones 1998). Therefore, by definition, the approach must be humane, these writers contend (Alberto & Troutman 1999).

The humanists persist in their criticism, however, by saying that the same ends could be achieved by less damaging means. This is the debate between controlling and guiding (Glasser 1998a, 1998b; Gordon 1991) which states that people can learn without direct experience of behavioural consequences, and so they can make valid behavioural choices for themselves without being manipulated by others.

Even rewards—often justified as being in the interests of students—manipulate students into doing as teachers want and so it is the adults who actually benefit (Kohn 1993). The status quo is thus preserved. This refutes ABA's claim to be amoral or apolitical (Kaplan & Carter 1995): it is, Kohn (1993: 30) claims, 'a profoundly conservative doctrine posing as a value-free technique'. In rebuttal, Edwards (1997) states that, while a lack of rewards may work for most people, students who are discouraged about learning may need some external reinforcers to encourage them to put in effort, especially on difficult tasks.

Other criticisms are directed at ABA's narrow view of the precursors to behavioural disruptions, which humanists say amounts to a callous and unethical disregard of the broader social context. This means that the underlying problem is not really treated (Kaplan & Carter 1995). Others disagree: they say that the problem *is* the behaviour, not its underlying cause and, in any case, inner needs are difficult to identify and so should not be of concern (Wheldall & Merrett 1984).

A fundamental problem with ABA is that teachers often refuse to enact behavioural interventions (Benes & Kramer 1989), in part because they disagree with ABA's philosophy that all behaviour is determined by outside forces (Bailey 1992; Miller 1991; Wolery et al. 1988) and in part because they may have played little part in deciding how to intervene. Their exclusion can come about because ABA is so complex that interventions need to be designed by specialists (Kutsick et al. 1991).

The partially democratic theories

Cognitive-behaviourism and neo-Adlerian theory share some of the strengths and weaknesses of their more authoritarian counterparts, and some of those of the more democratic theories. They still allow for a high degree of adult control, thus limiting the engagement of students (Ashman & Conway 1993). They overcome some of the ethical dilemmas of imposing controls externally, but are less purist in this aim than the democratic approaches.

Cognitive-behaviourism

Cognitive methods rely on assessing which aspects of students' problem-solving processes are going awry. This can be a difficult task. However, if achieved, cognitive strategies then directly and explicitly teach students the self-management skills— such as problem solving—that they will need as adults. These skills are more relevant than many others that we teach students, and are more likely to generalise (Kaplan & Carter 1995). Students can also develop an internal locus of control, attributing their performance to their own efforts rather than to external forces. Their improved self-control will, in turn, enhance their self-esteem.

This means that private behaviour, occurring in the absence of a teacher, can still be controlled, as students internalise control (Grossman 1995). There can be a difficulty, however, with motivating them to manage their own behaviour (Grossman 1995) or to abandon irrational thinking and replace it with more functional thoughts, particularly when their extremist thinking works for them (Kaplan & Carter 1995). Adolescents in particular might find the new thinking 'phony' and will need to persist until it no longer feels awkward (Kaplan & Carter 1995). Furthermore, if students cannot examine thinking logically, it will not be possible for them to dispute their illogical beliefs (Kaplan & Carter 1995). Thus age might play a part in children's readiness to learn cognitive strategies (Ashman & Conway 1997).

The benefits for teachers are that you do not have to solve all of your students' problems or oversee their behaviour constantly, as it is assumed that students have skills and can govern their own behaviour. You have the freedom to differ in your expectations of students, as the students themselves provide their own consistency by controlling themselves. Finally, you benefit from the fact that cognitive methods may more closely align with your own belief systems and educational goals for students. Nevertheless, cognitive treatments still have to be supplemented by behavioural interventions (James 1993) and you may feel uncomfortable with these.

Neo-Adlerian theory

This theory institutes democratic preventive methods, thus avoiding the disadvantages that are said to arise from authoritarian interactions. In particular, the practice of encouragement is consistent with this theory's democratic stance, conveying respect and avoiding competition.

However, its interventive practices are authoritarian, with the teacher diagnosing the students' goals and then acting 'in such a way that the behaviour does not achieve its intended goal' (Balson 1992: 94). Having said that, other authors (e.g. Nelsen et al. 1997, 1998) use the communication skills of listening and problem solving that are part of this theory's preventive component to respond more respectfully to 'mistaken' behaviour and its underlying goals. This suggests that the authoritarian response of the earlier writers is neither essential nor universal to all neo-Adlerians.

This theory's view of children's motives is narrow: it believes that all individuals are striving to belong; others argue that social acceptance is only a foundation for personal development, rather than being an end in itself (Gartrell 1998). Despite claiming to deal with students' social needs, neo-Adlerian theory is very individually focused and does not take the social context into account. For instance, an observer may not have seen the sequence of events that gave rise to the behaviour and so misdiagnosis is possible.

Second, this theory's expectations about children's behaviour are unrealistic. The neo-Adlerians require children not to respond to provocation, to return kindness for hurt and to ignore belittling remarks. If they cannot, then their behaviour is deemed to be antisocial and to have one of four negative goals. These expectations reflect middle-class values, are unrealistic and are probably undesirable, as teachers do not want children to become passive victims of bullying or even incidental insults.

Third, this theory's view of children's motives is negative (Thompson & Rudolph 1996), despite Adler himself and also Dreikurs contending that individuals' goals are a natural and valid response to discouragement. The negative descriptions of their motives give rise to authoritarian interventions. Perhaps instead, each goal could have been given a more positive connotation—for example:

- attention seeking could have been called a quest for *confirmation*;
- power seeking could be referred to as a need for *self-determination*;

- the goal of revenge could instead be seen to reflect a belief that one is *unaccepted* and *unloved*;
- withdrawal could be framed as a feeling of *hopelessness*.

This lack of respect for student needs is mirrored in a lack of respect for parents, who are said to cause their children's difficulties by not accepting their children as they are, by correcting their mistakes and not allowing children to demonstrate their skills (Balson 1992). The belief that problems will be resolved if parents are offered the 'right' training conveys an undemocratic disrespect for the skills parents already possess and may undermine parents' confidence.

The attempt to diagnose students' goals violates the standpoint of three competing theories: first, cognitivism claims that your students do not cause your feelings and so your emotions are a poor indicator of students' motives. This is demonstrated aptly in the instance when one teacher finds the behaviour acceptable and another does not, or when the same teacher feels differently about the behaviour on different occasions: it is illogical to claim that the students' goals vary with these differing reactions.

Second, Gordon (1970) accuses this approach of amounting to mind-reading, which is one of his communication blockers. In an apparent paradox, even the neo-Adlerians themselves describe such an approach as playing the amateur psychologist, which they too say is a roadblock to communication. In contrast, Glasser for instance would seek to help students become aware of their own goals and to decide *for themselves* whether their behaviour is likely to get them what they want.

The third theory to object to neo-Adlerian diagnosis of students' goals is systems theory. Its advocates would argue that diagnosing students' goals is based on a confusion between the *intent* of their actions and their *outcome*.

Nevertheless, having diagnosed students' goals, you now have very clear guidelines for action. One of these includes the use of logical consequences; however, the purer humanists describe these as a euphemism for punishment, claiming that they attract all of the same disadvantages (Gordon 1991; Kohn 1996).

The democratic theories

The democratic theories attract the glowing reports of adherents about their positive benefits for students' learning, self-esteem and democratic participation (Kohn 1996; Rogers & Freiberg 1994). At the same time, humanism in particular is prey to accusations by detractors that it is unscientific (Skinner 1989).

Some accuse these theories of not really being democratic at all, as teachers still act as leaders (McCaslin & Good 1992). However, while the humanists would agree that teachers are authoritative (because of their expertise), they nevertheless have the same rights as students to have their needs met. The democratic label for the humanist, choice and systems theories is not a statement about equal roles, but about equal rights.

Humanism

The main focus of humanism is the prevention of academic and behavioural difficulties in schools. The humanists believe that it is more humane to prevent a problem from occurring than it is to deal with it once it has arisen. Although students can arrive at school with disadvantaging home backgrounds, the role of school is to help them overcome these by considering its own contribution to disruptive student behaviour.

The humanists are not unanimous about whether to use logical consequences, although those who do support them agree that they should be a last resort only. If logical consequences are omitted, some could contend that, aside from reciprocal contracts and collaborative problem solving, the humanists offer no direct interventions for disruptive behaviour.

The communication skills of active listening, assertion and conflict resolution demand of teachers considerable interpersonal sophistication, while both students and teachers require good language abilities, which may preclude students with intellectual or language disabilities.

Gordon may also have given insufficient guidance on framing assertive messages, giving only the 'When you . . . I feel . . . because . . .' formula for assertive messages. This may be unduly limiting. Jakubowski and Lange (1978) list other forms, which are described in Chapter 13.

Choice theory

Choice theory endorses the other humanist writers' contention that democracy must not be taught solely as a topic in politics, but must be lived within the classroom (Glasser 1969). As such, choice theory takes into account more than just the psychology of individual students, instead asking educators to consider the effect of the school system on students.

Glasser's theory extends humanism's notion of self-responsibility. Its emphasis on individuals' choices offers hope for those whose background would otherwise condemn them to school failure and unfulfilling relationships. Its focus on their present decisions, with optimism that they can change these to meet their own needs (without violating the rights of others), and gentle but firm guidance for doing so, provides a clear framework for change. This focus also ensures socialisation, as students are required to act in ways that do not interfere with other people.

Glasser (1998a) contends that many teachers respond to student disruptions with a righteous attitude that students shouldn't behave that way. Instead, teachers can remove some of the heat from their exchanges with students by not taking their rebellion personally, and remembering that students are only railing against the system, not against teachers specifically.

Choice theory adds the counselling approach to the interventions recommended by the humanists, providing a broader range of intervention options. Nevertheless, it too avoids punishments: Glasser (1992a: 277) refutes advice that teachers should get tough with disruptive students because 'that's all they understand', saying: 'If we continue to get tough with them, it is all they will ever understand.'

It may be difficult for teachers to communicate with students about their unacceptable behaviour without resorting to controlling methods or imposing their own solutions. It is also difficult to avoid responding in a way that allows students to make excuses for their behaviour (Edwards 1997). Furthermore, students' own authoritarian ideas can undermine the effectiveness of Glasser's interventions (Lewis 1997).

Systems theory

Unlike the previous democratic theories with their specific attention to education, systems theory arises from clinical practice and so gives less attention to the role of the school organisation and structure in provoking the disruptive behaviour of students.

Like the previous two democratic theories, systems theory builds on individuals' strengths rather than diagnosing their deficiencies. This communicates respect for students, their parents and their teachers. It has the effect of normalising stigmatised students by not blaming them but instead simply assuming that the complaint is a result of an unintentional mismatch between the problem and the attempts at its solution (Amatea 1989). It also conveys optimism about the potential for change. Focusing on the present is particularly useful, because school teachers are looking for relief from present, not past, difficulties (Dicocco et al. 1987).

Reframing is fundamental to seeing problems as changeable. However, some writers have criticised this method for being insincere, for deliberately distorting information, and for being covertly manipulative (Amatea 1989; Duncan 1992; Murphy 1992). This is answered by the contention that there *are*, in fact, many different views of events, and the positive ones are just as likely to be correct as negative ones, and so there is nothing dishonest in selecting the most positive view on offer, as long as participants are comfortable with it (Molnar & Lindquist 1989).

When students are behaving disruptively, teachers tend to lose confidence in themselves and appear to be at the mercy of students (Amatea 1989). Teachers' confidence is also undermined by diagnostic labels that define students as needing specialised expertise which they believe they do not have (Dicocco et al. 1987). Systems theory aims instead to work with participants by not displacing old ideas, but simply offering alternatives. This ensures participants do not feel criticised for their earlier attempts, and so increases their openness to new approaches.

Just as it motivates teachers to promote change, so too it empowers students. It uses the principle of neutrality to ensure that teachers do not undermine students' motivation for change, and it encourages creativity, light-heartedness and open-mindedness in the face of chronic problems (Molnar & Lindquist 1989), making its approaches particularly attractive to children (Combrinck-Graham 1991; Heins 1988).

But, in its enthusiasm for solutions, solution-focused therapy might induce denial or the minimisation of problems (Nichols & Schwartz 1995), although the concept of cooperation is important insurance here, as it implies that you must listen to those you are helping and take a new tack if your optimistic focus is causing them discomfort (Rhodes 1993).

A key strength of systems theory is its breadth. If interventions with individual students have not produced improvements, you can look beyond them to their interactions with yourself, with peers, with the school as a whole, or even further by looking at the family's relationship with the school and with other social agencies (Dowling 1985). In so doing, it expands your options for finding a solution.

Summary

In line with the advice of Johnson and colleagues (1994), the above critique (and summary in Table 9.2) attempts to reveal the values, assumptions and contradictions that underlie school discipline practices. The critique itself assumes that you must consider not only the impact of recommended practices on student discipline, but also the secondary impact of your practices on students' sense of themselves as worthy, responsible, capable learners who can solve problems and exercise self-control (Curwin & Mendler 1988).

Table 9.2 Strengths and weakness of each theory of student behaviour management

Strengths	Weaknesses
Limit-setting approaches	
Practical recommendations	Authoritarian
	Some recorded negative effects on students
	Not based on pedagogical theory
Applied behaviour analysis	
Unbiased observation	Authoritarian
Precise methods	Narrow preventive component
	Disregard for causes of behaviour
	Uses complex jargon
	Less feasible for groups than for individuals
	Negative effect on learning
	Maintenance of gains is doubtful
	Ethical problems
Cognitive-behaviourism	
Increased student motivation	Has authoritarian undertones
Improved educational and behavioural outcomes	More vague than ABA
Overcomes some of the ethical dilemmas of ABA	Continued reliance on behavioural methods
	Students may not be motivated to participate in self-management
	Requires students to be competent verbally
Neo-Adlerian theory	
Democratic preventive methods	Authoritarian interventions
Encouragement	Narrow list of emotional needs
Clear prescriptions for action	Unrealistic expectations of children
Parent training	No evidence for goals of mistaken behaviour
	Subjective diagnosis of goals
	Disrespect for students' self-knowledge
	Negative labelling of individuals
	Use of logical consequences/punishments
	Criticism of parents
	Lack of social focus
Humanism	
Preventive focus	Few immediate behavioural interventions
Positive view of individuals	Students may initially test the teacher's integrity
Promotes self-responsibility	Requires teachers to have sophisticated communication skills
Enhanced learning	Students need competent verbal skills
Addresses underlying causes of student discontent	
Living democracy	

Table 9.2 continued

Strengths	Weaknesses
Choice theory	
Promotes self-responsibility	Requires teachers to have sophisticated
Takes context into account	communication skills
Removes heat from student–teacher conflicts	Students need competent verbal skills
Wide applicability	
Adds counselling intervention to a humanist	
base	
Living democracy	
Effective whole-school approach	
Systems theory	
Applied to chronic problems	Complex theory
Respect for individuals	Individual interventions are difficult for new
Breadth of focus	practitioners to design
Optimistic about potential for change	Open to insincerity
Facilitates new solutions	
Uses humour	

Discussion questions

Select a theory that most interests you, or take each theory in turn, and answer the following questions about it:

1   How well do the philosophical assumptions of the theory stand up to scrutiny from the standpoint of the other theories and from your own knowledge of child development?
2   What do you regard as this theory's strengths and weaknesses?
3   How could any weaknesses be overcome? If your answer involves borrowing approaches from other theories, are the philosophical assumptions and practical recommendations that you have combined compatible with each other?

Suggested further reading

Kohn, A. 1993 *Punished by rewards: the trouble with gold stars, incentive plans, A's, praise and other bribes* Houghton Mifflin, Boston, MA
——1996 *Beyond discipline: from compliance to community* Association for Supervision and Curriculum Development, Alexandria, VA

Part Two
Motivating students

> *Being a spectator not only deprives one of participation but also leaves one's mind free for unrelated activity. If academic learning does not engage students, something else will.*
>
> Goodlad (1983, in Jones & Jones 1990: 163)

Motivation refers to students' willingness to invest time, effort and skills in the tasks that we set for them (Ben Ari & Rich 1992; Cole & Chan 1994). Glasser (1998a) contends that when we say that students are not motivated, this is clearly untrue: all individuals are motivated to meet their needs. (A composite list of needs from all the writers could comprise: survival, autonomy, a sense of competence (or self-esteem), relatedness and fun.) Thus what we are actually saying when students choose not to work is:

- they are not motivated to do the particular work they are being given; because
- this work is not meeting their needs.

Motivation—or a lack of it—is not, then, an inherent part of children's personalities. If some students are choosing to invest their energies elsewhere, this will be because what we are asking them to do does not meet their personal needs (Glasser 1998a).

Thus motivation has the following aspects (Cole & Chan 1994; DiCintio & Gee 1999; Glasser 1998a; Jones & Jones 1998):

- students' *expectation* that they can be successful, which requires that they experience an optimal (not too high and not too low) degree of challenge so that they are confident that they can meet demands;
- their assessment of the benefits that success will bring in terms of the fulfilment of their personal needs. This assessment will cause students to place a *value* on being successful;

- the extent to which the environmental *climate* meets their physical, emotional and social needs.

Jones and Jones (1998) regard these elements as multiplicative, which implies that all three components are necessary for motivation. Thus, their formula (Jones & Jones 1998: 179) is:

Motivation = Expectation of success x expected benefits of success x work climate

Because motivation is learned rather than being inherent in students (Jones & Jones 1998), you have two tasks in motivating students: first, to make them more *willing* to put in the effort to learn; and second, to structure your teaching so that it is *easier* for them to learn.

It is not my intention in this section to detail the voluminous research into effective classroom management techniques such as pacing, offering variety and enacting procedures for the smooth flow of activities. These are the topics of whole texts in themselves (see, for example, Emmer et al. 1997; Evertson et al. 1997; Good & Brophy 1997; Grossman 1995; Jones & Jones 1998). Instead, the four chapters in this section are guided by the theories in Part One and by research into teaching practice which says that schools are obliged to cater for students' needs both for the students' own ultimate emotional development, and also to empower them to succeed at school. In turn, when they feel that success is not only possible but probable, there will be less cause for them to disrupt classes.

10 Safeguarding students

Students' descriptions reveal that in some schools a feeling of tension permeates the air—and, in some cases, generates fear . . . In these environments, students are uneasy and watchful. They frequently believe that the worry and anxiety they feel are unobserved by teachers and other adults.

Phelan et al. (1992: 702)

Key points

- Learning will not be a high priority for students whose physical needs are not met.
- You can take steps to ensure that the class and overall school environment promote high achievement and considerate behaviour.
- These measures include establishing an ethos that honours diversity in students and protects them from intimidation by others.

The physical environment

The democratic theories (see Chapters 6 and 7) and evidence from educational research concur that students behave more thoughtfully and learn more effectively when their basic needs are met in the classroom (Jones & Jones 1998).

Comfortable setting

Basic physical needs include the requirements for food, drink, rest and protection. This category also includes the needs for physical safety, activity (Lipsitz 1984, in Jones & Jones 1998), adequate lighting, limited background noise, safe touch, space to move, a visually attractive, comfortable and warm environment, easy pace, and time to relax and reflect. Not only must the classroom environment be comfortable, but so too must the school's eating and play areas. These must offer respite so that students can equip themselves for the next learning session; if they do not, the students' ability to learn will be reduced.

Sufficient activity

The constraints on physical movement that are often imposed in classrooms are unnatural and restrictive; students will vary in their ability to cope with this (Grossman 1995). Kohn (1996) tells the story of a teacher who allowed her students to sit, lie or stand anywhere while they were reading and found that they achieved more; Kohn observes that it is sad that schools do not usually even allow students this basic control over their own bodies and that doing so seems such a departure from normal practice.

You will need to note how much activity the school day offers students and supply enough activity for them to be able to operate quietly when necessary. Physical activity offers many benefits: it can give students confidence in their ability to control their bodies, exercises both the body and the brain (enhancing academic success), teaches children that they can meet physical challenges, and offers an outlet for stress, as long as it does not become another avenue for serious competition.

Physical safety

To promote student safety, you need to be present to supervise students at all times so that they are not at physical risk from injury or abuse (including bullying). You will also need to be familiar with the signs of child abuse that may be occurring outside school, as you are legally obliged to report any concerns about abuse to child welfare agencies.

Safe touch

Young primary or elementary school students need some touch and, occasionally, physical comfort from their teachers. Older students, however, may feel uncomfortable with physical contact, while touching students could expose you to accusations of inappropriate conduct. Thus, both to protect students from discomfort and to protect yourself legally, it may be safer to restrict your contact with older students to a pat on the back, a brief arm across their shoulder while standing alongside them, a high-five or a handshake (Jones & Jones 1998).

The emotional environment

The term *climate* refers to the learning atmosphere and the students' feelings about themselves, each other, the teacher and the subject matter (Kindsvatter et al. 1992). A positive classroom tone reflects the way you organise the class to maximise students' self-esteem and learning (Rogers 1998). It has the following dimensions (Schmuck & Schmuck 1997: 25–6):

- *affiliation*—how well the students feel that they know each other and how willing they are to cooperate with each other;
- *involvement*—how interested the students are in academic learning and how much they participate;
- *teacher support*—how much help and personal involvement you give to students, how much you trust students;
- *competition*—the extent to which students compete with each other for grades and personal recognition in the classroom;
- *task orientation*—how much emphasis you place on the content of tasks—getting them done, or being correct—compared with a focus on the learning process;
- *innovation*—the extent to which you encourage student creativity and use new teaching practices;
- *organisation*—how much you emphasise order for its own sake, versus supplying sufficient structure to enable students to achieve;
- *expectations*—the extent to which you emphasise rules versus emphasise considerateness;
- *control*—whether you monopolise control versus working with students to shape a productive and accepting setting.

School climate

A US study found that the following features influence how safe students feel at school (Phelan et al. 1992):

- the visibility and accessibility of the principal;
- the level of support students receive from teachers;

- how safe they feel from violence;
- the level of interaction between student groups;
- whether they are protected from the behavioural excesses of each other;
- the availability of extracurricular activities;
- mechanisms for student input into decisions;
- the condition of the school's facilities;
- permission to use their first language at school.

These features of the school appear to have more impact on students' academic performance and behaviour than home backgrounds (Phelan et al. 1992). As these are directly under your control, this gives you a substantial influence on the engagement of even disaffected students.

An anti-bias curriculum

While bigotry assumes that differences between people mean that they are unequal, 'colour-blindness' assumes that the differences do not matter (Stonehouse 1991). Neither perspective is accurate. The aim of an anti-bias curriculum is for students to experience difference as interesting rather than something to be feared or shunned. It acknowledges and celebrates differences openly and honestly (Saifer et al. 1993) by giving students straightforward information about gender, race and ethnicity.

You can help students to accept difference by inclusive projects, activities and discussions about how members of other cultures live. At the same time, it is important that this does not degenerate into a 'tourist curriculum' that focuses on a culture's exotic customs rather than daily life, as this can perpetuate stereotypes (Derman-Sparks & the ABC Task Force 1989). You can support your anti-bias curriculum by inviting parents, community members and other staff to share with students some of their cultural experiences.

Glasser (1998b) says that the most basic rule in any school must be that no one is allowed to put anyone else down. When incidents of racist, sexist or disability-based teasing, name-calling or harassment occur, you could give the perpetrator some simple information that counters the stereotype or slur, as long as you keep this brief and do not preach (Crary 1992). Sometimes students genuinely believe their stereotypes; at other times, they are simply using another child's differences as a pretext for bullying. In the latter case, you can deal with it as you would any bullying, regardless of the specific content of the abuse.

Teacher self-discipline

So that students feel safe with you, you will need to express your feelings appropriately and not humiliate or denigrate students (Phelan et al. 1992). You may still express anger and frustration, but should do so by stating your own feelings rather than by blaming students. Ginott believes that teachers cannot afford to make scenes, and should *never* use sarcasm. In the same vein, Bill Rogers (1998) observes that disciplining from emotion rather than reason is self-indulgent and unhelpful.

Discourage bullying

Tattum (1993a: 3) does not mince words when he calls bullying, 'the most malicious and malevolent form of antisocial behaviour practised in our schools'. Almost one in five students is subjected to bullying at least once a week in schools and half experience it during their school lives, with a third of students saying that it makes them feel unsafe at school (Pepler et al. 1993; Rigby 1996; Slee 1994b, 1998; Smith & Sharp 1994; Tattum 1993a).

Bullying comprises an unjustified and deliberate intent to inflict hurt by repeatedly taking advantage of one's own superior physical or psychological strength (Olweus 1993; Slee 1995; Slee & Rigby 1994). It is the systematic (deliberate, planned and repeated) abuse of power (Smith & Sharp 1994). The use of the word *repeated* in this definition signals that the duration of the bullying influences its cumulative effects on victims. Bullying can range in duration from a few days to many months with longer durations being typical for upper primary students (Slee 1995; Slee & Rigby 1994).

Types of bullying

Bullying comprises direct physical attacks; direct verbal attacks such as taunting; extortion; and indirect methods such as spreading vicious rumours or excluding someone from the social group (Olweus 1993; Rigby 1996; Smith & Sharp 1994; Tattum 1993a). For both sexes, the most common form of bullying is name-calling and abuse (Salmivalli et al. 1998), while males in the last two years of high school and females of all ages tend to employ less direct approaches such as exclusion from the peer group or spreading malicious rumours (Rigby 1996, 1998; Salmivalli et al. 1998).

Sexual harassment is a form of bullying that involves verbal comments, physical touch and visual harassment such as using pornography or defacing school posters of women to embarrass or intimidate girls (Drouet 1993). Girls may be required to perform favours (not necessarily sexual) at the threat of rumours affecting their sexual reputation being circulated, and they may feel obliged to avoid areas in which males congregate.

Location of bullying

Bullying occurs at roughly equal rates in city and rural schools, in large and small schools, and across socioeconomic classes (Olweus 1993). Some studies find that it is most prevalent in the middle years of primary school (Slee 1994b), peaking again in the first two years of high school (Rigby 1996; Slee 1994a); other studies report highest rates in the early years of primary school (grade 2), with a steady decline thereafter (Olweus 1993).

Half of all bullying occurs in a one-to-one relationship and half involves a larger group (Smith & Sharp 1994). This gives rise to the suggestion that the word *bullying* be replaced with *mobbing* to emphasise the group dynamics involved in many instances (Olweus 1993; Roland 1993).

Both girls and boys report being bullied more in coeducational than in single-sex schools, with girls in coeducational settings also being sexually harassed more than in single-sex schools (Rigby 1993, 1998). This finding contradicts earlier research that indicated a higher incidence of bullying in single-sex boys' schools (Rigby 1998).

Gender differences

At all ages, boys are most frequently the perpetrators of bullying (Olweus 1993; Salmivalli et al. 1998). Boys and girls in primary schools are (roughly) equally victimised by bullying, but by high school there is double the rate of male versus female victims (Rigby 1998). Teachers and peers usually under-identify girls as victims, perhaps because female bullying more commonly involves exclusion from the friendship group, which is difficult to detect (Cowie & Sharp 1994; Rigby 1998; Smith & Sharp 1994).

In terms of their reactions to being bullied, boys are likely to report feeling angry about it or deny that it bothers them, whereas girls are more likely to feel sad and to stay away from school in response (Rigby 1998). Also, girls' more intimate friendship patterns would make betrayal by the group more painful than is the case for boys (Salmivalli et al. 1998). As sadness is associated with self-blame and lowered self-esteem, the consequences of peer victimisation may be more serious for girls (Rigby 1998). On the other hand, girls are more likely to report the incident (and suffer fewer negative consequences for doing so), whereas boys are less likely to ask for help when they need it (Rigby 1998).

Finally, the reasons why boys and girls bully are similar—namely, to exercise power over others (Rigby 1998). However, they do this not in anger but in what could be termed a 'proactive' rather than reactive form of aggression (Salmivalli et al. 1998). It is gratuitous and unjustified violence (Rigby 1996). Having said this, there are two forms of bullying that are not malicious, even though their effect on the victim is the same. These forms include teasing without being aware that it is hurting the other person, and parading your superior skill (at academics or sport, maybe) to the humiliation of a less skilful performer (Rigby 1996).

Effects of bullying

Victims of bullying are often neglected or disliked by their peers (Slee 1998), ostensibly because they possess certain devalued personal characteristics. But, rather than provoking the bullying in the first place, these traits may be devalued after the event, in an attempt by perpetrators and onlookers to justify the harassment (Olweus 1993). On the other hand, a sensitive demeanour on the part of children often signals that they would not retaliate if attacked, making these children attractive targets for abuse (Olweus 1993).

The bullying itself, victims' rejected status, and their lack of social supports can create unhappiness at the time as well as long-term adjustment problems (Smith & Sharp 1994). Its effects can be compounded when students also suffer violence at home (House of Representatives Standing Committee on Employment, Education and Training 1994). Particularly when students lack emotional supports from else-where, bullying is likely to lead to absenteeism from school, increased health complaints, impaired capacity to relate to others, low self-esteem, depressive tend-encies, and feelings of isolation, unhappiness and loneliness in victims (Olweus 1993; Rigby 1996; Slee 1995; Slee & Rigby 1994). At the same time, victims' learning can suffer (Rigby 1996). Finally, as might be expected, victims become intimidated and lack confidence, and so are unlikely to report the abuse.

The bullies themselves, contrary to myth, are usually outgoing and confident, showing little anxiety or remorse owing to a lack of empathy for others; they are impulsive and they believe in dominance and in being violent to gain status (Olweus 1993; Smith & Sharp 1994; Tattum 1993a). Male bullies are frequently rejected by the majority of their classmates but are well accepted by their friendship group, members of which all tend to display similar levels of aggression; female bullies often have a controversial peer status, being rejected by some classmates and accepted by others, perhaps because girls' bullying is less direct and because it may alternate with displays of affection (Salmivalli et al. 1988). There are links between persistent school bullying and later delinquency, and possibly even depression (Olweus 1993; Rigby 1996; Slee 1998; Smith & Sharp 1994; Tattum 1993c), and between bullying and aggression towards teachers, school property and siblings (Tattum 1993a).

The third affected group is bystanders. Some collaborate with the bullying because of group pressure or to avoid becoming victims themselves and experience shame as a result; passive observers often experience distress and anxiety and feel guilty for not helping (Rigby 1996; Pepler et al. 1993). Others, of course, don't care (Rigby 1996). Those who defend victims generally have high status; perhaps these children feel free to come to others' defence as they are already popular, or their high status is a result of appreciation for their support (Salmivalli et al. 1998).

An anti-bullying program

In order to deal with bullying, we need to understand it (Rigby 1996). It arises from a desire to hurt someone, the need to dominate and the enjoyment of another's distress (Rigby 1996). Children probably learn these emotions early in life through a history of neglect and a good deal of frustration, and are permitted to act on them by a school ethos that colludes with rather than discourages bullying (Olweus 1993; Rigby 1996).

Nevertheless, to understand the bully's perspective in this way is not to excuse the behaviour. Thus, in an effort to reduce its incidence, Slee and Rigby (1994) propose that schools enact an anti-bullying program which they describe by the acronym PEACE:

P   is for a school *policy* against bullying that includes a philosophy statement and clear grievance procedures.
E   stands for *education* about what is meant by bullying and which procedures to use to deal with it.
A   means *action* at all levels, involving close supervision in the yard, class discussions, and individual talks with bullies and victims, backed up with clear sanctions that the students play a part in determining.
C   stands for helping victims and bullies *cope* with their difficulties, which may include a social skills training program.
E   stands for *evaluation* of the effectiveness of the program.

School-wide policy

Bullying is a complex problem that is embedded in systems (family, classroom and school) that inadvertently model, maintain and reinforce domination and intimidation (Pepler et al. 1993; Tattum 1993c). Therefore, any response to school bullying needs to address its wider context.

The first step is to formulate a whole-school policy on bullying as part of an overall policy about aggression and discipline in general, which is guided by the school's social justice, pastoral care and protective behaviours policies (Rigby 1996; Roland 1993; Sharp & Thompson 1994). Your policy will have the same components as any of these other policies, beginning with a definition; your philosophical commitments to a moral climate in which bullying is not tolerated; statements about the rights and responsibilities of teachers and students with respect to bullying; and procedures for intervening. This school-wide policy would set the scene for classroom discussions about bullying (Olweus 1993).

Education

This is the second aspect of the school's anti-bullying program (Slee & Rigby 1994). It includes the following elements.

Student support and education. Students who bully may not have learned prosocial values such as integrity and cooperation and may not have been taught empathy and cooperation (Rigby 1996). Therefore, you need to teach these values and skills in school as part of an overall social skills program. Meanwhile, bystanders need to know how they can intervene while remaining safe themselves (Slee 1998).

A second level of student education involves including anti-bullying issues within traditional subject areas. Drama, role-playing, videos and general discourses about bullying can be included within many subjects. Discussion needs to focus both on the content and on the emotional aspects of bullying and being bullied (Tattum 1993b) and on how it affects both individuals and groups (Herbert 1993).

Teacher education. Teachers are seldom trained about school bullying and so the school will need a commitment to providing ongoing staff training on discipline in general and bullying in particular.

Parent information. As parents are seldom made aware that their child is a victim or perpetrator of bullying and, as few talk with their children about bullying in general, offering a parent information session can raise their awareness and gain their support for your measures for counteracting bullying at school (Olweus 1993).

Action

The third aspect of Slee and Rigby's (1994) anti-bullying program is taking action. The following factors are involved.

Increased opportunities for collaboration. This is so that students get to know each other well.

Increased supervision. Most bullying in schools occurs in playgrounds, which may be due to the low levels of supervision there compared with other areas of the school (Boulton 1994). This implies that adult presence is an important deterrent to bullying (Olweus 1993). However, as it is unlikely that more supervisors will be appointed to playground duty, supervisors need to be more effective (Boulton 1994). This requires training in detecting and then responding to all forms of bullying.

As a preventive approach, you could organise cooperative play activities that give students something prosocial to do, or join in the children's games, while enriching the playground can also help avoid antisocial play (Boulton 1994; Whitney et al. 1994).

Supporting victims. Two aspects are necessary to support the victims: the first is listening empathically to their concerns and the second is teaching them some skills to protect themselves.

It is seldom helpful to teach victims to ignore bullying, as this can cause its escalation and makes victims feel powerless. It is only sometimes useful to teach them how to be more assertive; of greater benefit is giving them 'resistance training' comprising teaching and rehearsal of the protective behaviours of recognising an unreasonable request; being assertive about it in the form of 'brave talk'; and enlisting support from bystanders (Rigby 1996; Sharp & Cowie 1994).

Mobilising peers. Targeting bystanders is crucial in the light of reports that almost half of students report that they would not come to the aid of a victim (Pepler et al. 1993; Slee & Rigby 1994) which, we must also remember, means that half would (Rigby & Slee 1993). You can capitalise on the empathy of the majority of students by teaching them that bullying is everyone's responsibility and that bullies are not to be admired (Boulton 1994). As well as encouraging bystanders to help victims, the aim of such discussions is to discourage peers from joining in the bullying (Pepler et al. 1993).

Direct intervention. One disturbing feature of bullying is the perception by a quarter of students that teachers seldom act to protect them (Slee 1994a). Although you must protect students, you must also avoid the temptation to meet bullying with aggression, as this will reinforce dominance (Boulton 1994). You will need to employ a hierarchy of sanctions which bullies accept as reasonable; otherwise they may exact revenge on their victim.

At younger ages (below nine years), and for individual rather than gang bullying, you might simply tell the bully to stop (Smith et al. 1994). For students over the age of nine, and for those who are bullying in gangs, you could use Pikas's method of shared concern or Maines and Robinson's non-blame approach (Smith et al. 1994; Tattum 1993b). These approaches are built on the concept that some members of the gang go along with the bullying because of peer pressure and because diffusion of responsibility allows them to evade awareness of their part in causing the victim's distress (Olweus 1993).

The steps involved in the two methods differ in their sequence although, in essence, they involve listening to the victim and then conveying his or her feelings to the bullies, either individually or as a group. In so doing, you need to describe non-judgmentally that the victim is in a bad situation, without accusing the bullies or asking for an admission of guilt. Then you can invite the aggressors to participate in finding a solution and ask them for a commitment to the agreed option. A group meeting could be extended to include a discussion of bullying in general, so that the group does not switch its bullying to another victim.

Evaluation

In a follow-up meeting, you must check whether the solution is working—that is, helping victims to feel safer. As for the aggressors, research shows that bullies are more likely to maintain improvements in their aggression if the problem is solved collaboratively, as detailed above (Rigby 1996).

At a wider level, you must check that the anti-bullying program as a whole is having the desired effect on all school members.

Summary

Only when students can trust that they are physically and emotionally safe at school will they be empowered to participate in academic work; only when they care about others will they be motivated to be considerate of them. Both the school ethos and practical measures will promote their feelings of well-being, to the mutual benefit of individuals and the whole school community.

Discussion questions

1 What does your school's physical environment convey to students about how well regarded they are?
2 What measures do you adopt to ensure a positive climate in your classroom?
3 How does the school extend these measures?
4 What measures does your school use to prevent and respond to bullying? How effective are these?

Suggested further reading

For details of school approaches to bullying:

Rigby, K. 1996 *Bullying in schools: and what to do about it* ACER, Melbourne
Rigby, K. and Slee, P. 1992 *Bullying in schools: a video with instructional manual*, Institute of Social Research, Videotape, University of South Australia, Adelaide
Sharp, S. and Smith, P.K. eds 1994 *Tackling bullying in your school: a practical handbook for teachers* Routledge, London

11 Satisfying students' need for autonomy

Students' motivation was significantly associated with the amount of control perceived by them over their learning situations. Students reported being more involved and more competent when they perceived greater control over decisions and choices; conversely, they reported being less bored, less confused, and less interested in doing something else.

DiCintio & Gee (1999: 234)

Key points

- Fundamental to all human beings is the need to be in control of ourselves.
- You can meet this need in your students, both through how you teach and through your responses to their behaviour.

Introduction

This chapter is guided by the democratic theorists' argument (see Chapters 6 and 7) that students will not think for themselves or be motivated to learn in an environment that attempts to control them (DiCintio & Gee 1999). Yet much of the research into teacher effectiveness in classroom management (e.g. Jones 1987a, 1987b; Kounin 1970) defines effectiveness in terms of whether the teacher's management methods allow him or her to dominate the flow of the activities (Kohn 1996). The democratic theories argue that this is counter-productive and can provoke behavioural difficulties as students attempt to seize back some of the autonomy that is being denied them.

Authoritative teaching

This democratic stance applies to both your instructional and managerial roles. That is to say, it is important that you give students control of their own learning and behaviour so that they do not become hostile about the violation of their basic need to be self-determining (Ginott 1972).

Promote independence

A major benefit of democratic management methods is that they promote students' self-reliance. Because being independent is such a basic human need, achievement of it will in turn enhance students' self-esteem. When you allow students to work alone and to attempt tasks independently, and encourage emotional self-control, you will be furthering their sense of competence and self-pride. B. Brown (1986: 26) notes that often our good intentions mean that we do things for children instead of allowing them to achieve things for themselves and feel good about themselves, and he goes on to say:

> Perhaps it is time to change our priorities from direct control aimed at stuffing the maximum possible amount of knowledge, skills and values into children to motivating them to manage their own lives—shifting the balance of our work with children from helping to enabling, from support to promoting self-reliance.

Self-reliance is of particular importance to children with disabilities, who may have restricted opportunities to be independent; any opportunity that remains must be capitalised on.

Guide students to select personal goals

Their need for autonomy means that, as well as understanding your goals for them, students will be more motivated when they can select their own goals. You will need to guide them to establish specific, short-term learning goals (as distinct from performance goals that are aimed at gaining a reward for completed work). Students' decisions may centre on what material to work on, when and how it will be completed, and how to self-monitor the work (Jones & Jones 1998).

Attribution training

An important belief that young people learn through experience is whether they themselves can control outcomes (this is termed having an *internal* locus of control, or *self-efficacy*) or whether luck, fate or other people control what happens to them. People are said to have an external locus of control or to display 'learned helplessness' (Seligman 1975) when they believe that events outside their control are responsible for what happens to them.

When they believe that they are responsible for the outcomes of their actions (i.e. when they have an internal locus of control), students (Knight 1995):

*   are more likely to learn from their mistakes;
*   have more incentive to invest effort and strive for success;
*   have more effective communication skills and better interpersonal relationships;
*   have superior concentration skills;
*   are more persistent;
*   are more reflective learners.

It is important to teach students to see themselves and interpret their actions accurately so that they can accept responsibility for what they do (Seligman 1995). In this way, they learn that they have control over their own lives. To encourage them to persist in the face of setbacks, you will need to teach them to attribute their achievements to their own efforts, rather than to uncontrollable factors such as inability or luck.

Thus, when students are unsuccessful, you do not have to confront them with failure, but to deny it is not helpful either. You will need to guide them to:

*   define the failure as *temporary* rather than permanent;
*   see failure as *specific* to the event rather than a sign of a general or all-pervasive failing on their part; and
*   explain the failure in terms of their *behaviour*, not personality: they need to take personal responsibility without taking blame (Seligman 1995).

Specifically, when you hear students blame their personality for failings (such as when they say 'I'm hopeless at this'), and when they assume that the problem is permanent ('I'll *never* be able to do it'), you can gently correct their statements (with something like, 'It hasn't worked out, has it? What could you do to make it better?').

Provide choice

Martin Seligman (1975) states that adults can 'inoculate' children against learning to be helpless, by giving them repeated experiences of control over even small aspects of their environment. Giving students some choice about their activities during lesson time also increases their engagement and reduces disruptive behaviour (Dunlap et al. 1994). Therefore, students must be offered choices at any opportunity. Even if they have no choice about doing an activity, you can give them a choice of how to go about it. On the other hand, it is also important not to offer fake choices, asking students if they want to do something when there is no option.

Authoritative discipline

If you want students to experiment intellectually, you must be ready for them to experiment behaviourally as well, even when this sometimes results in mistakes. If your response to those mistakes quashes their explorative spirit, it may repress their intellectual exploration as well. Thus, as an authoritative manager, you would respond to students' behavioural errors by looking for a solution rather than punishing a culprit.

Establish behavioural guidelines

Guidelines will be necessary to protect individuals' rights. It is important that students understand what is expected of them (Knight 1991) so that they can remain in charge of their own learning and behaviour and so that they can exercise their rights as well as their responsibilities. The authoritative system of discipline makes demands that are fair and reasonable rather than arbitrary, making it more likely that students will accept and voluntarily observe the standards expected of them.

These rights and corresponding responsibilities are summarised in Table 11.1 on the following page (Knight 1991; Lovegrove et al. 1989; Rogers 1989, 1998).

Negotiate rules with students

Students should participate in formulating guidelines so that they understand what is expected of them and are willing to observe the standards to which they have

Table 11.1   Rights and responsibilities of students, teachers and parents

Students' rights	Students' responsibilities
Physical and emotional safety and protection	To care for themselves and others
Access to materials and resources	To share equipment
To learn and to understand how learning will help them live in the world now and as adults	To care for equipment and use it safely
	Not to demand teacher attention excessively
To competent teaching that imparts vital knowledge	To be cooperative
To receive teacher assistance	To be considerate
To enjoy learning, gaining pleasure, interest and confidence from learning	To speak out
	To listen and not obstruct the opinion of others
To feel important as people, who have the right to be individual and to express opinions	Not to dominate individuals or the group
	Not to put other students down
To be treated with dignity	To be accountable for their actions
To receive fair treatment	To participate in the schooling process
To be protected from abuses by authority	
To receive specialist services as required	
To privacy and confidentiality	
To be free from unnecessary restrictions	
Teachers' rights	**Teachers' responsibilities**
To defend optimal learning environments for all students	To be competent
To be treated with courtesy	To provide an environment that is friendly, encouraging, supportive and positive
To expect students to cooperate with reasonable requests that will enhance their growth and respect teacher needs	To assist students who need help
	To model courteous behaviour
To respond to disruptive behaviour	To have reasonable expectations of students, in line with the task demands and students' developmental levels
To express an opinion and be heard	
To feel secure in the classroom, both emotionally and physically	To protect students from harm: from themselves, other students and school personnel
To achieve job satisfaction	To listen to students and colleagues
To receive support from school administration	To be fair
To receive support from colleagues	To take responsibility for their own feelings, not blaming students for them
To participate in inservice training	
To have access to consultants	To provide forums for student participation in decision making
To contribute to school policy	
	To take responsibility for their own actions that may detract from job satisfaction (e.g. stress management)

Table 11.1   continued

	Teacher's responsibilities (*continued*)
	To support colleagues
	To consult with colleagues and reach agreement
	To make an effort to be involved
Parents' rights	**Parents' responsibilities**
To participate in their children's education through:	To ask for information when needed
	To make the time to be involved
• gaining information on school processes and curricula	To be open and willing to listen
	To be willing to find workable solutions
• participation in decision-making	
• receiving and offering information about their children's learning and behaviour	
To expect consistent approaches by teachers	
To expect non-discriminatory practices	

agreed (Kohn 1996; Tauber 1990). The process of negotiating the guidelines is an exercise in social problem solving and, as such, is valuable in itself (Kohn 1996).

Obviously, some rules will be compulsory, and it would be hypocritical of you to manipulate students into nominating or agreeing with these (Grossman 1995). Therefore, you will need to nominate those rules—such as those relating to drug taking—that are non-negotiable because of school policy. At the same time, you can explain the rationale for these restrictions, and then negotiate remaining standards.

If you are a secondary teacher, you cannot operate with a different set of rules for each of your classes (Emmer et al. 1997; Grossman 1995) but, on the whole, all students will nominate the same sorts of rules and so it is likely that there will be a common standard across classes. If you find that you have to impose some strictures so that standards are the same for all your class groups, democratic values require individuals to abide by guidelines that have been decided by others, and this therefore may not be detrimental for students (Grossman 1995).

Concrete guidelines

Once the class has established its guidelines, it will help to frame them in concrete, specific, explicit and functional terms that make it obvious how they contribute to work accomplishment (Doyle 1986). You will need to avoid vague terms such as requiring students to 'be polite' and it will be useful for guidelines to state what you want students to do, rather than what they must *not* do. To maximise understanding and to avoid students feeling oppressed by a long list, there should be very few guidelines. Glasser (1998a) suggests that most rules come down to expecting courtesy, so most guidelines could be subsumed under this single heading.

Teach the rules

Effective managers integrate their rules and procedures into a workable system and teach them systematically to students so that they understand them (Doyle 1986). As well as teaching the rules, you can teach a variety of non-verbal signals that remind students when their behaviour contravenes the agreed standards (Doyle 1986).

Consistency

Once an agreed system is in place, some theorists say that you will need to be consistent in its application. Consistency refers to three aspects: first, maintaining constant expectations across time for students' behaviour; second, maintaining the same standards for all students; and third, applying any consequences consistently (Emmer et al. 1997; Evertson et al. 1997).

Inappropriate inconsistency will arise from three sources: first, when the rules are unreasonable, unworkable or inappropriate; second, when you are erratic in detecting misdeeds, leaving students who *have* been observed feeling disgruntled; and third, when you do not feel strongly enough about a rule or procedure to enforce it. In these cases, you will need to renegotiate the rules with the class so that you are willing to enforce the new standards reliably.

However, the humanists argue that the concept of consistency is built on the assumption that teachers must externally impose standards of behaviour on students. These and other writers say that demanding conformity to rigid standards is likely to alienate many students, resulting in behavioural difficulties (Kauffman 1997), whereas appropriate flexibility and informality increase your power as a decision maker (Doyle 1986). The humanists suggest instead that you simply explain when your own needs or the needs of other students are being infringed or when a student's behaviour violates an agreement. In this way, you would be consistent about upholding your needs, but the need itself (and your resulting response) may vary according to the circumstances at the time.

Review

Procedures and rules must be reviewed regularly to check that they are workable.

Model self-control

You will need to demonstrate how to remain in control of yourself so that students will learn from you how they can exercise self-control. This will be particularly important for students from violent backgrounds, as they will not have learned how to regulate their own feelings.

Teach self-management

If you want students to develop the skills that they will need in adult life, you will need to teach them how to use those skills in the present. Thus you will need to teach students who are experiencing behavioural difficulties to plan, monitor and evaluate their own behaviour so that they become less impulsive in their thinking and more methodical about solving problems (Schraw & Graham 1997). They will need to become aware of their own behaviour and the reactions it elicits from others.

Mostly, this will involve regulating their emotions. When students behave thoughtlessly, it is seldom that they lack information about the alternatives; it is more likely that they temporarily lack control over their own emotions (Porter 1999a). Just as adults do not need to know how many calories (or kilojoules) there are in snack food, but instead need more self-control so that they do not eat when they are not hungry, student disruptions are usually due to a lack of self-control. In these instances, this understanding implies, first, that you do not need to teach the actual skill involved in, say, prosocial behaviour; second, that instead you need to support and teach students to manage their emotions when under stress; and third, that you should not punish them for being overwhelmed when this is a natural childhood event and so would amount to punishing them for *being* children (Porter 1999a).

What about consequences?

Rather than teaching students what will happen *to them* if they violate an agreed standard, inductive reasoning involves explaining to students the effects of their actions *on other people* (Berk 1997). This is crucial for teaching children to behave

KING ALFRED'S COLLEGE
LIBRARY

compassionately and can prevent thoughtless behaviour (Kohn 1996). This means that guidelines do not need to specify 'consequences' for misdemeanours, but will detail the procedures for resolving the issue. Some possible steps might be:

- Look for a solution, rather than a culprit (Porter 1999a). In so doing, *listen* to what the students tell you about what is going on, rather than demanding to know in a tone of voice that implies you simply want to find out who to punish (Porter 1999b).
- Develop a warm *relationship* with students so that they are willing to work with you to solve problems (Kohn 1996).
- Examine *your own role* in the disruption—both in the immediate circumstances and in the wider context of the quality of instruction.
- *Avoid lecturing* students about their mistakes: in the perpetrator's hearing, talk to the victim of an aggressive outburst about how it hurt, but do not preach to the perpetrator. Without blaming or shaming the perpetrator (so that discouragement does not lead to another outburst), negotiate how he or she could make restitution, maybe through apologising, cleaning up or otherwise restoring any damage (Kohn 1996).
- Once a solution has been negotiated, *check back later* to see if it is working (Kohn 1996).

Summary

Students will learn best when they understand what is required of them and when curricular content and teaching processes encourage them to be actively involved in learning. Ensuring that they have some autonomy and that learning is fun will help to motivate them to learn to be considerate of others.

Discussion questions

1 Is motivating students to learn different from motivating them to behave considerately?
2 What is your conclusion on the debate about consistency? Does it fit with a democratic approach, and how does it compare with flexibility?

Suggested further reading

For a discussion of the rationale for student autonomy:

Glasser. W. 1998 *The quality school teacher* rev edn, Harper Perennial, New York

Kohn, A. 1996 *Beyond discipline: from compliance to community* Association for Supervision and Curriculum Development, Alexandria, VA

12 Fostering competence

Self-esteem is not a trivial pursuit that can be built by pepping children up with empty praise, extra pats, and cheers of support. Such efforts are temporary at best, and deceptive at worse. Our children need coaches, not cheerleaders.

Curry & Johnson (1990: 153)

Key points

- Students will be motivated to participate in learning and to behave considerately when they anticipate that they can be successful at school.
- When they become competent at worthwhile skills, their self-esteem will rise, which in turn will make them more willing to take intellectual risks in future.
- Feedback that informs them about their achievements is more likely to encourage continued effort than are judgments about them or their work.

Introduction

A history of concern with self-esteem has, in some ways, led to some misunderstandings about what helps students to feel good about their skills (Seligman 1995). To explain this assertion, I shall describe what I mean by 'self-esteem'.

What is self-esteem?

Self-esteem is a measure of how much we value our personal skills and qualities. By referring to Figure 12.1, you can think of it as a comparison between our

240

Figure 12.1   Diagram of self-esteem

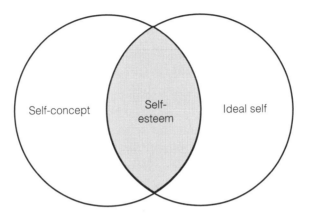

self-concept, which lists our attributes, and our ideal self, which ranks those attributes according to how highly we value them (Burns 1982). Our self-descriptions span five dimensions: social, emotional, academic, family and physical (Porter 1999c). As our self-knowledge grows with age, so our self-concept becomes more comprehensive in each of these aspects. Meanwhile, the messages that we receive from the significant people in our lives tell us how much they value our qualities, creating in us a sense of which attribute and abilities are ideal. Our self-esteem, then, is a measure of how many of our ideals we believe we attain. When we believe that our qualities and achievements are worthwhile, our self-esteem is healthy.

This implies that an unhealthy or low self-esteem can come about in three ways. First, we might in fact *not be competent* at the skills that we value. Second, we might be competent but do not realise it because we do not notice enough of our positive attributes: our *self-concept* is inaccurate. Third, our expectations of ourselves (our *ideals*) could be too high, and as a result we are disappointed even in our high achievements and personal virtues. This understanding yields some recommendations for ensuring that students develop a healthy self-esteem by achieving at tasks that they value.

Promote competence

Competence will breed confidence and enjoyment of learning; on the other hand, repeated failure will cause students to alternate their attention between the task and their worries about failing and being criticised (Tobias 1979, in Jones & Jones 1998).

Children's academic self-esteem is largely a function of how successful they are in school, regardless of all other variables, even disadvantaging home backgrounds (Chapman et al. 1990). As evidence of this claim, one study found that school had six times more effect on reading progress than did the students' backgrounds (Mortimore & Sammons 1987, in Jones & Jones 1998).

If students lack confidence because they are being unsuccessful in important ways, you do not want to boost their self-esteem artificially, but instead build their skills (Curry & Johnson 1990). Their low self-esteem is both valid and functional, because it might motivate them to achieve. Thus you need ways to promote *genuine* success in your classroom.

Provide sufficient structure

Structure in the classroom provides clarity and predictability for students and will maximise their chances of being successful. A class will function most smoothly when you (Brophy & Good 1986; Charles 1999; Edwards 1997; Emmer et al. 1997; Evertson et al. 1997):

- have a comfortable environment (see Chapter 10);
- can see all the students in order to check that they are finding the activities engaging;
- give clear directions;
- have organised procedures for handing out materials, making transitions between activities, having students ask for help and giving students help;
- effectively cope with multiple demands while teaching (Kounin 1970).

Thus effective classroom management techniques comprise how you organise, deliver, monitor and communicate your instructional program (Charles 1999). However, the structure must be responsive to student needs, rather than turning you into a slave to efficiency and procedures. Also, you must keep in mind that the aim of these management techniques is not to make it easier for students to behave according to your standards, but to make it easier for them *to learn* (Kohn 1996).

Relevant curriculum

The humanist and cognitive theories tell us that students are more motivated to learn—and correspondingly less motivated to disrupt in class—when they value what they are being asked to do—that is, when it is relevant to their lives and produces something useful (Knight 1991). Students will feel best about themselves and their abilities when they are meeting meaningful challenges and putting in some real effort (Katz 1995). In contrast, if they do not understand the concept and do not value the task, they will come to believe that learning is meaningless and full of traps that they cannot predict (Katz 1988). They will learn by rote instead of understanding the material, which will not work in the long run. And, in turn, their skills, interest in learning and confidence in their abilities will deteriorate.

The measures for making work relevant to students generally begin with using their interests as a vehicle for expanding their skills and knowledge; when you teach something that does not appear immediately to be relevant, you can explain your rationale for teaching it. These and other suggestions are offered by the humanists (see Chapter 6).

Match teaching to students' skill levels

Students will be motivated to attempt a task when they believe (from previous experience) that they can be successful at it. However, you cannot fool students by making tasks too easy for them: achievement of a trivial task will not make any difference to their self-esteem (Bandura 1986). In fact, it might actually do harm by teaching them *helplessness*: that no matter what they do, they will always get it right because the task has been made so easy.

Instead, students need tasks that increase their perception of their personal skills (Seligman 1975). On the other hand, tasks with too much challenge can cause them to worry that they might not be successful and they will not want to invest energy in them (Chan 1996; DiCintio & Gee 1999; Vallerand et al. 1994). That is, motivation has an 'expectancy component' (Chan 1996).

If you give the same activities to all students, some will become frustrated and unmotivated, because the material is either too easy or too difficult for them. This makes it imperative to know at what level students are functioning. Obviously, knowing students' skill levels rests on assessing these both formally and informally. Therefore, schools will need policy, procedures and the resources to assess the academic skills of students, as long as the goal is to identify the resources students need to improve their skills, rather than to label and disenfranchise them from learning (and excuse teachers from teaching).

As well as quantifiable differences in ability, students differ in their preferred mode for receiving information (verbally or visually), the pace at which they most comfortably learn, and the physical conditions (such as seating, noise, level of distractions and lighting) under which they learn best. You could use questionnaires that ask students about their preferences and can observe the conditions that promote each student's learning; then, where possible, incorporate these into your instructional program. Additional measures include the following.

- *Minimise performance anxiety and stress.* While some challenge is necessary to excite learning, too much challenge can turn into stress and compromise students' achievement. Competition between classmates is a major cause of school stress (Humphrey & Humphrey 1985; Kohn 1996). You can minimise such stress for students by not putting them under time pressure to achieve; letting their achievements (including grades) remain private rather than praising or criticising them in front of others; and focusing on how to solve problems, rather than on arriving at a 'correct' answer (Humphrey & Humphrey 1985). When you have to award grades for students' work, you can minimise the stressful effects by explaining the grading criteria in advance, and afterwards by giving individual feedback to students about their accomplishments (Jones & Jones 1998).
- *Give students time to integrate learning.* Learning includes both the acquisition of new skills and the consolidation of skills already gained. Thus students need the chance to practise and consolidate their skills; otherwise they may lose confidence in their grasp of the material and in turn become less motivated to persist.
- *Teach students how to learn.* To encourage them to achieve to their maximum ability, you will need to teach students how to apply themselves, to work independently at times, and to explore and solve problems (Curry & Johnson 1990; Knight 1995; Yong 1994). You can also portray that making an effort is a way of investing in learning, rather than a way to risk failure (Good & Brophy 1997).
- *Maintain students' expectations of success.* Ensure that students have a sufficient history of success, so that they are willing to attempt a task that carries a risk of failure (Whitmore 1980).

Give specific feedback

When students receive little positive feedback, their off-task behaviour increases and liking for school diminishes (Jones & Jones 1998). Especially when they are becoming discouraged about their performances, it will be necessary for you to acknowledge and support their efforts, keeping in mind that critical remarks do not invite but rather discourage improvement.

This issue has three elements: first, feedback must be authentic (Curry & Johnson 1990), which means that you must be honest with students to allow them to recognise accurately when they are successful and when they are not. Much teacher praise is unrelated to the quality of students' work, but instead is determined by teachers' view that particular students 'need' or are making bids for encouragement (Brophy 1981). But students cannot become competent unless they have information about what needs improving; and their self-esteem will not improve if they are aware (as most will be) when their performances are of low quality.

Second, teacher feedback is often too vague and does not specify success or failure accurately. Students need feedback that is specific, immediate, genuine and constructive, especially when they are concerned about possible failure (Jones & Jones 1998). Some students might also need help to notice positive feedback and not to take negative feedback too much to heart.

Third, the intent of praise is to reinforce studiousness and acceptable behaviours. However, we need to be aware that much teacher praise (Brophy 1981):

- is given to low-ability students, even when their work is incorrect, in which case if it functioned as a reinforcer, it would be reinforcing poor-quality performances;
- is accompanied by non-verbal behaviour that contradicts the positive verbal message;
- occurs at such low rates for individual students that it cannot function as a reinforcer. This is so even when teachers give high rates of praise to the group overall—which itself is rare, particularly in high schools, and is especially uncommon when directed at students' behaviour as opposed to their academic performances;
- is not directed at reinforcing students' performances at all, but has other functions. These are listed in the box on the following page.

The list in the following box implies that, when talking about the effects of praise, we need to distinguish which forms we are referring to.

Praise as a reinforcer

If we want praise to act as a reinforcer, we need to know that any reinforcing effects abate with age. In the junior primary or elementary years, children want to please

Common uses of praise

- As *reinforcement* for desirable behaviour or academic achievement. This, surprisingly, is rare in classrooms and is mostly non-contingent or indiscriminant, in which case it will not reinforce desirable behaviour in ABA terms.
- A *spontaneous expression of surprise or admiration*. This is probably the most reinforcing for students, although your surprise could communicate that you believe that a praised student is ordinarily less competent.
- To *offset earlier criticism*. To the extent that this has undertones of 'I told you that you could do better', this type of praise may actually be punitive.
- *Attempted reinforcement of onlookers*. Teachers often praise model students in the hope that others will imitate their behaviour. However, model students are seldom popular, in which case others will not choose to imitate them, and singling out 'teachers' pet' types may scapegoat students into that role.
- *An attempt to use positive guidance*, so that you do not feel that you are always nagging and issuing commands.
- A form of *student-elicited stroking*—cheerful and extroverted students will approach you for praise, but knowledge that they 'pulled' it may make the praise less potent for them.
- A *transition ritual*—here, you may comment positively on students' work as a way to indicate that they have finished that unit and can now move on to the next activity. Students are unlikely to attribute this sort of praise to anything special that they have done and so it will have little effect on their perceptions of themselves as learners.
- A *consolation prize*—the least able and most discouraged students tend to receive the most praise, even when their work has been incorrect. However, if this praise is too effusive, it might humiliate less able students who know that when other students achieve at similar levels, they do not receive the same amount of praise.

Brophy (1981)

their teachers and so praise has a mild reinforcing effect; in later years, it is usually neutral or negative in its effects on student achievement and behaviour (Brophy 1981). Also, praise will have different effects when it is delivered privately versus in public, when it is most likely to be detrimental (Brophy 1981). Thus, as a reinforcement, praise is very weak.

Rewards as manipulation

Humanists object to the intention of praise to manipulate children into repeating a behaviour of which we approve, as if they would not otherwise choose to behave considerately (Porter 1999a). For this and other philosophical reasons listed in Chapter 5, these educators decry praise and other rewards (Kohn 1993, 1996).

Interference with mastery orientation

Some writers conclude that rewards can detract from students' own natural motivation (Kohn 1996; Ryan & Deci 1996). Students who want to master the curriculum value learning for its own sake and so will persist when faced with setbacks; those who seek approval from others will apply themselves only to those tasks where success is likely (Cole & Chan 1994). This latter is called a performance goal orientation, and is related to wanting to *be* the best rather than to do one's best. To encourage the alternative mastery orientation, you need to avoid comparing students' achievements with each other's and instead provide feedback that acknowledges each student's own progress (Cole & Chan 1994).

A contrary opinion is advanced by many (Cameron & Pierce 1994, 1996; Eisenberger & Armeli 1997). These writers say that, although many school tasks will be intrinsically reinforcing, some students will need some extrinsic reinforcers to motivate them to persist at tasks that are complex, difficult or tedious for them.

Nevertheless, Brophy (1981) concludes that, while it is essential that students receive feedback (information) about their achievements, it is seldom appropriate or necessary to praise or reward (positively judge) these. Informative feedback tells students about their qualities and achievements, and so expands their self-concept; praise and rewards, on the other hand, are a judgment or an evaluation, either of students or their work. Evaluations feed their ideals. Whenever you raise ideals, there is a risk that individuals will be disappointed in themselves, as no one can be perfect: in terms of Figure 12.1, their self-esteem will be lowered.

Exercise: Translating praise into acknowledgment

Examples of differences between acknowledgment and praise are given in Table 12.1. Because praising can be a very hard habit to break, it can be useful to plan in advance how to translate your typical praising statements (evaluations) into informative feedback. To help you do this, take a sheet of paper, and divide it vertically down the middle. On the left-hand side, write down some of the praising statements that you commonly use with your students. Next, on the right-hand side, translate each statement into an acknowledgment. In doing so, it might help to think about what you would say to an adult who had just achieved something.

Table 12.1 Translating praise into acknowledgment

Praise	Acknowledgment
You're a good helper.	Thanks for your help. I appreciate your help. Thanks: that's made my job easier.
I'm proud of you for doing so well in your maths exam.	Congratulations. I'm proud for you. Looks like you're enjoying maths. I hope you're pleased with your work. What do you think of *that*?
That's a beautiful painting.	I like the colours you've used. You look pleased with that! Are you pleased with yourself? Looks like that was fun. Looks to me like you planned your picture before you started.
Your school play was excellent.	I enjoyed your play very much. I'm impressed at the work you put into your play.

Source: adapted from Porter (1999a: 60)

Expand students' self-concept

The second way in which students can develop low self-esteem is when they have the qualities that they desire, but are not aware of them. Thus you will need to expand their self-awareness.

Facilitate self-acknowledgment

Students can expand their self-concept by noticing their own successes through immediate self-acknowledgment. They can also be guided in writing a personal record of their improvements in class, and how to report their success to parents (Charles 1999). Murals, class diaries, newsletters that document class progress, notes home to parents and public performances can also give students acknowledgment of their successes.

As well as expanding their self-concept, a second fundamental reason to teach students to notice their own successes is that doing so improves their ability to notice the effects of their own actions. This same skill can be used to recognise when their behaviour is less thoughtful. If they can accept responsibility for their achievements, it will be easier for them to accept responsibility for their less successful actions.

Incorporate activities that increase students' self-knowledge

You can incorporate some activities that make your students aware of their qualities, such as making and regularly updating lists of their skills. (see, for example, Borba & Borba 1978, 1982; Canfield & Wells 1994). Such activities will not improve their self-esteem directly but, with an expanded self-concept, students may realise that they have many of their ideal qualities and so will appreciate them more.

Allow students to share their feelings

Their feelings at school are a legitimate cause of concern for students (Jones & Jones 1998). Some develop negative views of themselves because they believe that what they feel is wrong (McGrath & Francey 1991). When you accept students' feelings and experiences, you tell them that feelings do not have to be judged by a standard. Also, when students are able to discuss their feelings with each other, this may reveal that they are not alone.

Promote realistic ideals

A third way to enhance students' self-esteem is to help them to have realistic ideals for themselves.

Positive expectations

When you expect students to be capable, they are more likely to behave capably (Kauffman 1997). Thus you will need to communicate your faith in every student's ability to improve, grow and develop, and expect all to achieve high standards of work (Jones & Jones 1998; Kauffman 1997; Kindsvatter et al. 1992; Rogers 1998). This is not the same, however, as expecting normal performances from students who have learning disabilities, as requiring them to behave in ways they cannot will cause frustration and avoidance (Kauffman 1997).

Diagnostic labels can help you to understand the difficulties under which certain students are functioning, but you should not allow labels to excuse students from learning or you from teaching. When you use labels such as 'ADHD' or 'learning disabled' as *explanations* of children's difficulties, rather than mere shorthand *descriptions*, you are likely to lower your expectations for labelled children academically and behaviourally; equally, when you do not recognise gifted learners—particularly those with atypical patterns of talent such as gifted-learning disabled children or gifted children from minority cultural backgrounds—then you can exacerbate the challenges that they face and perhaps incite behavioural problems and under-achievement.

You can ensure that your responses to low-achieving students do not feed into their own negative impressions of their abilities. For instance, Jones and Jones (1998) report that teachers commonly place low-achieving students further away from them, pay less attention to these students, call on them less often, give less specific feedback, criticise them more often, and give them insufficient time and support to complete their work successfully. Rather than being the logical response to these students' needs, it actually can add to their learning difficulties (Jones & Jones 1998).

Encourage risk taking

It is crucial that you encourage students to take risks, set their own goals, organise their own activities and negotiate learning contracts (McGrath & Francey 1991). Fostering creativity is essential for positive learning (Knight 1991) and will give students permission to strive for their ideals.

Accept mistakes

One reason to avoid rewarding students for their successes is that this implies that making mistakes is not good. However, if students are not making mistakes, they already know the work and are just practising; mistakes signify that they are learning something new and therefore are only a sign that they need to keep working.

Balson (1992) notes that most adults instruct children by focusing on their mistakes, in the erroneous belief that this will help them to learn. Instead, it discourages effort and contributes to continued failure by focusing on children's deficiencies and not noticing their strengths. Therefore, you could teach and live by the mottos:

Strive for excellence, not perfection (Brown 1991).
Don't let failure go to your head (Ginott 1972: 188).
Have the courage to be imperfect (Dinkmeyer et al. 1980).
On worthwhile tasks, strive to *do* your best, not to be *the* best (Porter 1999c: 133).

250

Similarly, behavioural mistakes are inevitable. No one is thoughtful and considerate all of the time. Thus, when students' behavioural mistakes result in a disruption, you will need to see this as an occasion for problem solving. It is important not to judge students, even when you do not like their behaviour.

Guide realistic standard setting

You can help students to evaluate whether their skills are appropriate for their personal circumstances, rather than when compared with others. When placed in high-ability streams, the academic self-esteem of gifted students is sometimes lowered by having more able peers with whom to compare themselves (although their social self-esteem raises and so the two balance out) (Chan 1988; Craven & Marsh 1997; Gross 1997). The same reduction in academic self-esteem can occur for students with disabilities in regular streams. This implies that you will need to guide students to compare themselves to those who are similar to themselves in age, ability levels and interests, so that their expectations of themselves are not too demanding.

Undo negative prescriptions

Sometimes, your students will come to you with a history of being judged to be 'hopeless' in one way or another. Put-downs from adults become like seeds in children's minds, teaching them how to think negatively about themselves and their capacities (Biddulph 1993). This implies that you need to avoid using insults, sarcasm and emotional blackmail when talking with students (Biddulph 1993) and that, instead of colluding with such labels, you must actively counteract them by (Faber et al. 1995):

- looking for opportunities to highlight exceptions to these labels: when the 'scatterbrain' remembers his or her spelling list; when the 'inattentive' student pays attention; when the 'lazy' student puts in effort;
- giving students opportunities to depart from a limiting role by giving them a new role to perform;
- letting students overhear you say something positive about them;
- reminding students of their past accomplishments.

Accept yourself: Teacher self-esteem

By hearing how you talk to yourself, children learn how to talk to themselves. Given that they probably hear more negative than positive self-statements from the adults in their lives, they learn to talk to themselves in these negative terms too. To counteract this, you need to show them how to congratulate themselves when they have achieved their goals. As long as you feel safe doing so, you might say something positive about yourself, such as 'I think that activity went very well. I'm very glad that I planned it so carefully' or 'Aren't we all stars!' or 'I am feeling very pleased with myself today'.

At a wider level, Maples (1984) and the cognitivists attest to the importance of your own healthy self-esteem in equipping you to cope with the challenges of a classroom. They suggest that if you doubt your ability to respond appropriately to student behaviour, you may become defensive, which in turn will exacerbate management problems.

Summary

A considerable body of research points to the value of meeting students' needs, both for the sake of their emotional and academic development and also as a means to prevent disruptive behaviour in schools (Grossman 1995; Jones & Jones 1998). Nevertheless, the strategies for creating a positive classroom climate remain insufficient by themselves: you must supplement them with your wise and informed academic and social guidance (Kindsvatter et al. 1992) so that students can accomplish their goals and develop worthwhile skills. This, in turn, will promote their healthy self-esteem.

Discussion questions

1   In your view, what is the link between students' competence, their self-esteem, their academic motivation and their behaviour at school?

2   What is your conclusion on the debate between informative and evaluative feedback? Do you agree with Brophy's statement that, while informative feedback is essential, evaluative feedback seldom is?

3   For what reasons do we give evaluative feedback to children but usually give only informative feedback to adults? Are the humanists right that it is because we do not respect children as much as we do adults and so we think that it is alright to patronise them by judging them?

Suggested further reading

Curry, N.E. and Johnson, C.N. 1990 *Beyond self-esteem: developing a genuine sense of human value* National Association for the Education of Young Children, Washington, DC

For activities to expand students' self-concept:

Borba, M. and Borba, C. 1978 *Self-esteem: a classroom affair: 101 ways to help children like themselves* Winston Press, Minneapolis, MN
Borba, M. and Borba, C. 1982 *Self-esteem: a classroom affair: more ways to help children like themselves* Winston Press, Minneapolis, MN
Canfield, J. and Wells, H.C. 1994 *100 ways to enhance self-concept in the classroom* 2nd edn, Allyn & Bacon, Boston, MA

13 Meeting students' social needs

Students say that they like classrooms where they feel they know the teacher and the other students . . . In classrooms with their friends, students feel less isolated and vulnerable . . . The number of student references to 'wanting caring teachers' is so great that we believe it speaks to the quiet desperation and loneliness of many adolescents in today's society.

Phelan et al. (1992: 696–8)

Key points

- Schools need to rearrange their priorities to focus on students' relationships with each other, as well as their present emphasis on student–teacher relationships.
- You can establish warm relationships with your students by being open with them and by communicating your care for their achievements and personal development.
- You can facilitate the social inclusion of isolated students by instituting cooperative activities and by offering a social skills curriculum.

Students' relationship needs

Students' most basic relationship need is for *emotional safety and protection*, both from peers and teachers while at school, and also on the way there and back. This is the reason for taking action to limit bullying, for example (see chapter 10).

Second is a need for *personal involvement and trust* (Coopersmith 1967; Lipsitz 1984, in Jones & Jones 1998).

A third relationship need is for love or *acceptance from others* and a feeling of *belonging*, which refers to the extent to which students feel personally accepted, respected, included and supported by others (Goodenow 1993) and their willingness to give affection in return.

Young people also need *flexibility in relationships* with adults, in line with their developing skills. This implies that you will need to adjust your relationship style according to your students' ages (Grossman 1995).

Relationships with teachers

Students say that they like their teachers to care about their academic progress and to listen to their ideas and opinions (Phelan et al. 1992).

Respect

Communicating respect does not mean that you have to like every student, or even to pretend that you like them all, but that you must behave in a professional manner with all students regardless of your personal feelings (Rogers 1998).

Reciprocal relationships

Gordon (1974) says that your relationships with students need to be characterised by:

- *openness*, which refers to being direct and honest with each other;
- *care*, which signals that you value each other;
- *interdependence*, in which you support but do not rely on each other;
- *separateness*, so that you can each grow and learn;
- *mutual needs satisfaction*, so that all class members can meet their needs without violating those of others.

Openness with students about your reactions to events at school and limited aspects of your personal life, values and interests allows students to know you and therefore to value your good opinion of their work and behaviour (Jones & Jones 1998). This degree of relatedness, however, is in contrast with disclosing your unfulfilled needs and becoming involved in students' lives: you can be friendly without being your students' friend.

Your care is crucial to students' involvement in their learning and attitude to themselves as learners (Phelan et al. 1992). You can communicate to students that you care about them by helping them to succeed at their work; by taking a few minutes to relate personally to individual students; and by seeking and valuing their opinions (Phelan et al. 1992). One way to elicit the latter would be to have a suggestion box and class meetings in which you discuss students' suggestions, among other issues (Jones & Jones 1998).

You can help students get to know you by using natural events to tell them about who you are, what you stand for and will not stand for, and what you will and will not be asking them to do (Glasser 1998b). You can write them introductory letters about yourself, allow them to interview you, or participate in their play time, extracurricular and special school activities (Jones & Jones 1998).

More about communication skills

Bill Rogers (1998) believes that any rules that uphold rights for students, teachers or parents are 'fair'. You therefore are justified in upholding these rights and responsibilities through assertive (but not hostile) messages. Gordon (1974) describes the 'When you . . . I feel . . . because' formula for assertive messages, but this format may not be adequate for all occasions. Jakubowski and Lange (1978) suggest the following alternatives:

- *'I want' statements.* When you tell others what you need, they can often mistake this for a demand. To avoid this, you can qualify what you say by asking if students are able to grant your request, by stating how strongly you need it, or by limiting it in some way—for instance: 'I would like that area cleaned up soon. But if you're still working, you can finish off first and then clean up later if you'd rather.'
- *Mixed feeling statements.* With this assertion method, you name more than one feeling and explain the origins of each. For example: 'I appreciate that you were working quietly for a while. It helped me to hear your individual reading. I'm disappointed now, though, that you're getting noisier because I still need to be able to hear two more children's reading.'
- *Empathic assertion.* I find this form of assertive message the most useful of all, as it tells students that you understand them and are willing to listen to their needs and, in exchange, it asks that they listen to yours. For example: 'I know that you're excited about the holidays and it's hard to work when they're so

close. But we still have work to finish and I need you to settle yourselves down so that it can be done.'

- *Confrontive assertion.* This is useful when students have violated an agreement that they made with you about their behaviour. The message has three parts:

1 In a non-judgmental way, you describe what was agreed to.
2 Describe what the student has done in contradiction of the agreement.
3 Express what you want to have happen.

For example: 'We agreed that you could stay back to practise for the concert but that you'd clean up the hall afterwards. I see that you've left lots of gear out. I would like you to think about what you could do to keep our agreement.'

When being assertive, it pays to restrict your focus to the present, as it is unfair and ineffective to bring up past behaviour (Jones & Jones 1998). Even with chronic behavioural problems, your first step in each instance should be to talk directly to students rather than involving their parents or other staff; that way, they know what is being said about them and you communicate that you respect them and believe that they can cope with your feelings. Finally, avoid questions such as 'Where have you been?' and instead tell students about yourself: 'I was concerned that you would miss the bus' (Jones & Jones 1998).

Peer relationships

Many authors (such as Glasser 1986; Johnson & Johnson 1991; Johnson et al. 1993) have observed that our schooling system has focused almost exclusively on the influence that teachers have on students and has neglected the positive and powerful influences that peers have on each other's learning, socialisation and personal satisfaction.

To harness the benefits of peer relationships, you will need to foster cohesiveness in your class and school. Cohesiveness is a characteristic of groups rather than of individuals and reflects students' feelings of membership, identification with others in their class, and good feelings about participating (Schmuck & Schmuck 1997). Highly cohesive groups are more conducive climates in which to make friends (Schmuck & Schmuck 1997). A sense of cohesiveness allows students to accept others and trust their peers with their ideas and feelings. When students feel supported at school, they like school more, value learning and are willing to put in effort and take intellectual risks (Goodenow 1993; Kohn 1996).

The other side of the coin is that isolated and unhappy students can negatively affect the atmosphere in the classroom, provoke discipline issues and limit the activities that you can offer (Mize 1995). Thus positive peer relationships can avoid disruptions in the class.

Elements of friendships

Friendship is a voluntary, ongoing bond between individuals who have a mutual preference for each other and who share emotional warmth. In relating to peers, three issues are involved:

- *inclusion/exclusion*—the extent to which students feel included or excluded from their peer group;
- *control*—who within the group has a given status as a leader and who a follower; and
- *affection*—whether the individuals in the group feel any lasting affection for each other (Schutz 1958, in Webb et al. 1991).

As Webb et al. (1991: 146) observe: 'Typically you feel affection only for those whom you can count on, and whose behaviour is predictable.' This makes aggressive and impulsive children unpopular with their peers, particularly past the age of eight years, by which age their peers expect them to behave more maturely.

Benefits of friendships

Peers can make unique contributions to children's development in many domains (Asher & Parker 1989; Asher & Renshaw 1981; Rubin 1980). Friendships provide a venue for developing and practising social skills; teach self-control; give children experience at problem solving; provide practice at using language; allow children to exchange skills and information that they do not readily acquire from adults; and teach children reciprocity and cooperation (Asher & Parker 1989; Asher & Renshaw 1981; Burk 1996; Hartup 1979; Johnson & Johnson 1991; Kemple 1991; Kohler & Strain 1993; Perry & Bussey 1984; Rubin 1980). These cognitive and social benefits in turn enhance other skill domains as well (Swetnam et al. 1983).

On the emotional side, friendships supply reassurance, promote a healthy self-esteem, enhance children's confidence in stressful situations, avoid loneliness, provide fun and foster individuals' happiness. Friends also offer practical and emotional support by giving information, advice and counsel. By adolescence, peer relationships teach young adults about intimacy, empathy, compassion, loyalty, collaboration, altruism and self-disclosure, as well as give them support for their developing sexuality (Asher & Parker 1989). Such intimacy is necessary to sustain students' drive to excel and contributes significantly to how satisfied they feel about their lives (Gross 1996).

Identifying socially at-risk students

You might be concerned about students' social needs on a number of grounds: their play or friendship patterns; their lack of facility with prosocial skills; their apparent skill deficits; or because sociometric measures indicate that certain students are neglected or rejected by their classmates.

Friendship patterns

In terms of students' play and friendship patterns, you might be concerned if:

- some students appear to have very few friends;
- they spend very little time playing with their peers;
- their type of play is inappropriate for their age;
- they appear to be unhappy with their friendships or say that they feel lonely.

None of these measures is perfect. First, the number of friends can be misleading; most people of all ages have just one or two friends (Porteous 1979), and the number of students' friendships is less important than their quality. Students might have few friends but appreciate and enjoy the ones that they have (Webb et al. 1991).

Second, children might spend little time playing with others but, when they do, they play entirely appropriately. In contrast, socially engaged children might be aggressive (Perry & Bussey 1984). In other words, the important measure is *how*—not *how much*—children play socially.

Observational assessment of prosocial skills

Students need both the skills to behave prosocially and the ability to use those skills in the right time and place. It is not enough to be pleasant: students need to be sensitive to the context and to their peers so that they respond appropriately in the circumstances. This is the difference between having knowledge or skills,

259

versus being competent socially (Cartledge & Milburn 1995). Thus, to work cooperatively and competently together, students need to be able to:

- communicate their feelings;
- give information;
- ask for information or help;
- manage their own feelings;
- negotiate differences in opinion with their friends;
- deal with conflict constructively;
- achieve what they want without hurting anyone else;
- respond to provocation such as teasing or bullying;
- evoke favourable responses from other people;
- deal with people in authority.

In short, students need the skills for dealing with the impact of the world on themselves and for influencing that world (Peterson & Leigh 1990). They need to be able to achieve desired social responses from others without being harmful to them (Foster & Ritchley 1979, cited by Rose 1983; Peterson & Leigh 1990), to evoke approving responses from others, and to respond to the demands of the adult world (Swetnam et al. 1983).

It is likely that the subskills that comprise social competence change as children get older (Asher & Renshaw 1981). Preschool-aged children need the specific social skills to establish and maintain contact, the language and communication skills for accurate exchange of information (past the age of two and a half), and the motor skills to engage in the favourite activities of the peer group (Finch & Hops 1983), while ability to share feelings will be paramount at later ages.

The most crucial social skill is entering a group (Cartledge & Milburn 1995). Entry skills provide a useful assessment of overall social competence (Putallaz & Wasserman 1990). Having gained entry to a group, children need the skills to maintain the relationship.

- *Entry skills.* Children need to recognise the appropriate time and place to initiate entry and use appropriate non-verbal messages to signal their wishes. Competent children typically follow a series of steps to enter a group: they approach other children at play; quietly observe their game (hover); wait for a natural break to occur; begin to behave in ways that relate to the group members' activity; and only then do they comment on the activity (Perry & Bussey 1984; Putallaz

& Wasserman 1990). That is, they join the group's frame of reference and are unlikely to disrupt the game (Putallaz & Wasserman 1990).

In contrast, less competent children disrupt the group process, perhaps by calling attention to themselves, criticising the way the children are playing, or introducing new games or topics of conversation. As a result, their initiations are rebuffed and, in their attempts to save face, they behave in ways that are more likely to lead to repeated rejection (Putallaz & Wasserman 1990).

- *Skills for maintaining friendships*. Once within the group, children need to be supportive of their peers by complementing, smiling at, imitating, cooperating with, helping and sharing with their peers. These behaviours signal that they are keen to cooperate and can be trusted. They also need to be sensitive to their peers' needs and wants and moderate their behaviour to suit their peers. They need skills at being persuasive and assertive when making suggestions about the group's play, and need ways to solve disputes fairly.

Observation of antisocial behaviours

As well as possessing prosocial entry and maintenance skills, competent children generally lack irritating behaviours that lead to rejection by other children—such as interrupting an ongoing activity, disrupting games, being aggressive or abusive, arguing, making contentious statements, displaying impulsive and unpredictable behaviour, having tantrums and monopolising equipment. These behaviours are irrelevant, inappropriate to the context and out of tune with peers. These difficulties might represent *ineffective* social actions—they do not result in students receiving what they need—or they could be *unacceptable*—they might work but are undesirable (Slaby et al. 1995).

In some cases, direct observation will be the best measure of whether children's social skills are appropriate for the context (Kemple 1991; Pellegrini & Glickman 1990), as it lets you appreciate the conditions that gave rise to the behaviour. On the other hand, many social behaviours are subtle and difficult for an external observer to interpret accurately (Asher & Renshaw 1981).

Sociometric measures

In contrast to the above measures that involve assessment by adults, sociometric measures involve assessment by peers. They are the most common measure of social acceptance for school-aged children and are of three types (Asher & Renshaw 1981; Coie et al. 1989; Hops & Lewin 1984). The first is *peer nominations* of those classmates with whom each student would most (or least) like to be friends or with whom they would like to play or work. Children who receive a high number of positive nominations are usually popular; children with a high number of negative nominations are rejected; children with few of either type of nomination are said to be neglected (or ignored).

The second method, termed *peer ratings*, gives students a list of classmates and asks them to rate every individual on a likeability scale. Peer ratings give an indication of acceptability or likeability, which is not the same as popularity. Ratings can be more sensitive than peer nominations to changes in students' social status, and they overcome the problem of some students being forgotten or overlooked with a nomination approach (Hops & Lewin 1984).

The third method is a *paired comparison* procedure in which each student is asked to choose the preferred child out of every possible pair in the class. This is more sensitive to reciprocity in relationships, although it is lengthy to administer.

There are some difficulties with whatever form of sociometric measure is used. First, some children might be popular with the *group* but do not feel that they have close friendships with *individuals* (Kemple 1991). Second, children might nominate other students who they *want* to be their friends but who in fact are not (Hops & Lewin 1984). Third, the measures seldom identify reciprocity of choices, which is the basis of a true friendship.

A fourth issue is that peer ratings give little information about the specific behaviours that have excited rejection or neglect of particular students (Johnson et al. 1990) and therefore what skills to include in a social skills program (Kerr & Nelson 1998). Nevertheless, we do know that rejection usually results from aggression and behavioural difficulties, while neglected students often have internalising difficulties such as anxiety or depression (Cartledge & Milburn 1995). These behaviours, then, could become the targets for social skills intervention.

Isolated students

Most children will experience some temporary isolation at one time or another during their school lives (Asher & Renshaw 1981), often as a result of being new to a group or having just lost their favourite friend. For some students, however, their isolation is long-lasting, with the result that they lack the relationships to practise their skills and so they may become less socially capable over time.

The most common reason for peer rejection is aggression, especially after the ages of seven or eight, although students who are physically unattractive or who display strange behaviours may also be rejected by their peers (Coie et al. 1989). These children are not isolated out of choice; despite this, they tend to be no more lonely than popular children (Asher & Parker 1989). However, this may mean only that they have hardened themselves to their rejected status.

Effects of isolation

Low peer acceptance may have more damaging consequences than low academic achievement (Frosh 1983). Children who are isolated miss out on the important benefits that friendships offer, and are lonelier and less satisfied with those relationships they do have. Socially isolated children adjust less well to school, have more chance of dropping out of school and have a higher incidence of school maladjustment and mental health problems as adults (Hartup 1979; Hill & Hill 1990; Hops & Lewin 1984; Kemple 1991; LeCroy 1983; Rose 1983), especially if their low acceptance is due to their aggression rather than to shyness and withdrawal (Asher & Parker 1989).

However, we cannot conclude that isolation or a lack of friendships *cause* children's later emotional problems (Asher & Parker 1989; Frosh 1983; Ladd 1985; Schneider 1989). Early forms of what will develop into an emotional disorder in adulthood may cause both peer rejection in childhood and the adult maladjustment.

A cognitive model of social skills

Social competence is no different from other cognitively based skills and, therefore, what we know about cognitive training can be applied to the social skills domain (Asher & Renshaw 1981; Dodge 1985; Dweck 1981; Ladd 1985; Ladd & Mize 1983). One added dimension to social skills, however, may be their emotive value to students, in that social rejection will mean more to them than failure at some other, academic, task. Also, social learning may be more complex and may require more practise than other cognitive skills (Dweck 1981).

The model in Figure 13.1 on the following page depicts the cognitive model of social skills. This model implies that students who display social skills difficulties might not lack skills as such: they may have the skills but are not using them for reasons of:

- external factors such as the lack of a true peer group (Dweck 1981) or class size (Frosh 1983);

Figure 13.1   Components of social competence

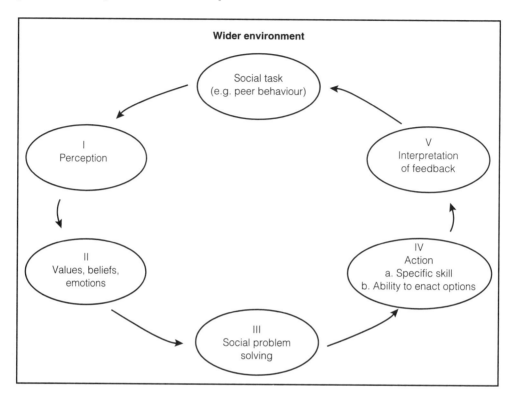

- their devalued peer group status (Asher & Renshaw 1981; Cillessen & Ferguson 1989);
- emotional difficulties (Dodge 1985);
- an inability to process social experiences and information (Oden 1988);
- an inability or unwillingness to act prosocially; or
- a problem with discriminating which behaviour to use in which settings.

That is, some students do not have a *knowledge* deficit as such, but a *performance* deficit (Schneider 1989).

The environment

The environment both affects students' acquisition of social knowledge (Bye & Jussim 1993) and can change their performance (Dodge & Price 1994). As adults, we can choose to take part in activities and to associate with people who bolster our self-esteem, but our students are at the mercy of the contexts in which we place them (Katz 1995). This means that your students rely on you to create an accepting social environment that gives them some freedom and the confidence to practise prosocial skills.

Use democratic behaviour management methods

Democratic discipline has some powerful effects on students' social inclusion. First, it models the communication skills—including listening, assertiveness, collaborative problem solving, understanding another person's point of view and recognising other people's qualities—that students will need for relating to others. Second, it teaches students personal attributes that their peers value, such as self-reliance, self-control, exploration, leadership and the ability to solve problems.

Third, as well as protecting students from the behavioural excesses of each other, democratic discipline also ensures that disruptive students are not scapegoated by how you respond to them, which would result in their rejection by peers.

Limit competition

Competition at school in the form of competitive activities and public grades and awards can create tensions between students (Glasser 1969; Humphrey & Humphrey 1985; Jones & Jones 1998). In one study, gifted students reported that competition tended to scapegoat them and promoted jealousy from classmates (Ford 1989). Thus competition can actually lower achievement levels, even of students who consistently win (Cropper 1998).

Foster inter-group relationships

Although they prefer to associate most with friends, students report that they feel more comfortable at school when they can also mingle with other students (Phelan et al. 1992). When students have numerous opportunities to become acquainted with each other, they will be able to overcome stereotypes about others from backgrounds that differ from their own, make new friends more easily and move between groups with ease (Phelan et al. 1992; Schmuck & Schmuck 1997).

Conduct class meetings

All theorists except the authoritarians are strong advocates of class meetings as a way of helping students to support each other. Their format for meetings is suggested in Chapters 6 and 7 and so I will not repeat that information here. However, it is worth mentioning that meetings do not always run smoothly, especially when first instigated. Therefore, Kohn (1996) recommends that you use the meetings themselves to solve initial problems such as students' acting out, making outrageous suggestions and resisting their increased autonomy.

Institute peer tutoring

Peer tutoring fosters the notion that asking for and giving help are positive behaviours (Jones & Jones 1998). It can improve the confidence of both tutor and learner and enhance their academic performance (Cushing & Kennedy 1997; DuPaul et al. 1998), as long as the tutors do not feel burdened by responsibility for their peer's progress and tutees have opportunities to act as tutors as well.

Structure cooperative games for young children

Earlier beliefs that young children are too egocentric to play cooperatively have been supplanted by the awareness that our understanding of children's egocentrism might be due to how we rear children in Western societies (Slaby et al. 1995). The implication is that we can anticipate increased cooperation skills if we actively encourage their development through activities such as joint projects and co-operative games.

Cooperative games aim to involve isolated children and to pair up children who ordinarily do not play with each other. In this way, they expand each child's pool of potential friends; help children to form a cohesive group; teach cooperation skills, turn-taking and sharing; decrease aggressiveness; and provide a non-threatening context for modelling and rehearsing social skills (Bay-Hinitz et al. 1994; Hill & Reed 1989; Orlick 1982; Sapon-Shevin 1986; Slaby et al. 1995, Swetnam et al. 1983).

Examples of cooperative games include non-elimination musical chairs which involves removing a chair—not a player—whenever the music stops, so that all the children end up having to fit on the one remaining chair. Another example is the frozen bean bag game that requires children to move around with a small bean bag on their heads, freezing when it falls off and remaining still until another child helps by replacing the bean bag on their head (Sapon-Shevin 1986). (For further examples of cooperative games, see Porter 1999a; Sapon-Shevin 1986.)

At the same time, it will pay to avoid competitive games, as these increase aggressive behaviours and reduce cooperation (Bay-Hinitz et al. 1994). Competitive games are those in which students aim to win and to see their opponents fail. They may involve taunting or teasing (such as 'King of the castle'), grabbing or snatching at scarce toys (as in musical chairs), monopolising or excluding other children (for instance, the piggy in the middle game), or games involving physical force (such as tag ball) (Orlick 1982; Sapon-Shevin 1986).

Employ cooperative learning

Cooperative learning involves highly structured group activities in which the students rely on each other to achieve a common goal and common reward (Robinson 1990). It aims to enhance their learning through developing a deeper understanding of the concepts involved; improve their thinking and problem-solving skills; improve their attitude to learning; increase acceptance of peers; reduce aggression; and enhance their self-esteem from feeling able to contribute at their skill level (Cole & Chan 1990; Hill & Hill 1990; Hill & Reed 1989; Johnson et al. 1993).

The purpose is for students to maximise their own and each other's learning as each member can achieve if, and only if, all other group members are successful and participate fully. This is contrasted with competitive activity, in which individual students' achievements are at the expense of others; and with independent tasks, in which their achievement is independent of others (Hill & Reed 1989; Johnson & Johnson 1991; Johnson et al. 1993).

However, cooperation is not the same as having students sit or work together and neither does it necessarily imply harmony. Cooperative groups will not just happen; it will take practice for them to work smoothly (Johnson & Johnson 1991; Putnam 1993).

Groups need to be small enough so that members can get to know each other personally and groupings should change regularly so that rivalry does not build up between groups.

You will need to structure activities so that coordinated effort from all members is necessary for success and teach students the social skills needed in cooperative work—namely forming the team, working together, problem solving as a group, and managing differences (Hill & Hill 1990).

Tasks requiring creative thinking and problem solving are especially suited to cooperative work (Johnson & Johnson 1991; Johnson et al. 1993). At the same time, you will need to be aware that some topics of study are more amenable to individual than to cooperative endeavour (Johnson et al. 1993). Also, heterogeneous grouping may not live up to its promise of fully including children with disabilities and other students who commonly have low status (Cole & Chan 1990).

Similarly, gifted students often complain that they have to carry the group (Matthews 1992; Phelan et al. 1992); advocates for gifted education claim that this 'Robin Hood' effect of robbing their time to teach others amounts to exploitation of gifted learners (Colangelo & Davis 1997; Montgomery 1996).

Finally, you and the students will need to find ways to evaluate how the groups are functioning and how successfully the students are meeting their goals, in terms of both cooperative effort and academic performance (Johnson & Johnson 1986, 1991).

Grouping practices

Given that children choose friends who are at their own developmental level, students with marked developmental delays or advances can find it difficult to locate a same-aged person at their developmental level and can feel under pressure to fit in with others whose development is dissimilar to their own.

Thus multi-age classes can help children to locate potential friends. But these are not the same as composite classes, in which children of different grade levels are 'housed' together but taught separately: in a true multi-age classroom, students are not seen to be members of a grade or year level, but instead are taught at their ability (not age) level.

Nevertheless, simply placing children of different ages together in composite classes will not be enough to ensure that they benefit from the experience (Mosteller et al. 1996; Veenman 1995, 1996): any social and academic benefits appear to come from your philosophical commitment to meeting individual students' needs without regard to age norms (Lloyd 1997).

Structured social skills teaching

The model in Figure 13.1 on p. 264 illustrates that only within a socially empowering school and classroom can students be socially successful (MacMullin 1998). Within facilitating environments, most students will naturally become socially skilful. However, the social difficulties of students who are neglected or rejected by their peers are unlikely to disappear spontaneously (Asher & Parker 1989; Hill & Hill 1989; Schneider 1989). Therefore, skills training may avoid their social problems becoming entrenched.

A second group to benefit from formal social skills training is students with developmental delays in mainstream settings, as they are at risk of being neglected (Guralnick et al. 1995). Simply placing together children with and without disabilities will not ensure that they relate with each other, which implies that social skills training may improve disabled students' chances of successful inclusion in mainstream schooling (MacMullin 1998).

Components of training

Structured social skills training involves teaching students to discard ineffective or unacceptable behaviours and replace these with more effective and prosocial actions (Cartledge & Milburn 1995). Most training involves (Cartledge & Milburn 1995; McGrath 1998):

- discussing specific skills and describing a rationale for learning them;
- identifying correct and incorrect ways of using each skill;
- simulated practice of the skill, usually with guidance and prompts;
- teacher and peer feedback about students' performance;
- reinforcement for using the skill in natural settings.

Phase I: Perception

Selective attention will limit the breadth of cues to which students attend (Bye & Jussim 1993). For instance, aggressive children are more likely to misinterpret social cues and will attribute hostile intent to others when their behaviour has been ambiguous (Feindler 1991; Lochman et al. 1991; Ladd 1985; Wragg 1989). The following factors must be taken into account in this phase:

- *Knowledge.* The first component of social skills training is knowledge of *general interaction principles*, such as cooperating, sharing, participating and validating peers; the *strategies* that can achieve these goals; the *contexts* in which each strategy may be used appropriately (Ladd & Mize 1983); and *self-knowledge* (Bye & Jussim 1993).
- *Values.* To improve training outcomes, you must clarify students' values systems to give them a rationale for acquiring new skills (Caplan & Weissberg 1989; Cartledge & Milburn 1995). Aggressive children, for instance, often value coercive behaviour and have competitive goals, with little appreciation of the negative effects of their aggression on others (Cartledge & Milburn 1995).

Phase II: Emotional influences

You must focus on *how* students think, not *what* they think about social difficulties (Ashman & Conway 1997).

- *Feelings*. Feelings can establish, maintain or disrupt relationships between students and others (Cartledge & Milburn 1995). Therefore, your social skills program must include teaching students to identify their own *feelings* and how to identify others' feelings by looking, listening and asking (see Gesten et al. 1979; MacMullin et al. 1992; McGrath & Francey 1991; Peterson & Ganoni 1989).
- *Self-efficacy and locus of control*. Some students give up when faced with social failure because they believe that they are incompetent, whereas more competent children tend to interpret failure as a temporary setback that they have the skills to overcome. Because occasional failure in social situations is inevitable, you will need to teach students to link their actions with their social outcomes (Dweck 1981). This is called attribution training (see Chapter 4).
- *Motivation*. Motivating and teaching students to be less impulsive and to make rational decisions about their behaviour may be a bigger task than simply broadening their behavioural options (Schneider 1989). Motivation can be enhanced when you let students choose their goals for their own social behaviour (Ashman & Conway 1997; LeCroy 1983) and supply a convincing rationale for adopting new skills (Cartledge & Milburn 1995). This will involve explaining how a new skill will have better outcomes (for them and others) than their present behaviours (Cartledge & Milburn 1995). Enhancing motivation will also require you to use a minimum of direct instruction and a maximum of active rehearsal or practice (Gesten et al. 1979; Ladd & Mize 1983; Rose 1983).

Phase III: Problem solving

Students will need to learn the self-management or *planning* skills of goal setting, gathering information, making decisions about alternative behaviours, problem solving and negotiation (Caplan & Weissberg 1989; Goldstein et al. 1995; LeCroy 1983). Generating specific behaviours requires *alternative* thinking (the ability to generate solutions), *means–end* thinking (planning steps needed to carry out a solution) and *consequential* thinking (consideration of the results before acting). If students lack these skills, their strategies are often situationally inappropriate (Ladd 1985).

Petersen and Ganoni's (1989) social problem-solving training teaches planning skills using the steps: stop, think and do. Role-plays and other activities allow students to generate solutions to social problems and to evaluate their consequences.

Phase IV: Action

Performing the social skill requires an ability to convert the information arrived at during the problem-solving phase into useful behaviours, and an ability to perform the actions skilfully.

- *Intrapersonal skills.* Having earlier discussed how to recognise common feelings such as anxiety or stress, embarrassment, responding to success and failure and dealing with provocation, you will need to teach students how they can deal with these feelings constructively (Cartledge & Milburn 1995).
- *Interpersonal skills.* A second component teaches a range of interpersonal skills including playing games well (being fair, and winning and losing gracefully); being positive (about yourself, other people and experiences); taking risks; cooperating; being interesting; and standing up for yourself.

  Programs that are targeted for adolescents have comprised training in:
  - scholastic competence (as this affects social acceptance) and responding to teacher expectations;
  - establishing accepting relationships with same- and opposite-gender peers;
  - resisting peer pressure to take dangerous risks;
  - gaining independence from adult authority;
  - giving and receiving both positive and negative feedback.
- *Developmental skills.* Because their play often centres around physical games, it helps social interaction for students to have similar abilities to their peers. Thus they need the chance to practise ball skills, skipping, hopscotch or whatever active pursuit their peers presently enjoy. Vision checks or referral to a physiotherapist for coordination difficulties can lead to improvements not only in their abilities but also their social inclusion.

Phase V: Interpreting feedback

Students need to be able to interpret accurately the feedback of their peers so that they can judge whether their own actions are suitable. Some students do not pay enough attention to relevant social cues, while others under-estimate how their behaviour will influence the reactions of others. For instance, aggressive children and adolescents tend to under-estimate their own aggressiveness and therefore do not attempt to control it (Feindler 1991; Lochman et al. 1991; Wragg 1989).

Therefore, the final part of social skills training involves *self-monitoring*, which can entail coaching students to notice other people's reactions to their behaviour and to interpret their reactions constructively.

Issues for social skills training

Knowing the appropriate skill and determining the right time to use it require sophisticated decision making and problem solving. This is the difference between having knowledge or skills, versus being competent socially (Cartledge & Milburn 1995). The latter is more difficult to teach.

Effectiveness

Direct social skills training produces many short-term improvements in students' peer acceptance rates and social behaviours, especially in the cognitive and motor aspects of social skills, although data about long-term effectiveness are less compelling (Asher & Renshaw 1981; McGrath 1998; Schneider 1989; Schneider & Blonk 1998). The less-than-resounding long-term results could be due to the programs targeting skills that were not relevant for children's acceptance (McGrath 1998); because children's reputations are hard to change even if their skills improve (Kemple 1991; Schneider & Blonk 1998); because programs targeted students with serious social skills problems and who were most resistant to change (Schneider & Blonk 1998); or because some students are rejected for reasons such as home background that they cannot control, in which case improving their social skills will not necessarily improve their friendship rate—although it may reduce their active rejection (Cillessen & Ferguson 1989).

Generalisation

So that students transfer the skills that they have been taught in sessions to natural social occasions, you will have to incorporate social skills concepts into other curriculum areas, not just in the social skills training sessions (Cartledge & Milburn 1995). Generalisation is also more likely when you conduct sessions for whole class groups rather than withdrawing targeted students only (McGrath 1998) and when you use natural consequences in the natural setting to acknowledge students' skill gains (Cartledge & Milburn 1995; Ducharme & Holborn 1997).

Age of the students

Early childhood is an ideal time to intervene with social difficulties because preschoolers are receptive to adult direction (Swetnam et al. 1983), and social skills naturally receive considerable adult attention during the preschool years (Mize & Ladd 1990). While a structured remedial program may not be necessary at young ages, you can use young children's numerous social interactions or structured cooperative games to shape their social skills. (For examples of early childhood programs, see Kohler & Strain 1993; Mize 1995.)

The personal and relationship changes that occur during adolescence (Bloom 1990) can provoke new social challenges, although adolescents also have increased ability to learn new coping responses, and therefore skills training in these years can be useful (Johnson et al. 1990).

Nevertheless, designing programs for adolescents is made difficult by this group's social diversity. A year or two's difference in development which at earlier ages could be accommodated in social settings makes for both qualitative and quantitative differences in adolescents' social skills. Furthermore, programs must be tailored to individual needs (Goldstein et al. 1995), yet this is difficult in secondary schools. Subject-based instruction leaves little time for non-academic activities and makes it difficult to nominate one teacher or one subject area that should be responsible for social skills training. This difficulty is exacerbated by the fact that the changing needs of individuals throughout the adolescent period mean that programs must be maintained and topped up throughout secondary school, rather than being a one-off event (Caplan & Weissberg 1989).

Summary

Students flourish within caring relationships with teachers who are willing to listen to them and encourage their ongoing growth. In such an emotional climate, they are likelier to achieve well at school and will be empowered to form close relationships with each other.

Friendships have many benefits, including the obvious salve against loneliness. Students who are isolated do not partake of the benefits of friendships and so are at risk of unhappiness in the present and future (although we must remember that this link is not necessarily causal). Although not all isolated children lack the social skills for forming close relationships, feeling neglected or rejected is likely to lower their confidence in the skills they do possess.

Social competence is more than mere knowledge of skills. It requires insight into the right time and place to use a skill, based on awareness of the social context and the needs of others. Therefore, social skills training requires more than instruction in a wider repertoire of behaviours: it involves ensuring that the environment facilitates prosocial behaviour, and enhancing emotional and cognitive skills as well. Training methods differ for students of different ages, although in the main they involve instruction, rehearsal, feedback, reinforcement of appropriate behaviour and repeated opportunities to practise social skills.

Discussion questions

1   Think about schools in which you have taught, or that you attended as a student. In what ways does their wider environment shape the social skills of their students?
2   Think about students in the age group you teach. With which social tasks do they have the most difficulty?
3   How could you teach impulsive students social-cognitive problem-solving skills? Which aspect (emotional, cognitive, behavioural or environmental) would you expect to be the most crucial for changing their social behaviour?
4   How could you go about teaching a social skills program to students in the age group in which you specialise?

Suggested further reading

For detailed suggestions about enacting cooperative learning:

Johnson, D.W. and Johnson, R.T. 1991 *Learning together and alone* 3rd edn, Allyn & Bacon, Boston, MA

Johnson, D.W., Johnson, R.T. and Holubec, E.J. 1993 *Circles of learning: cooperation in the classroom* 4th edn, Interaction Books, Edina, MN

For a detailed discussion of social skills assessment and training, I recommend:

Cartledge, G. and Milburn, J.F. eds, 1995 *Teaching social skills to children: innovative approaches* 3rd edn, Allyn & Bacon, Boston, MA

For practical suggestions for establishing a socially inclusive classroom:

McGrath, H. and Noble, T. 1993 *Different kids, same classroom: making mixed ability classes really work* Longman, South Melbourne

For programs and activities for social skills training in schools:

MacMullin, C., Aistrope, D., Brown, J.L., Hannaford, D. and Martin, M. 1992 *The Sheidow Park social problem solving program* Flinders University, Adelaide

McGrath, H. 1997 *Dirty tricks: classroom games for teaching social skills* Longman, South Melbourne

McGrath, H. and Francey, S. 1991 *Friendly kids; friendly classrooms* Longman Cheshire, Melbourne

Petersen, L. and Ganoni, A. 1989 *Teacher's manual for training social skills while managing student behaviour* ACER, Melbourne

For descriptions of cooperative games and activities:

Orlick, T. 1982 *The second cooperative sports and games book* Pantheon, New York

Porter, L. 1999 *Young children's behaviour: practical approaches for caregivers and teachers* MacLennan & Petty, Sydney

Sapon-Shevin, M. 1986 'Teaching cooperation' in *Teaching social skills to children: innovative approaches* 2nd edn, eds G. Cartledge & J.F. Milburn, Pergamon, New York

Part Three
Beyond the classroom

Teaching involves more than just working with students within the four walls of your classroom. Particularly when problems arise, you need to be able to draw on the resources of those around you, including your parent group and colleagues.

Thus, in this section, I look at how you can collaborate with parents to empower them to make choices for their children, and draw on the support of a whole-school discipline policy to empower yourself in your teaching.

Naturally, you will find it difficult to collaborate with parents and colleagues when you are treated as a pawn within the education system (Kohn 1996). Empowerment is not a one-way process. You will need the support of your school administration to engage in a truly collaborative way with your students' parents and with your colleagues. You need to feel that your role is valued and that you have support from beyond your classroom to provide high-quality education to your students.

14 Collaborating with parents

When a teacher talks to parents about their children, he [or she] inevitably intrudes on family dreams . . . What the teacher says about the child touches on deep feelings and hidden fantasies. A concerned teacher is aware of the impact of his [or her] words. He [or she] consciously avoids comments that may casually kill dreams.

Ginott (1972: 277–8)

Key points

- Collaboration with parents and other professionals is a state of mind not just another additional task to add to your many others.
- The goal of collaboration is to empower parents to act in their children's interests, to empower you to meet your students' needs at school, and to empower students to contribute to problem solving.
- Although, because of your professional status, it could be assumed that you will make all educational decisions, parents also have skills and knowledge to contribute to the planning of services for their children. Even when these skills are not readily apparent, systems theory reminds us that people always do the best they can in the circumstances; by respecting parents, you can improve their personal circumstances and correspondingly enable them to act more successfully.

Introduction

It is not easy to work collaboratively with parents, not least because, in the main, teachers lack training for doing so (McKim 1993). The skills that help us consult with parents are not the same as those that make us successful with students, but they can be learned.

A second limitation is, of course, many parents' restricted availability for participating actively in the school; still others do not want to become involved, preferring to leave educational decisions to educators (Kauffman et al. 1993). However, a high level of participation is not essential: collaboration is a frame of mind rather than a level of involvement.

Rationale for parental participation

Students who cope best with school are those whose home experiences are similar to their school experiences. They thrive best when their teachers and parents make an effort to understand and respect each other (Gartrell 1998). The drive towards parental participation is thus based on a number of assumptions (Sebastian 1989: 77):

- Parents have the most important and enduring relationship with their children.
- Children learn more from their home environment than from any other setting.
- Parents' involvement in their child's education contributes to students' attitudes to learning and to themselves as learners (Jones & Jones 1998; Raban 1997).
- Parental involvement in their child's education promotes mutual respect and understanding between the home and the school.
- Parents can make valuable contributions to school.
- Accountability is more open when parents are involved in their child's education.

Parents can contribute their expertise about their own children; their informed observations of their children over a long period of time and in many circumstances; knowledge of their children's needs; and their skill in reading and responding to their children's cues. When you can harness this information, your relationship with your students can only benefit.

Furthermore, systems theory tells us that whatever we do with students affects their whole family, and vice versa: any event in their families is felt by students. Keeping the lines of communication open with parents allows you to anticipate students' needs that arise from changes at home.

The evolving parent–teacher relationship

Although working with parents has been an aim of most professionals over time, the concept of a partnership with parents has changed. At first, the notion of professional expertise implied that schools should correct deficiencies in children's home experiences. Thus many teachers felt they had to rescue or 'save' children from 'inadequate' parents.

The next trend limited the responsibility of teachers to *communicating* with parents about their children's education. Teachers were seen to 'know what was best' for children and regarded parents as passive recipients of their advice (Sebastian 1989). This view is carried into the more authoritarian theories about school discipline, which tend to focus their parent-directed efforts on 'parent training' under the assumption that parents need to learn proper ways to parent their children (see, e.g. Schloss & Smith 1998).

The next phase in the relationship with parents was to involve them in their child's program if they were available. This *cooperative* relationship is more reciprocal than the one-way flow of information from the school to home, but it does not necessarily imply a high level of participation (Waters 1996), and might comprise only token involvement such as helping to raise funds or participating on committees.

The more recent emphasis is on *collaboration*, which means that teachers jointly determine goals and plan strategies along with the students' parents (Hostetler 1991). Parents' participation at this level does not necessarily mean day-to-day assistance in a school (Arthur et al. 1996), because many parents will be unavailable for this. Instead, collaboration is a philosophical stance that implies a shared responsibility for the education of children (Arthur et al. 1996; Fleet & Clyde 1993). It relies on being open to families' needs, values, aspirations and skills (Tinworth 1994). However, it is probably true to say that this family-centred perspective is more typical of early years education and care than it is of the more formal school years.

The goal of collaboration with parents

The goal of collaborating with parents is to empower both you and them to act in the interests of children, according to your separate roles (Turnbull & Turnbull 1997):

- Parents will feel empowered when they believe in their own ability to plan, select and enact their own choices for their child's services.
- You will feel empowered when you know how to meet your students' needs, either directly or in collaboration with parents and colleagues.
- Students can be empowered in this process also when you listen to their preferences and suggestions for ways to solve their difficulties.

In this way, *mutual* empowerment results from collaboration with parents. In order to participate as equally valued partners, parents need to feel that they have something valuable to contribute and thus they need:

- recognition of their skills;
- encouragement to contribute to their child's education;
- information about their options;
- a sense of control over their options;
- time and other resources—such as energy.

Parents' perceptions of teachers

Parents are vulnerable: they rely on you almost as much as their child does. They are painfully aware that they are seldom able to anticipate problems that arise after they have enrolled their child in school (Larner & Phillips 1996).

With respect to behavioural difficulties that are the focus of this text, parents' vulnerability will be most acute during the early days of identifying and beginning to address their child's school difficulties. Meanwhile, at this time, you might be feeling your way and might not yet be clear about their son or daughter's needs. This creates the potential for some miscommunication between you: we all misread other people's cues when we feel vulnerable.

It is likely that people who choose to become teachers have had fairly good experiences with school as children; parents, on the other hand, may be mistrustful of teachers because of their own negative school experiences. Furthermore, most will have had dealings with other professionals such as the family doctor or welfare agencies and, at times, felt dominated and patronised in these relationships, and so might approach you with the expectation that they will be similarly overwhelmed and out of control of their interactions with you. On the other hand, it may be that parents are more positively disposed to teachers than to other professionals, perhaps because you tend to have less status than, say, medical practitioners.

Your view of student difficulties

The main reason that teachers find it difficult to provide adequately for children with special needs or behavioural difficulties is that they lack the necessary supports and resources (MacMullin & Napper 1993). When you feel unprepared and under-resourced, you are likely to view special needs negatively because you feel helpless. Almost inevitably, you will communicate your frustration to parents who might misinterpret its source, mistakenly thinking that you blame their child.

Your view of parents

It is easy to be judgmental of parents (Tinworth 1994). This is recognised humorously in a sign in a school office that read:

> Dear parents: we will not believe half of the things the children tell us about you, if you don't believe half of the things they tell you about us.

Obviously, you become involved with parents over school-based problems when *there is a problem*, rather than when everything is going well. At times of difficulty, it is easy to assume that parents' personal deficiencies are the cause of their children's difficulties when, instead, parents' 'inadequacies' can *result* from living with a challenging child (Kauffman et al. 1993). Your exposure to parents when they are under stress can slant your perception of the skills of parents in general and of any particular family, and cause you to over-estimate the stressors with which they are dealing.

Just as you plan for a diversity of needs in your students, so too you need to work with different parents in a variety of ways (a'Beckett 1988). Whether the parents with whom you are consulting come from a different culture from your own, have a son or daughter with a disability, have a gifted child, or in any other way have different needs from the usual, you will need to avoid stereotypes about what they may be experiencing and instead *listen* to their aspirations for their child. Most do not want a better education for their child with special needs, only a more appropriate one.

Some widespread myths about families can interfere with forming respectful relationships with those who depart from the 'ideal' picture of the nuclear family with its two adults and their two biological children. These myths are so common-place that most of us do not even know that they are fallacies. For instance, you might not have known the following:

- The rate of single-parent households with dependent children is the same today (16.6 per cent) as it was in 1890 in Victoria (16.7 per cent). Throughout the intervening century, many fathers left their families during the depressions in search of work or went to war, in both cases sometimes not returning (McDonald 1993).

- The vast majority of today's single parents were in a stable relationship that subsequently disintegrated: they did not set out to be single parents. Whereas, in 1971, one in four Australian women had a child before her twentieth birthday, by 1990, this figure had decreased to one in ten.

- Although divorce is clearly far more common today than ever before, nevertheless life expectancy has increased, and so marriages are today *more* likely to last in excess of 30 years than they were a century ago (McDonald 1993).

- Marital separation does not trouble children as much as living in a conflict-ridden intact family (Burns & Goodnow 1985). If separation does trouble them, this is usually because the separation has not ended the parents' conflict or because it has exacerbated the family's already impoverished living circumstances.

- The rate of stepfamilies is the same now as it was in the sixteenth and seventeenth centuries (Whelan & Kelly 1986). Of course, stepfamily establishment these days usually follows divorce, whereas in the past it followed the death of a spouse. Although this difference may change the psychological impact, nevertheless these figures tell us that stepfamilies are not a new family form.

- Throughout Australia's history, women have always worked, because they were too poor to do otherwise, or to supplement the family income during the depression years, or while men were away at wars. The only exception was the decade of the 1950s when women exited the work force as the men returned from World War II, but this decade is held up today as the norm when in fact it was the exception.

Put together, these facts mean that departures from the idealised nuclear family are not new. Thus our reverence for the nuclear family as the only 'right' way to bring up children could well be somewhat misplaced: it is clear that many types of families can bring up happy children.

Recommended collaborative practices

You will need to find a way to convey that you intend to work alongside parents, relinquishing your dominant role by acknowledging their strengths and skills (Seligman & Darling 1997). This takes some well-attuned communication skills and a good deal of confidence about your own skills, and it means becoming less possessive about your own professional knowledge.

Friendliness

The notion that professionals must maintain 'professional distance' is often experienced by families as a lack of empathy and an unwillingness to offer them support (Summers et al. 1990). Thus, you will need to be personable with parents, rather than relating to them from your professional role, in much the same way you do with students (see Chapter 13).

Respect parents

Naturally, most of us find it easy to accept families whose backgrounds are similar to our own (Galinsky 1990). But the result is that the families who are least well equipped to care for their children are the least likely to receive the support they need (Arthur et al. 1996; Galinsky 1988). You cannot expect yourself to like every parent, but you can respect them for their efforts to bring up their children, recognising that they want the best for their children and have skills and expertise (Gartrell 1998).

Nevertheless, there are parents whose skills *are* difficult to respect; in such cases, remember that respect does not mean having to agree with parents, but simply means recognising their values and perspective (Caughey 1991). A collaborative approach requires that you understand how families are experiencing their lives. So a new way of looking at families who are under stress is to acknowledge that they can survive crises and manage a challenging family situation (Rosenthal & Sawyers 1996).

Alongside professionals' changing attitudes to collaborating with parents has come a change in our attitudes to family assessment. Whereas, in the past, professionals assessed families' weaknesses and helped overcome these, today you are more likely to be told to highlight their strengths. However, both represent the patronising attitude that it is up to you to assess what parents need (Sokoly &

Dokecki 1995). Instead, your job is to *listen* as you explore with them what services they require.

True respect also means avoiding labels that denigrate parents or their children (as in an 'over-involved' parent, or a 'stubborn' child), as labels such as these apportion blame. The view of parents as less observant, less perceptive, less intelligent or overly emotional leads to discounting their views of their child and his or her needs, and will undermine a successful relationship with them. Such labels not only criticise parents, but also allow us to avoid taking responsibility for making the parent–teacher relationship work.

Maintain parental control

All families have a natural hierarchy in which the role of parents (singly or jointly) is to oversee family functioning and be family leaders or decision makers (Foster et al. 1981). In other words, the parents must be in executive control of the family, being the central figures around whom the family is organised, rather like the hub of a wheel. All family members are accorded equal rights to having their various needs met, but their roles within the family differ.

Even before you do anything, the fact that parents have had to ask for assistance with their son or daughter can undermine their confidence. If you subsequently give them the impression that you do not think they are competent or that you know more than they do, they may become more helpless or dependent than they already feel. When instead you work with them to find a solution to their child's difficulties, ask them about past difficulties that they have managed to overcome and ask what they do now that makes some days better than others, you will confirm their status as family leaders, as the people who are able to solve their own problems.

Balance individual and family needs

While the roles of parents and teachers complement and supplement each other, your functions are not the same: you are paid to devote your attention to the welfare of individual students, while parents must address the needs of their entire family, both in the present and over the course of their children's lives. Parents need to pace themselves for this long-term task: they are on a marathon rather than a 100-metre dash, and need time to relax and to meet everyone's needs (Turnbull & Turnbull 1997). Thus, if you are asking parents to act on a child's school-based difficulties, you will need to balance what you expect them to do in light of their overall commitments. This both avoids parent burn-out and prevents making the child the focus of all family attention. This point is expanded by Seligman (1979: 177), who says:

> Some parents may genuinely want to be helpful and co-operative and have every intention of pursuing activities decided upon with the teacher, but somehow they find them impossible to initiate. For some parents, the demands of other members of the family and jobs may be so great that good intentions are difficult to implement. For others, engaging in mutually agreed upon activities with their child serves to highlight their child's deficiencies thereby increasing their anxiety.

In the short term during crises, it is natural for a child with difficulties to become the centre of the family's efforts, but if that exclusive focus is maintained in the long term, it will undermine the parents' ability to lead the family (Frey 1984). The hierarchy is turned upside-down, with the child in control. This is unhealthy for overall family functioning, for children and for parents' confidence.

Limit your responsibilities

Obviously, it is important to be sensitive and responsive to parents' needs. However, if you make yourself endlessly available to parents or attempt to 'rescue' them in times of distress, you will unwittingly be telling them that you do not think that they can solve their own problems. In turn, they will become increasingly dependent on your support and advice. It may also delay their becoming uncomfortable enough to do anything about their problems: discomfort is a necessary stimulus for change.

Refer on

No one knows everything about everything and it is not usually a teacher's responsibility to provide ongoing counselling for students or parents. Part of your role, therefore, will involve referring parents to other professionals whose job it is to focus on a problem that is outside your field of expertise. In order to do so, you will need to know about the services that are available. This is where your group of parents can act as a very useful resource: by asking their recommendations for practitioners in a range of fields, you can compile a list of local and recommended specialists to whom you can refer parents and children who need specialist help.

Collaborate with other professionals

It is important that the various professionals in young people's lives work with each other, as otherwise you can undermine each other's efforts at assisting students. Therefore, when a student in your class is receiving from another professional services that could affect the student's education, it will be helpful for you to make contact with that service provider—as long as, of course, you have parental permission to do so. This not only ensures that the various professionals are 'pulling in the same direction' but the two-way exchange of information empowers other service providers with your knowledge of the student and empowers you as you gain first-hand knowledge of their views of your student's situation.

Communicating with parents

There are many occasions when you can exchange information with parents. These include day-to-day informal contacts; brochures about the school's policies and procedures; formal meetings aimed at solving problems or routinely reviewing students' progress; newsletters and bulletin boards. The remainder of this chapter will focus on problem-solving meetings, as these will be the most personally challenging for you.

Before moving on to that topic, it should first be said that these meetings will be much more productive when you have maintained ongoing contact with parents over positive and interesting things their son or daughter has done at school. Your initial contacts can begin with a letter of introduction where you describe the curriculum at that grade level, introduce yourself and your background, summarise your philosophy about education, and state your aims for the year, while also asking parents about their own goals for their son's or daughter's education (Jones & Jones 1998).

Delivering sensitive information

There will be occasions when you have concerns about students' progress at school and need to convey these concerns to their parents. When conveying such poten-tially upsetting information, it is crucial that you are honest and do not try to shield the parents from the facts out of some misguided desire to protect them. However, you can still remain positive. You might achieve this balance by starting with a report about their child's progress and then qualifying that with a statement about how this compares to the level you would expect at that age.

You will need to plan your meeting very carefully, in order that the parents will feel comfortable and that there is enough time to discuss your concerns, listen to them and answer their questions (Abbott & Gold 1991). You can begin by giving them some positive feedback about their son or daughter and then, instead of listing their child's limitations, point out what he or she needs to do differently.

Next, listen to their response so that you can understand how they view their son or daughter. This information will also help you choose terms that they will understand when you are giving your impressions (Gartrell 1998). You will need to avoid jargon where you can, and define those terms that you cannot avoid (Turnbull & Turnbull 1997).

It will help two-parent families if you can speak with both parents about your concerns. If this cannot be arranged, then you could tape your conversation so that the parent who could not attend can at least listen to the taped conversation. You will need to pass on the invitation for that parent to contact you with any questions that arise from hearing the tape. Another useful strategy is to take notes about your conversation and give these to the parents so that they can absorb more of what you have been telling them.

Before the meeting, ensure that you have updated your knowledge of which agencies are available to provide any specialist services that the student might require. This information will include waiting time, costs and contact phone numbers. The more specific your information can be, the easier it will be for the parents to follow up your concerns promptly.

Problem solving with parents

When a student is experiencing a difficulty at school, parents are likely to feel resentful if you assume that they need to be taught how to respond to their child (Foster et al. 1981). Thus it is wise to avoid giving them advice (Coleman 1991); rather, collaborate with them to find a solution. You might use the collaborative problem-solving steps that were outlined in Chapter 6.

You might describe what has worked at school and ask parents what they find works at home. Together, then, the two of you can formulate a plan that does not impose solutions on parents, but which combines your various expertise.

However, Heath (1994) asks, 'What if the parents' suggested solutions—such as smacking a child—cannot be implemented?' If you argue against their suggestion, you might undermine them, but neither can you follow their advice. In this case, Heath suggests that, before selecting the course of action you will follow, you and the parents could:

- identify the types of solutions that are possible in the circumstances;
- restate your goals for the student;
- identify the relevant characteristics of the child—temperament, age, size, abilities, interests, responses to earlier disciplinary attempts, and so on;
- identify the needs of the people involved;
- identify the feelings of those who are involved.

In this way, the solution remains compatible with your broader goals for the student.

Handling complaints

As consumers of an important (and—in terms of private school fees or tax contributions—expensive) service, parents would be irresponsible if they did not closely question what you offer their child (Greenman & Stonehouse 1997). More than being mere consumers or even equal participants in a partnership with you, parents are actually your employers. This makes you directly accountable to them for your practices.

This means that, regardless of their manner, you need to meet with courtesy the questions that parents ask and the demands that they make. Even 'difficult' parents are not being demanding just to make you jump through hoops: they both *need* and have a *right* to ask questions.

Nevertheless, there will be occasions when parents are belligerent, uncooperative, abusive, or otherwise disrespectful or overpowering (Boutte et al. 1992). Although at first glance these behaviours can be intimidating, generally the parents feel that they have a valid reason for their behaviour. It will help not to take their behaviour personally, as it will be triggered by their situation, rather than by yourself. The notion of collaboration implies that you understand that, from their perspective, their frustration is valid.

Thus you will need to listen, acknowledge their frustration or anger, and reflect what they are saying. When they are expressing their complaints offensively, however, you might want them to moderate how they are talking to you, in which case it can pay to direct them to want they want to accomplish (Jones & Jones

1998)—for example: 'I accept that you are angry that Simon was sent out of class. Perhaps now we can focus on what you would like to see happen next time there is a problem with his behaviour?'

The next step is to state that you have a common interest—namely, providing the best possible education for their son or daughter. You might restate how the meeting is intended to advance that purpose: 'I wonder how we could ensure that he can calm down in class rather than having to be sent out to do so.'

When your time is limited, it helps to tell the parents so at the outset and suggest that all you can do now is make a start on solving the problem but can schedule another meeting for later (Jones & Jones 1998). At other times, it can be useful to impose a time limit deliberately, so that you can give yourself time to evaluate the complaint (Heath 1994). A delay will also give the parents time to calm down. They will not be able to listen to even the most reasonable explanation while they are angry (Stanley 1996). Therefore, you could take the information, offer to think about it or to gather more facts from others who were involved, and then get back to the parents for a follow-up meeting.

Conclusion

Despite the many barriers to empowering relationships between parents and teachers, you share a common bond: you both want what is best for individual students. You may have differing opinions about what would be 'best' or how to attain that 'best', but, ultimately, goodwill and skilled communication will go a long way towards establishing relationships in which the skills of both the parents and yourself can inform each other, enrich your relationship and promote better outcomes for students.

Discussion questions

1   If you have been successful in collaborating with parents when their son or daughter was having difficulties at school, what helped make those approaches work for you? For the parents? For the students?

2   What supports do you need within the school for working with parents?

Suggested further reading

For discussion of how to collaborate with parents whose child has a disability:

Porter, L. and McKenzie, S. in press *Professional collaboration with parents of children with disabilities* Whurr, London

Seligman, M. and Darling, R.B. 1997 *Ordinary families; special children* 2nd edn, Guilford, New York

For discussion of the needs of families whose child may be gifted:

Davis, G.A. and Rimm, S.B. 1998 *Education of the gifted and talented* 4th edn, Allyn & Bacon, Boston, MA

Porter, L. 1999 *Gifted young children: a guide for teachers and parents* Allen & Unwin, Sydney. Simultaneously published by Open University Press, Buckingham, London

15 Formulating a discipline policy

Any intervention can be misused and abused if the person using it lacks an ethical system of personal and professional values. Practitioners must never forget that knowledge is power and that with power comes the responsibility to apply that power for the benefit of all persons.

Walker & Shea (1999: 15)

Key points

- Whether at a personal or a school-wide level, a policy on discipline in schools needs to have clear philosophy, goals, theory base and guidelines for practice.
- Proactive measures will be given most emphasis in such a policy because prevention of problems is more powerful than intervention.
- Policies must take into account the requirements of teachers, students, parents and school administrators.

Introduction

A professional is someone who not only knows what to do, but can also say why she or he uses a particular practice. The aim of understanding theory is to empower you with a wide repertoire of responses to students' behavioural difficulties and to enable you to give a clear rationale for your selected approach. Thus it is fitting that this text ends with a discussion of policy on school discipline, as enabling you to formulate such a plan was its purpose.

In general, policies are statements about what services you will offer and how you will deliver them. A school-wide policy on discipline expresses how school members are expected to behave towards each other so that they can work productively together (Cowin et al. 1990). It offers students, teachers and parents safeguards and clear expectations of their roles, rights and responsibilities.

Discipline is a process for helping students to learn and to gain personal skills: it is not an end in itself (Jones & Jones 1998). Therefore, a policy statement about student behaviour will include more than a direct focus on intervening with disruptive behaviour.

Mandate

When writing either a school-wide policy or a personal plan for discipline in your own classroom, you will need to take account of higher-level policies that govern your practice. A school might have an over-arching policy dictated by its governing body or local education authority; while individual teachers will be constrained by your school's policy.

Nevertheless, most general policies at these levels offer broad guidelines only, frequently leaving day-to-day decisions about implementation to individual teachers. This is wise, as teachers are more effective when they can exercise such discretion compared with when they are obliged to adopt a discipline style that does not suit them (Lewis 1997).

Philosophy

Many schools express a democratic philosophy about behaviour management of students and yet detail procedures that come from the authoritarian approaches (Lewis 1997). A philosophical statement is a positive place to start a policy, as it can focus you on what you want to achieve (Jones & Jones 1998). With your philosophical stance spelled out, you can later check that your espoused practices are consistent with your philosophy of education and of life (Edwards 1997).

Personal needs

Your individual plan will need to take account of your own personal needs, as distinct from your professional goals (Charles 1999). These might include your need for:

- a pleasant physical environment in which to work;

- a measure of order in the classroom;
- courteous behaviour between all members of the class;
- job satisfaction;
- parental and school support.

At the same time, you must take account of students' needs (Charles 1999). Later steps will be designed to meet both your own and your students' personal needs, as well as your educational goals for students.

Educational goals

The main focus of your discipline plan is meeting the goals that you want your students to achieve as members of the classroom and of the wider society (McCaslin & Good 1992). A discipline policy will express the aim of fostering a well-disciplined environment in which you can work and students can learn.

Your goals will need to be feasible, clearly written and incorporating both educational and social-emotional goals. You might plan how you will:

- establish a safe and caring physical and emotional environment that supports and protects the rights of all students to learn and grow personally, and safeguards your right to teach;
- facilitate students' success through offering a worthwhile and enjoyable curriculum (Charles 1999);
- recognise students' achievements, which will involve making a judgment about the debate on informative versus evaluative feedback and the use of external reinforcers;
- empower students to participate in decisions that affect them;
- promote prosocial behaviour through proactive and interventive means;
- give students strategies for coping with stress;
- maintain collaborative relationships with parents.

Teacher satisfaction

As well as meeting student needs, a school policy must establish a system for meeting teachers' needs (Good & Brophy 1986; McCaslin & Good 1992). These needs fall into two areas: developing the skills to motivate and manage students so that you experience success and job satisfaction; and receiving personal and professional

KING ALFRED'S COLLEGE
LIBRARY

support through ongoing contact with colleagues, practical assistance with particularly challenging students and inservice training (Jones & Jones 1998; Rogers 1998). These measures are built on a recognition that chronic problems need a team approach.

Theory

Your chosen theory must be consistent with your philosophy. When selecting a guiding theory, you will need to evaluate its assumptions and practices on the basis of whether they are consistent with your views about education and child development, and whether they are known to be effective and ethical. Although you might blend theories somewhat eclectically, only those with a similar philosophy will fit coherently together. If there are apparent contradictions between your guiding theories, you will have to find a way to overcome them.

Practice

Next, you will need to detail some efficient, self-sustaining rules and procedures for achieving your goals, with ways to include students in formulating and managing these. Procedures will focus on how you can organise your school or classroom so that most behavioural difficulties are prevented and those that do occur receive a constructive response (Cowin et al. 1990). As prevention is far more powerful than intervention (Doyle 1986), this aspect will be the largest part of your practices section.

At a school-wide level, this section should describe the responsibilities of students, teachers, parents and administrators. This will include describing who is responsible for acting in particular situations, what the procedure will be, and what school and other resources can be called on to support the action that is taken.

Having arrived at some recommended practices, you will have to check that they are realistic, that staff are willing and have the resources to carry them out, that they conform to guidelines of higher-level policies, and that the school can overcome any special problems that could affect implementation.

Intervention

Rogers (1998) believes that four Rs should underpin any school discipline policy. These are rights, rules and responsibilities which relate to the quality of relationships—see Figure 15.1.

Figure 15.1   Policy framework for rights, rules, responsibilities and relationships

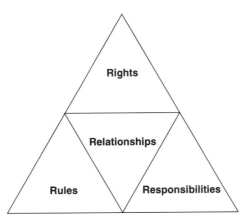

Source: Rogers (1998: 133)

Clarify your assumptions

Jones and Jones (1998) argue that it is contradictory for educators to punish students for behavioural mistakes while teaching them appropriate responses with academic errors. They suggest that this contradiction arises because we have differing assumptions about the two types of error, as described in Table 15.1 on the following page.

School rules

A list of rules runs the risk of degenerating into a list of misdemeanours, as if you expect students to try to get away with whatever they can. Thus, if you want to include a list of rules in a policy document, I suggest including only those behaviours that are prohibited at school, such as drug use. This brief set of mandatory rules will be imposed on students without negotiation, while the policy could direct individual teachers to formulate additional classroom rules in collaboration with their students.

Considerate behaviours

Because chronic behavioural difficulties have serious consequences for students, you must avoid exacerbating problems and instead give considerate behaviour far greater attention than you give to infractions of the rules. However, the humanists argue that any such acknowledgment should occur in a private exchange between you

Table 15.1   Assumptions about academic versus behavioural mistakes

Common assumptions about academic errors	Common assumptions about behavioural mistakes
Students are trying to make the correct response	Students are trying to be disruptive—that is, to make an *incorrect* response
Errors are accidental	Errors are deliberate
Errors are inevitable	Students are refusing to cooperate
Learning requires exploration	Students should not explore limits; they should obey them
Students who are having difficulties need additional or modified teaching	Students who are having difficulties should be punished
Students who achieve good work deserve some recognition	Students should behave appropriately without needing recognition (Brophy 1981)

Source: adapted from Jones and Jones (1998: 276)

and individual students, rather than a public recognition that might embarrass students or be seen as an attempt to manipulate others into copying them.

Disruptive behaviours

Inconsiderate behaviour requires a response that protects the rights of students to learn, supports the rights of teachers to teach and offers the student involved a chance to learn how to make a more considerate choice in the future. You will need to specify those behaviours that you plan to discourage, which will usually include any acts that violate someone's rights by: preventing the student from participating; interfering with other students' learning or emotional safety; or interfering with your teaching or otherwise violating one of your rights. This includes any behaviour that violates a prior agreement.

Behaviours that do not violate anyone's rights are less serious. Some are accidental or are the result of normal childhood exuberance (Emmer et al. 1997; Evertson et al. 1997). While these behaviours can be inconvenient at times, even angering you, Grossman (1995) advises that you will cope better when you can adjust and accommodate to the nature of young people, accepting that at times their behaviour is 'par for the course' given their age and stage of development.

Even if an irritating behaviour becomes more frequent or begins to involve others, nevertheless the majority of writers recommend dealing with this in a problem-solving mode rather than a punishment mode. Gartrell (1998), for instance, says that you can have three levels of intervention: at level one, students take themselves aside and solve their problem with no input from you; at level two, they solve the problem themselves, although you might guide their problem solving by clarifying the issue and suggesting potential solutions; and at level three, you actively assist students to formulate a solution.

Your response to disruptions must aim to minimise embarrassment and hostility, maximise students' choices about their behaviour, develop and maintain respect, maintain a sense of humour, and ensure follow up and follow through (Rogers 1998). Taking Rogers' distinction between primary and secondary behaviours, it is in your own interests to respond to a primary disruption in the most minimalist—and yet effective—way so that you do not provoke a secondary reaction, which can be more troublesome than the original behaviour.

Keep in mind that it is sometimes necessary to delay dealing with a disruption if you do not have all the facts, when there is not enough time to resolve the issue right then, when it would have to be dealt with in public, or when the student is too upset to respond rationally at the time (Grossman 1995). Thus, if you cannot deal with the situation immediately, make an appointment to do so.

Student participation

Your policy will detail ways to empower students to participate in school decision making about their behaviour and learning. You should specify their rights and responsibilities, particularly that they have a right to due process in the case of infractions of the rules (Knight 1991). This means that students should be presumed innocent until proven guilty, permitted to state their side of events, and have available channels of appeal against what they might perceive to be injustices.

Collaboration with parents

Your policy should include a systematic procedure for eliciting parents' advice and support with academic and behavioural issues. This is likely to extend beyond informing parents about the school and their child's conduct there, instead encompassing a two-way exchange of information (see Chapter 14).

Use of consultants

It would be useful to include in your policy a statement about the use of consultants: how and to whom to refer students for help and in which circumstances students might be referred. Clear and uncomplicated procedures for referring students and their families to specialists who will help them and yourself.

Special issues

It may be useful for the school policy to mention specific issues such as bullying (see Chapter 10), sexual harassment procedures and child abuse. Teachers are legally obliged to report any suspicions of child abuse to the local child welfare agency. Advising parents of this obligation and giving information about child abuse will raise awareness of the issue which, in turn, might prevent some abuse, or at least can set a foundation for some constructive intervention by school staff on those occasions when abuse is suspected.

Evaluation of the plan

Any plan will need some modification once you become familiar with the specific needs of your students, or when the plan seems to be ineffective. You might find it useful to ask the following questions, negative answers to which will provoke a change in practices (Borland 1997; Cowin et al. 1990; Davis & Rimm 1998; Sharp & Thompson 1994):

- Is your discipline plan consistent with theory?
- Are the procedures being enacted as originally conceived? Do your recommendations reflect actual practice or are they a 'wish list' (Eyre 1997)?
- Are the outcomes congruent with what you set out to accomplish—that is, your original goals?
- Are there other important unanticipated outcomes?
- Are there students for whom the procedures are more or less successful than others?
- What additional resources (including materials and personnel) are necessary to make the policy more effective? Are these available?

As well as assessing the outcomes of your procedures, you will need to evaluate the effectiveness of inputs—such as the resources being used, the efficient use of teachers' time and the involvement of parents (Davis & Rimm 1998).

Although evaluation can seem burdensome, it can be professionally fulfilling to be able to demonstrate to yourself—if to no one else—that what you are doing is effective. Reflecting on your practice can only enhance your confidence in what you do.

Constraints on discipline plans

While formulating your own personal discipline plan, you will be aware that constraints are inevitable. Classrooms are complex places in which many activities are going on simultaneously, students' responses to even the best-planned activities can be unpredictable, you are called on to make hundreds of decisions per day, and most of your responses are public (Doyle 1986). These characteristics mean that you continuously have to monitor and protect teaching and learning from distractions, intrusions and unpredictable events (Doyle 1986).

Contextual factors

Your response to a disruption will be influenced by contextual factors such as when the behaviour occurs and who is present at the time (Lewis 1997). For instance, safety reasons would suggest prompt intervention with exuberant behaviour during a science experiment, while the same behaviour could be tolerated in another class. Your own personal resources and available time will also influence your decision and action.

When debating how to respond, you will make complex judgments about the act itself, the individual student's history, and the circumstances in the classroom at the time (Doyle 1986). You must also consider whether contextual factors are provoking the student's behaviour, and whether alteration of these would prevent its recurrence.

Your personality

Your personality will affect what behaviour you choose to intervene with, and how (Grossman 1995; Lewis 1997). Teachers vary in the amount of movement and noise they tolerate, what activities they allow students to do without asking for permission, their emphasis on interpersonal skill development (process) versus knowledge acquisition (content), the types of instruction they use, the extent to which they allow students to participate in the development of classroom rules, their status with respect to students, their emphasis on intrinsic versus extrinsic motivation, and their emphasis on cooperation versus competition (Grossman 1995).

Nevertheless, your expectations of students need to be realistic, taking into account their abilities and the demands of the task at hand.

Your tenure

When your relationship with students is a short-term one, such as when you are relief teaching, you might feel obliged to adopt the approaches used by their regular teacher. The longer your relationship is anticipated to last, the less this becomes an issue, as students can adjust to different expectations from a range of teachers. However, McCaslin and Good (1992) caution against a series of changes from democratic to authoritarian management styles and back again.

Your stress levels

Many teachers find that, while they believe in fostering student autonomy, they sometimes instead find themselves responding to students in authoritarian ways (Lewis 1997). Lewis reports that new teachers begin with concerns about their own needs and their suitability for the role of teacher; then with experience they become focused on the teaching process; and finally they are able to attempt to meet student needs. When stressed, however, even experienced teachers can regress to being concerned about their own survival and may revert to authoritarian discipline. In answering the question of 'why teachers misbehave', Lewis suggests that some reasons include:

- You may know the authoritarian methods best (because as a child you were subjected to them yourself) and so when you feel stressed, you resort to them as if by reflex.
- When individuals feel out of control, their natural tendency is to try harder to exert control, both over themselves and others, which means using authoritarian methods.
- Teachers receive varying degrees of training in how to respond to student behaviours. What you do receive is often authoritarian in nature and so you are obliged to use these approaches by default, even when your personal philosophy endorses more democratic values.
- Students will at times push you to see if you will use punitive methods under

pressure. It is as if they are testing your integrity and commitment to the more democratic philosophies, and are searching for any sign of hypocrisy.

- Schools are organised hierarchically, with you being subjected to external discipline yourself. Within this environment, it is natural that you apply this control downwards to students.
- Your own thinking can be counter-productive, as examined in Chapter 4. You might attribute blame to students, which in turn will cause you to feel personally threatened (Lewis 1997) and to respond emotionally instead of rationally.

Despite these temptations to revert to dysfunctional management methods, Rogers (1989) reminds us that, while an old dog cannot learn new tricks, with effort and support *people* can. You *can* develop a plan for your practice that, while not a panacea, offers some guidelines. You *can* seek out colleagues who will discuss issues with you, and you *can* use your feelings to inform, not deform, your practice.

The students' ability levels

Highly motivated and achieving students are likely to be task-focused and are less likely to be distracted when you issue behavioural reminders to other students, even when these interrupt the flow of the activity; on the other hand, low-achieving students are more easily distracted and so you might choose to avoid reprimanding them in order to maintain their focus on the lesson content (Doyle 1986).

Age of students

Kohlberg (in Grossman 1995) described three main stages of moral development in young people, with children up to the ages of six to eight being motivated to do what is expected of them because adults have the power to reward or punish them. In the second stage (from seven to eleven years) children are said to be more able to understand why rules are necessary and will observe those rules that make sense to them. During adolescence, young people's decisions about right and wrong hinge on what feels right, and they exercise judgment accordingly. In light of these stages, some writers (e.g. Grossman 1995; Lewis 1997) suggest adjusting the management method to the students' age and related stage of moral reasoning, on the assumption that younger children cannot respond to self-directive approaches of management.

However, six arguments rebut this suggestion. First, there is very little research verifying the effectiveness of teachers adjusting their management approach to the students' stage of moral reasoning (Grossman 1995).

Second, older students who are suddenly expected to exercise self-discipline may find the experience uncomfortable, and therefore need earlier opportunities to practise self-regulation (Lewis 1997).

Third, once students have reached the legal age for leaving school, there are few threats that schools can carry out to ensure the compliance of disaffected students. If procedures for self-direction are enacted before students become alienated from school, behavioural problems in this senior group could be prevented.

Fourth, it is worth remembering that, for instance, while four-year-olds have only four-year-old social problem-solving abilities, they usually only have four-year-old problems to solve, and so they can be guided to apply their skills to age-appropriate problems.

Fifth, preschools and child care centres successfully teach very young children self-management (Porter 1999b), yet by high-school age, teachers are reluctant to use democratic approaches (Johnson et al. 1994; Lewis 1997). This is the reverse of what would be expected if the type of discipline depended on the children's capacity for moral reasoning. It appears to have nothing to do with the developmental abilities of the children and adolescents, but with the authoritarian culture that exists within traditional education systems. The context, not the students' ages, dictates management style.

Finally, rather than creating the need for that discipline style, Kohlberg's stages of moral reasoning may *result* from the typical ways that we discipline children at various ages (Kohn 1996). When, instead of imposing control on young children, we explain the effects of their actions on others, they are able to develop moral reasoning from as young as eighteen months of age (Berk 1997; Buzzelli 1992).

The students' frame of mind

There are no guarantees: there are times when certain students do not respond to even the best planned, most sophisticated and best executed approach. Their disaffection might not reflect any deficiency on their part, but a social problem: we raise students' expectations that hard work will be rewarded with good jobs, when they have neither the supports (such as nutrition, health and safety) to continue to work hard at school nor the likelihood of work when they leave (McCaslin &

Good 1992). Some who come to realise this grow disillusioned and refuse to work within a system that seems to have let them down.

Conclusion

Although formulating policy is time-consuming, the process gives all participants the opportunity to clarify their values, roles and responsibilities (Stonehouse 1991). A formal school-wide policy has the advantages of ensuring that teachers' disciplinary action is not capricious, while ideally still allowing them some autonomy (Cangelosi 1997; Farmer 1995; Good & Brophy 1986). The process of developing policy allows you to plan how to act rather than having to make hasty decisions in response to a problem that has already happened.

While schools with an overall policy do not have better results in terms of student behaviour than when teachers are left to formulate their own approach, a school-wide policy does help those teachers who have been experiencing disciplinary problems (Charles 1999). Written documentation also helps with familiarising new staff and parents with the philosophy and workings of the school.

When the policy is arrived at through wide consultation, it is more likely to receive widespread support from the highest level of the school and by the parent group. Awareness of their support can only assist your day-to-day functioning within your class.

Discussion questions

1   What are your beliefs about the purpose of discipline? How are these influenced by your understanding of childhood and how children learn, the reasons for disruptive behaviour and the status of teachers with respect to students? What do these imply for your role as a teacher?
2   What goals would you seek to include in your discipline policy?
3   Which theory (or blend of theories) of discipline is consistent with your beliefs?
4   Which practices would you consider ideal in your present or intended teaching context?
5   What constraints can you identify that may affect the use or success of those practices?

6   If your school (or a school you attended on placement) adopted the policy you espouse, would its present practices change? If so, in what ways?

Suggested further reading

For overviews of the range of theories and practices outlined in this text, you could consult:

Edwards, C. 1997 *Classroom discipline and management* 2nd edn, Merrill, Upper Saddle River, NJ
Lewis, R. 1997 *The discipline dilemma: control, management, influence* 2nd edn, ACER, Melbourne

For a description of personal discipline plans, you might refer to:

Charles, C.M. 1999 *Building classroom discipline: from models to practice* 6th edn, Longman, New York
Rogers, B. 1995 *Behaviour management: a whole-school approach* Ashton Scholastic, Gosford
——1998 *'You know the fair rule' and much more: strategies for making the hard job of discipline and behaviour management in school easier* ACER, Melbourne

References

a'Beckett, C. 1988 'Parent/staff relationships' in *Trusting toddlers: programming for one to three year olds in child care centres* ed. A. Stonehouse, Australian Early Childhood Association, Watson, ACT

Abbott, C.F. and Gold, S. 1991 'Conferring with parents when you're concerned that their child needs special services' *Young Children* vol. 46, no. 4, pp. 10–14

Adler, A. 1957 *Understanding human nature* Fawcett, New York

Agran, M. and Martin, J.E. 1987 'Applying a technology of self-control in community environments for individuals who are mentally retarded' in *Progress in behavior modification* eds M. Hersen, R. Eisler & P. Miller, Sage, Newbury Park, CA

Alberto, P. A. and Troutman, A.C. 1999 *Applied behaviour analysis for teachers* 5th edn, Merrill, Upper Saddle River, NJ

Amatea, E.S. 1988 'Brief strategic intervention with school behavior problems: a case of temper tantrums' *Psychology in the Schools* vol. 25, no. 2, pp. 174–83

——1989 *Brief strategic intervention for school behavior problems* Jossey-Bass, San Francisco, CA

Amatea, E.S. and Sherrard, P.A.D. 1989 'Reversing the school's response: a new approach to resolving persistent school problems' *The American Journal of Family Therapy* vol. 17, no. 1, pp. 15–26

——1991 'When students cannot or will not change their behavior: using brief strategic intervention in the school' *Journal of Counseling and Development* vol. 64, no. 4, pp. 341–3

Ansbacher, H.L. and Ansbacher, R.R. 1956 *The individual psychology of Alfred Adler* Basic Books, New York

Arthur, L., Beecher, B., Dockett, S., Farmer, S. and Richards, E. 1996 *Programming and planning in early childhood settings* 2nd edn, Harcourt Brace, Sydney

Asher, S.R. and Parker, J.G. 1989 'Significance of peer relationship problems in childhood' in *Social competence in developmental perspective* eds B.H. Schneider, G. Attili, J. Nadel & R.P. Weissberg, Kluwer Academic Publishers, Dordrecht

Asher, S.R. and Renshaw, P. D. 1981 'Children without friends: social knowledge and social-skill training' in *The development of children's friendships* eds S.R. Asher & J.M. Gottman, Cambridge University Press, Cambridge

Ashman, A. and Conway, R.N.F. 1989 *Cognitive strategies for special education* Routledge, London

——1993 *Using cognitive methods in the classroom* Routledge, London

——1997 *An introduction to cognitive education: theory and applications* Routledge, London

Axelrod, S. 1977 *Behaviour modification for the classroom teacher* McGraw Hill, New York

Bailey, J.S. 1991 'Marketing behavior analysis requires different talk' *Journal of Applied Behavior Analysis* vol. 24 , no. 3, pp. 445–8

——1992 'Gentle teaching: trying to win friends and influence people with euphemism, metaphor, smoke, and mirrors' *Journal of Applied Behavior Analysis* vol. 25, no. 4, pp. 879–83

Bailey, J. and Pyles, D. 1989 'Behavioral diagnostics' in *The treatment of severe behavior disorders: behavior analysis approaches* ed. E. Cipani, The American Association on Mental Retardation, Washington, DC

Balson, M. 1992 *Understanding classroom behaviour* 4th edn, ACER, Melbourne

——1994 *Becoming better parents* 4th edn, ACER, Melbourne

Bandura, A. 1986 *Social foundations of thought and action* Prentice Hall, Englewood Cliffs, NJ

Baumrind, D. 1967 'Child care practices anteceding three patterns of preschool behavior' *Genetic Psychology Monographs* vol. 75, pp. 43–88

References

Bay-Hinitz, A.K., Peterson, R.F. and Quilitch, R. 1994 'Cooperative games: a way to modify aggressive and cooperative behaviors in young children' *Journal of Applied Behavior Analysis* vol. 27, no. 3, pp. 435–46

Ben Arı, R. and Rich, Y. 1992 'Meeting the educational needs of all students in the heterogeneous class' in *To be young and gifted* eds P. S. Klein & A.J. Tannenbaum, Ablex, Norwood, NJ

Benes, K.M. and Kramer, J.J. 1989 'The behavioral tradition in schools (and miles to go before we sleep)' in *Cognitive-behavioral psychology in the schools* eds J.N. Hughes & R.J. Hall, Guilford, New York

Benson, A.J. and Presbury, J.H. 1989 'The cognitive tradition in schools' in *Cognitive-behavioral psychology in the schools* eds J.N. Hughes & R.J. Hall, Guilford, New York

Berg, I.K. and de Shazer, S. 1989 *Four useful questions in solution construction* Brief Family Therapy Center, Milwaukee, WI

Berk, L. 1997 *Child development* 4th edn, Allyn & Bacon, Boston, MA

Berk, L.E. and Landau, S. 1993 'Private speech of learning disabled and normally achieving children in classroom academic and laboratory contexts' *Child Development* vol. 64, no. 2, pp. 556–71

Berk, L.E. and Potts, M.K. 1991 'Development and functional significance of private speech among attention-deficit hyperactivity disordered and normal boys' *Journal of Abnormal Child Psychology* vol. 19, no. 3, pp. 357–77

Bernard, M.E. 1986 *Becoming rational in an irrational world: Albert Ellis and rational-emotive therapy* McCulloch, Melbourne

Biddulph, S. 1993 *The secret of happy children* rev edn, Bay Books, Sydney

Biederman, G.B., Davey, V.A., Ryder, C. and Franchi, D. 1994 'The negative effects of positive reinforcement in teaching children with developmental delay' *Exceptional Children* vol. 60, no. 5, pp. 458–65

Bloom, M. 1990 'The psychological constructs of social competency' in *Developing social competency in adolescence* eds T.P. Gullotta, G.R. Adams & R. Montemayor, Sage, Newbury Park, CA

Bolton, R. 1987 *People skills* Simon and Schuster, Sydney

Bonnington, S.B. 1993 'Solution-focused brief therapy: helpful interventions for school counselors' *The School Counselor* vol. 41, no. 2, pp. 126–8

Borba, M. and Borba, C. 1978 *Self-esteem: a classroom affair: 101 ways to help children like themselves* Winston Press, Minneapolis, MN

——1982 *Self-esteem: a classroom affair: more ways to help children like themselves* Winston Press, Minneapolis, MN

Borland, J.H. 1997 'Evaluating gifted programs' in *Handbook of gifted education* 2nd edn, eds N. Colangelo & G.A. Davis, Allyn & Bacon, Boston, MA

Boulton, M.J. 1994 'Understanding and preventing bullying in the junior school playground' in *School bullying: insights and perspectives* eds P.K. Smith & S. Sharp, Routledge, London

Boutte, G.S., Keepler, D.L., Tyler, V.S. and Terry, B.Z. 1992 'Effective techniques for involving "difficult" parents' *Young Children* vol. 47, no. 3, pp. 19–22

Brophy, J. 1981 'Teacher praise: a functional analysis' *Review of Educational Research* vol. 51, no. 1, pp. 5–32

Brophy, J. and Good, T.L. 1986 'Teacher behavior and student achievement' in *Handbook of research on teaching* 3rd edn, ed. M.C. Wittrock, Macmillan, New York

Brown, B. 1986 'We can help children to be self-reliant' *Children Today* Jan–Feb, pp. 26–8

Brown, H.J. Jnr 1991 *Life's little instruction book* Bookman Press, Melbourne

Brown, J.E. 1986 'The pretend technique: an intervention in the teacher–student system' *Family Therapy Case Studies* vol. 1, no. 2, pp. 13–15

Burden, R.L. and Fraser, B.J. 1993 'Classroom environment assessments' *Psychology in the Schools* vol. 30, no. 3, pp. 232–40

Burk, D.I. 1996 'Understanding friendship and social interaction' *Childhood Education* vol. 72, no. 5, pp. 282–5

Burns, A. and Goodnow, J. 1985 *Children and families in Australia* 2nd edn, Allen & Unwin, Sydney

Burns, R.B. 1982 *Self-concept development and education* Holt, Rhinehart & Winston, London

Buzzelli, C.A. 1992 'Young children's moral understanding: learning about right and wrong' *Young Children* vol. 47, no. 6, pp. 47–53

Bye, L. and Jussim, L. 1993 'A proposed model for the acquisition of social knowledge and social competence' *Psychology in the Schools* vol. 30, no. 2, pp. 143–61

Cameron, J. and Pierce, W.D. 1994 'Reinforcement, reward, and intrinsic motivation: a meta-analysis' *Review of Educational Research* vol. 64, no. 3, pp. 363–423

——1996 'The debate about rewards and intrinsic motivation: protests and accusations do not alter the results' *Review of Educational Research* vol. 66, no. 1, pp. 39–51

Canfield, J. and Wells, H.C. 1994 *100 ways to enhance self-concept in the classroom* 2nd edn, Allyn & Bacon, Boston, MA

Cangelosi, J.S. 1997 *Classroom management strategies: gaining and maintaining students' cooperation* 3rd edn, Longman, New York

Canter, L. 1988 'Let the educator beware: a response to Curwin and Mendler' *Educational Leadership* vol. 46 no. 2, pp. 71–3

——1989 'Assertive discipline: a response' *Teachers College Record* vol. 90, no. 4, pp. 631–8

Canter, L. and Canter, M. 1976 *Assertive discipline: a take charge approach for today's educator* Lee Canter & Associates, Los Angeles, CA

——1992 *Assertive discipline: positive behavior management for today's classroom* Lee Canter & Associates, Santa Monica, CA

Caplan, M.Z. and Weissberg, R.P. 1989 'Promoting social competence in early adolescence' in *Social competence in developmental perspective* eds B.H. Schneider, G. Attili, J. Nadel & R.P. Weissberg, Kluwer Academic Publishers, Dordrecht

Carlsson-Paige, N. and Levin, D.E. 1992 'Making peace in violent times: a constructivist approach to conflict resolution' *Young Children* vol. 48, no. 1, pp. 4–13

Carter, J.F. 1993 'Self management: education's ultimate goal, *Teaching Exceptional Children* vol. 25, no. 3, pp. 28–32

Cartledge, G. and Milburn, J.F. (eds) 1995 *Teaching social skills to children: innovative approaches* 3rd edn, Allyn & Bacon, Boston, MA

Caughey, C. 1991 'Becoming the child's ally—observations in a classroom for children who have been abused' *Young Children* vol. 46, no. 4, pp. 22–8

Chan, L.K.S. 1998 'The perceived competence of intellectually talented students' *Gifted Child Quarterly* vol 32, no. 3, pp. 310–14

——1996 'Motivational orientations and metacognitive abilities of intellectually gifted students' *Gifted Child Quarterly* vol. 40, no. 4, pp. 184–94

Chang, J. and Phillips, M. 1993 'Michael White and Steve de Shazer: new directions in family therapy' in *Therapeutic conversations* eds S. Gilligan & R. Price, W.W. Norton & Co, New York

Chapman, J.W., Lambourne, R. and Silva, P. A. 1990 'Some antecedents of academic self-concept: a longitudinal study' *British Journal of Educational Psychology* vol. 60, part 1, pp. 142–52

Charles, C.M. 1999 *Building classroom discipline: from models to practice* 6th edn, Longman, New York

Cillessen, T. and Ferguson, T.J. 1989 'Self-perpetuation processes in children's peer relationships' in *Social competence in developmental perspective* eds B.H. Schneider, G. Attili, J. Nadel & R.P. Weissberg, Kluwer Academic Publishers, Dordrecht

Coady, M. 1994 'Ethical and legal issues for early childhood practitioners' in *Issues in early childhood services: Australian perspectives* eds E.J. Mellor & K.M. Coombe, William C. Brown, Dubuque, IO

Coie, J.D., Christopoulos, C., Terry, R., Dodge, K.A. and Lochman, J.E. 1989 'Types of aggressive relationships, peer rejection, and developmental consequences' in *Social competence in developmental perspective* eds B.H. Schneider, G. Attili, J. Nadel & R.P. Weissberg, Kluwer Academic Publishers, Dordrecht

Colangelo, N. and Dettman, D.F. 1983 'A review of research on parents and families of gifted children' *Exceptional Children* vol. 50, no. 1, pp. 20–7

Cole, P. G. and Chan, L.K.S. 1990 *Methods and strategies for special education* Prentice Hall, New York

——1994 *Teaching principles and practice* 2nd edn, Prentice Hall, New York

Coleman, M. 1991 'Planning for the changing nature of family life in schools for young children' *Young Children* vol. 46, no. 4, pp. 15–20

Combrinck-Graham, L. 1991 'On technique with children in family therapy: how calculated should it be?' *Journal of Marital and Family Therapy* vol. 18, no. 4, pp. 373–7

Conoley, J.C. 1989 'Cognitive-behavioral approaches and prevention in the schools' in *Cognitive-behavioral psychology in the schools* eds J.N. Hughes & R.J. Hall, Guilford, New York

Conway, R. and Gow, L. 1990 'Moderate to mild disability: teaching and learning strategies to improve generalisation' in *The exceptional child* ed. S. Butler, Harcourt Brace Jovanovich, Sydney

Cooper, P. and Upton, G. 1990 'An ecosystemic approach to emotional and behavioural difficulties in school' *Educational Psychology* vol. 10, no. 4, pp. 301–21

——1991 'Controlling the urge to control: an ecosystemic approach to problem behaviour in schools' *Support for Learning* vol. 6, no. 1, pp. 22–6

Coopersmith, S. 1967 *The antecedents of self-esteem* W.H. Freeman, San Francisco, CA

References

Corey, G. 1996 *Theory and practice of counseling and psychotherapy* 5th edn, Brooks/Cole, Pacific Grove, CA

Corno, L. 1989 'Self-regulated learning: a volitional analysis' in *Self-regulated learning and academic achievement: theory, research, and practice* eds B.J. Zimmerman & D.H. Schunk, Springer-Verlag, New York

Cowie, H. and Sharp, S. 1994 'Tackling bullying through the curriculum' in *School bullying: insights and perspectives* eds P. K. Smith & S. Sharp, Routledge, London

Cowin, M., Freeman, L., Farmer, A., James, M., Drent, A. and Arthur, R. 1990 *Positive school discipline: a practical guide to developing policy* Narbethong Publications, Boronia, Vic.

Crary, E. 1992 'Talking about differences children notice' in *Alike and different: exploring our humanity with young children* rev. edn, ed. B. Neugebauer, National Association for the Education of Young Children, Washington, DC

Craven, R.G. and Marsh, H.W. 1997 'Threats to gifted and talented students' self-concepts in the big pond: research results and educational implications' *The Australasian Journal of Gifted Education* vol. 6, no. 2, pp. 7–17

Cropper, C. 1998 'Is competition an effective classroom tool for the gifted student?' *Gifted Child Today* vol. 21, no. 3, pp. 28–31

Curry, N.E. and Johnson, C.N. 1990 *Beyond self-esteem: developing a genuine sense of human value* National Association for the Education of Young Children, Washington, DC

Curwin, R.L. and Mendler, A.N. 1988 'Packaged discipline programs: let the buyer beware' *Educational Leadership* vol. 46, no. 2, pp. 68–71

——1989 'We repeat, let the buyer beware: a response to Canter' *Educational Leadership* vol. 46, no. 6, p. 83

Cushing, L.S. and Kennedy, G.H. 1997 'Academic effects of providing peer support in general education classrooms on students without disabilities' *Journal of Applied Behavior Analysis* vol. 30, no. 1, pp. 139–51

Davis, G.A. and Rimm, S.B. 1998 *Education of the gifted and talented* 4th edn, Allyn & Bacon, Boston, MA

de Shazer, S. 1993 'Creative misunderstanding: there is no escape from language' in *Therapeutic conversations* eds S. Gilligan & R. Price, W.W. Norton and Co., New York

de Shazer, S., Berg, I.K., Lipchik, E., Nunnally, E., Molnar, A., Gingerich, W. and Weiner-Davis, M.

1986 'Brief therapy: focused solution development' *Family Process* vol. 25, no. 2, pp. 207–22

de Shazer, S. and Molnar, A. 1984 'Four useful interventions in brief family therapy' *Journal of Marital and Family Therapy* vol. 10, no. 3, pp. 297–304

Derman-Sparks, L. and the ABC Task Force 1989 *Anti-bias curriculum: tools for empowering young children* National Association for the Education of Young Children, Washington, DC

Dewey, J. 1943 *The school and society* 2nd edn, University of Chicago Press, Chicago, IL

Diaz, R.M. and Berk, L.E. 1995 'A Vygotskian critique of self-instructional training' *Development and Psychopathology* vol. 7, no. 2, pp. 369–92

DiCintio, M.J. and Gee, S. 1999 'Control is the key: unlocking the motivation of at-risk students' *Psychology in the Schools* vol. 36, no. 3, pp. 231–7

Dicocco, N.E., Chalfin, S.R. and Olson, J.M. 1987 'Systemic family therapy goes to school' *Social Work in Education* vol. 9, no. 4, pp. 209–21

Dinkmeyer, D. and Dreikurs, R. 1963 *Encouraging children to learn: the encouragement process* Prentice Hall, Englewood Cliffs, NJ

Dinkmeyer, D. and McKay, G. 1989 *Systematic training for effective parenting* 3rd edn, American Guidance Service, Circle Pines, MN

Dinkmeyer, D., McKay, G. and Dinkmeyer, D. 1980 *Systematic training for effective teaching* American Guidance Service, Circle Pines, MN

Dinkmeyer, D. Snr, McKay, G.D., Dinkmeyer, J.S., Dinkmeyer, D. Jnr, McKay, J.L. 1997 *Parenting young children: systematic training for effective parenting (STEP) of children under six* American Guidance Service, Circle Pines, MN

Dixon, M.R., Hayes, L.J., Binder, L.M., Manthey, S., Sigman, C. and Zdanowski, D.M. 1998 'Using a self-control training procedure to increase appropriate behaviour' *Journal of Applied Behavior Analysis* vol. 31, no. 2, pp. 203–9

Dobson, J. 1992 *The new dare to discipline* Tyndale House, Wheaton, IL

Dobson, K.S. and Pusch, D. 1993 'Towards a definition of the conceptual and empirical boundaries of cognitive therapy' *Australian Psychologist* vol. 28, no. 3, pp. 137–44

Dodge, K.A. 1985 'Facets of social interaction and the assessment of social competence in children' in *Children's peer relations: issues in assessment and intervention* eds B.H. Schneider, K.H. Rubin and J.E. Ledingham, Springer-Verlag, New York

Dodge, K.A. and Price, J.M. 1994 'On the relation between social information processing and socially competent behavior in early school-aged

310

children' *Child Development* vol. 65, no. 5, pp. 1385–97

Dowling, E. 1985 'Theoretical approach—a joint systems approach to educational problems with children' in *The family and the school* eds E. Dowling & E. Osborne, Routledge and Kegan Paul, London

Doyle, W. 1986 'Classroom organization and management' in *Handbook of research on teaching* 3rd edn, ed. M.C. Wittrock, Macmillan, New York

Dreikurs, R. and Cassel, P. 1990 *Discipline without tears* 2nd edn, Dutton, New York

Drouet, D. 1993 'Adolescent female bullying and sexual harassment' in *Understanding and managing bullying* ed. D. Tattum, Heinemann Educational, Oxford, UK

Ducharme, D.E. and Holborn, S.W. 1997 'Programming generalization of social skills in preschool children with hearing impairments' *Journal of Applied Behavior Analysis* vol. 30, no. 4, pp. 639–51

Duke, D.L. and Meckel, A.M. 1984 *Teacher's guide to classroom management* Random House, New York

Duncan, B.L. 1992 'Strategic therapy, eclecticism, and the therapeutic relationship' *Journal of Marital and Family Therapy* vol. 18, no. 1, pp. 17–24

Dunlap, G., dePerczel, M., Clarke, S., Wilson, D., Wrights, S., White, R. and Gomez, A. 1994 'Choice making to promote adaptive behavior for students with emotional and behavioral challenges' *Journal of Applied Behavior Analysis* vol. 27, no. 3, pp. 505–18

DuPaul, G.J., Ervin, R.A., Hook, C.L. and McGoey, K.E. 1998 'Peer tutoring for children with attention deficit hyperactivity disorder: effects on classroom behavior and academic performance' *Journal of Applied Behavior Analysis* vol. 31, no. 4, pp. 579–92

Durrant, M. 1995 *Creative strategies for school problems* Eastwood Family Therapy Centre, Sydney

Dweck, C.S. 1981 'Social-cognitive processes in children's friendships' in *The development of children's friendships* eds S.R. Asher & J.M. Gottman, Cambridge University Press, Cambridge, UK

Dyck, M.J. 1993 'New directions in cognitive-behaviour therapy' *Australian Psychologist* vol. 28, no. 3, pp. 133–6

Education Department of South Australia, 1989 *School discipline: the management of student behaviour: policy and guidelines for practice*, Adelaide

Edwards, C.H. 1997 *Classroom discipline and management* 2nd edn, Merrill, Upper Saddle River, NJ

Eisenberger, R. and Armeli, S. 1997 'Can salient reward increase creative performance without reducing intrinsic creative interest?' *Journal of Personality and Social Psychology* vol. 72, no. 3, pp. 652–63

Ellis, A. 1962 *Reason and emotion in psychotherapy* Lyle Stuart, Secaucus, NJ

Emmer, E.T. and Aussiker, A. 1990 'School and classroom discipline programs: how well do they work?' in *Student discipline strategies: research and practice* ed. O.C. Moles, State University of New York Press, Albany, NY

Emmer, E.T., Evertson, C.M., Clements, B.T. and Worsham, M.E. 1997 *Classroom management for secondary teachers* 4th edn, Allyn & Bacon, Boston, MA

Evertson, C.M., Emmer, E.T., Clements, B.T. and Worsham, M.E. 1997 *Classroom management for elementary teachers* 4th edn, Allyn & Bacon, Boston, MA

Eyre, D. 1997 *Able children in ordinary schools* David Fulton, London

Faber, A., Mazlish, E., Nyberg, L. and Templeton, R.A. 1995 *How to talk so kids can learn at home and in school* Fireside, New York

Farmer, S. 1995 *Policy development in early childhood services* Community Child Care Cooperative Ltd, Sydney

Fawcett, S.B. 1991 'Some values guiding community research and action' *Journal of Applied Behavior Analysis* vol. 24, no. 4, pp. 621–36

Feindler, E.L. 1991 'Cognitive strategies in anger control interventions for children and adolescents' in *Child and adolescent therapy: cognitive-behavioral procedures* ed. P. Kendall, Guilford, New York

Fields, M. and Boesser, C. 1998 *Constructive guidance and discipline* 2nd edn, Merrill, Upper Saddle River, NJ

Finch, M. and Hops, H. 1983 'Remediation of social withdrawal in young children: considerations for the practitioner' in *Social skills training for children and youth* ed. C.W. LeCroy, Haworth Press, New York

Fine, M. 1992 'A systems-ecological perspective on home–school intervention' in *The handbook of family-school intervention: a systems perspective* eds M. Fine & C. Carlson, Allyn & Bacon, Boston, MA

Fisch, R., Weakland, J.H. and Segal, L. 1982 *The tactics of change: doing therapy briefly* Jossey-Bass, San Francisco, CA

Fleet, A. and Clyde, M. 1993 *What's in a day? working in early childhood* Social Science Press, Wentworth Falls, NSW

References

Fontana, D. 1985 *Classroom control* British Psychological Society & Methuen, London

Ford, M.A. 1989 'Students' perceptions of affective issues impacting the social emotional development and school performance of gifted/talented youngsters' *Roeper Review* vol. 11, no. 3, pp. 131–4

Foster, M., Berger, M. and McLean, M. 1981 'Rethinking a good idea: a reassessment of parent involvement' *Topics in Early Childhood Special Education* vol. 1, no. 3, pp. 55–65

Foxx, R. 1982 *Decreasing behaviors of severely retarded and autistic persons* Research Press, Champaign, IL

Frey, J. 1984 'A family/systems approach to illness-maintaining behaviours in chronically ill adolescents' *Family Process* vol. 23, no. 2, pp. 251–60

Frosh, S. 1983 'Children and teachers in schools' in *Developments in social skills training* eds S. Spence & G. Shepherd, Academic Press, London

Galinsky, E. 1988 'Parents and teacher-caregivers: sources of tension, sources of support' *Young Children* vol. 43, no. 3, pp. 4–12

——1990 'Why are some parent/teacher partnerships clouded with difficulties?' *Young Children* vol. 45, no. 5, pp. 2–3, 38–9

Gartrell, D. 1987a 'Assertive discipline: unhealthy for children and other living things' *Young Children* vol. 42, no. 2, pp. 10–11

——1987b 'Punishment or guidance?' *Young Children* vol. 42, no. 3, pp. 55–61

——1998 *A guidance approach for the encouraging classroom* 2nd edn, Delmar, Albany, NY

Geldard, D. 1998 *Basic personal counselling* 3rd edn, Prentice Hall, Sydney

Gesten, E.L., De Apodaca, R.F., Rains, M., Weissberg, R.P. and Cowen, E.L. 1979, 'Promoting peer-related social competence in schools' in *Social competence in children* eds M.W. Kent & J.E. Rolf, University Press of New England, Hanover, NH

Ginott, H.G. n.d. *Between parent and teenager* Cookery Book Club, London

——1969 *Between parent and child* Crosby Lockwood Staples, London

——1972 *Teacher and child* Macmillan, New York

Glasser, W. 1969 *Schools without failure* Harper & Row, New York

——1976 *The ten step discipline program* videotape, USA

——1977 'Ten steps to good discipline' *Today's Education* vol. 66, pp. 61–3

——1992a *The quality school: managing students without coercion* 2nd edn, Harper Perennial, New York

——1992b 'The quality school curriculum' *Phi Delta Kappan* vol. 73, no. 9, pp. 690–4

——1998a *The quality school: managing students without coercion* rev. edn, Harper Perennial, New York

——1998b *The quality school teacher* rev edn, Harper Perennial, New York

——1998c *Choice theory: a new psychology of personal freedom* Harper Collins, New York

——1998d *Choice theory in the classroom* rev. edn, Harper Perennial, New York

Goldstein, A.P., Sprafkin, R.P. and Gershaw, N.J. 1995 'Teaching the adolescent: social skills training through skillstreaming' in *Teaching social skills to children: innovative approaches* 3rd edn, eds G. Cartledge & J.F. Milburn, Allyn & Bacon, Boston, MA

Good, T.L. and Brophy, J.E. 1986 'School effects' in *Handbook of research on teaching* 3rd edn, ed. M.C. Wittrock, Macmillan, New York

——1997 *Looking in classrooms* 7th edn, Longman, New York

Goodenow, C. 1993 'The psychological sense of school membership among adolescents: scale development and educational correlates' *Psychology in the Schools* vol. 30, no. 1, pp. 79–90

Goodman, J. 1992 *Elementary schooling for critical democracy* State University of New York Press, Albany, NY

Gordon, T. 1970 *Parent effectiveness training* Plume, New York

——1974 *Teacher effectiveness training* Peter H. Wyden, New York

——1991 *Teaching children self-discipline at home and at school* Random House, Sydney

Greenberg, P. 1992a 'Why not academic preschool? (part 2): autocracy or democracy in the classroom?' *Young Children* vol. 47, no. 3, pp. 54–64

——1992b 'Ideas that work with young children: how to institute some simple democratic practices pertaining to respect, rights, roots and responsibilities in any classroom (without losing your leadership position)' *Young Children* vol 47, no. 5, pp. 10–17

Greenman, J. and Stonehouse, A. 1997 *Prime times: a handbook for excellence in infant and toddler programs* Longman, South Melbourne

Gross, M.U.M. 1996 'The pursuit of excellence or the search for intimacy: the forced-choice dilemma for gifted youth' in *Gifted children: the challenge continues: a guide for parents and teachers* eds A. Jacob & G. Barnsley, New South Wales Association for Gifted and Talented Children, Sydney

——1997 'How ability grouping turns big fish into little fish—or does it? of optical illusions and optimal environments' *The Australasian Journal of Gifted Education* vol. 6, no. 2, pp. 18–30

Grossman, H. 1995 *Classroom behavior management in a diverse society* 2nd edn, Mayfield, Mountain View, CA

Guess, D. and Siegel-Causey, E. 1985 'Behavioral control and education of severely handicapped students: who's doing what to whom? and why?' in *Severe mental retardation: from theory to practice* eds D. Bricker & J. Filler, Division on Mental Retardation, Council for Exceptional Children, Reston, VA

Guralnick, M.J., Connor, R.T., Hammond, M., Gottman, J.M. and Kinnish, K. 1995 'Immediate effects of mainstreamed settings on the social interactions and social integration of preschool children' *American Journal on Mental Retardation* vol. 100, no. 4, pp. 359–77

Haley, J. 1973 *Uncommon therapy: the psychiatric techniques of Milton H. Erickson, M.D.* W.W. Norton, New York

——1980 *Leaving home: the therapy of disturbed young people* McGraw-Hill, New York

——1984 *Ordeal therapy* Jossey-Bass, San Francisco, CA

Hall, R.J. and Hughes, J.N. 1989 'Cognitive-behavioral approaches in the school: an overview' in *Cognitive-behavioral psychology in the schools* eds J.N. Hughes & R.J. Hall, Guilford, New York

Hammel, B. 1989 'So good at acting bad' in *Control theory in the practice of reality therapy* ed. N. Glasser, Harper & Row, New York

Harrison, J. 1996 *Understanding children* 2nd edn, ACER, Melbourne

Hartup, W.W. 1979 'Peer relations and social competence' in *Social competence in children* eds M.W. Kent & J.E. Rolf, University Press of New England, Hanover, NH

Hayes, H. 1991 'A re-introduction to family therapy: clarification of three schools' *Australian and New Zealand Journal of Family Therapy* vol. 12, no. 1, pp. 27–43

Heath, H.E. 1994 'Dealing with difficult behaviours: teachers plan with parents' *Young Children* vol. 49, no. 5, pp. 20–4

Heins, T. 1988 'Relearning childthink' *Australian and New Zealand Journal of Family Therapy* vol. 9, no. 3, pp. 143–9

Herbert, G. 1993 'Changing children's attitudes through the curriculum' in *Understanding and managing bullying* ed. D. Tattum, Heinemann Educational, Oxford, UK

Herbert, M. 1987 *Behavioural treatment of children with problems: a practice manual* 2nd edn, Academic Press, London

Heward, W. and Cooper, J. 1987 'Definition and characteristics of applied behavior analysis' in *Applied behavior analysis* eds J. Cooper, T. Heron & W. Heward, Merrill, Columbus, OH

Hill, S. and Hill, T. 1990 *The collaborative classroom: a guide to cooperative learning* Eleanor Curtin, Melbourne

Hill, S. and Reed, K. 1989 'Promoting social competence at preschool: the implementation of a cooperative games programme' *Australian Journal of Early Childhood* vol. 14, no. 4, pp. 25–31

Hinshaw, S.P. and Erhardt, D. 1991 'Attention-deficit hyperactivity disorder' in *Child and adolescent therapy: cognitive-behavioral procedures* ed. P. Kendall, Guilford, New York

Hitz, R. and Driscoll, A. 1988 'Praise or encouragement?: new insights into praise: implications for early childhood teachers' *Young Children* vol. 43, no. 5, pp. 6–13

Honig, A.S. and Wittmer, D.S. 1996 'Helping children become more prosocial: ideas for classrooms, families, schools and communities' *Young Children* vol. 51, no. 2, pp. 62–70

Hops, H. and Lewin, L. 1984 'Peer sociometric forms' in *Child behavioral assessment* eds T.H. Ollendick & M. Hersen, Pergamon, New York

Horner, R.H. 1994 'Functional assessment: contributions and future directions' *Journal of Applied Behavior Analysis* vol. 27, no. 2, pp. 401–4

Hostetler, L. 1991 'Collaborating on behalf of young children' *Young Children* vol. 46, no. 2, pp. 2–3

House of Representatives Standing Committee on Employment, Education and Training, 1994 *Sticks and stones: report on violence in Australian schools* Australian Government Publishing Service, Canberra,

Humphrey, J.H. and Humphrey, J.N. 1985 *Controlling stress in children* Charles C. Thomas, Springfield, IL

Iwata, B.A., Pace, G.M., Cowdery, G.E. and Miltenberger, R.G. 1994 'What makes extinction work: an analysis of procedural form and function' *Journal of Applied Behavior Analysis* vol. 27, no. 1, pp. 131–44

Jakubowski, P. and Lange, A. 1978 *The assertive option: your rights and responsibilities* Research Press, Champaign, IL

James, J.E. 1993 'Cognitive-behavioural theory: an alternative conception' *Australian Psychologist* vol. 28, no. 3, pp. 151–5

Johnson, B., Whittington, V. and Oswald, M 1994

References

'Teachers' views on school discipline: a theoretical framework' *Cambridge Journal of Education* vol. 24, no. 2, pp. 261–76

Johnson, D.W. and Johnson, R.T. 1986, 'Mainstreaming and cooperative learning strategies' *Exceptional Children* vol. 52, no. 6, pp. 553–61

——1991 *Learning together and alone* 3rd edn, Allyn & Bacon, Boston, MA

Johnson, D.W., Johnson, R.T. and Holubec, E.J. 1993 *Circles of learning: cooperation in the classroom* 4th edn, Interaction Books, Edina, MN

Johnson, J.H., Jason, L.A. and Betts, D.M. 1990 'Promoting social competencies through educational efforts' in *Developing social competency in adolescence* eds T.P. Gullotta, G.R. Adams & R. Montemayor, Sage, Newbury Park, CA

Jones, F.H. 1987a *Positive classroom discipline* McGraw-Hill, New York

——1987b *Positive classroom instruction* McGraw-Hill, New York

Jones, V.F. and Jones, L.S. 1990 *Comprehensive classroom management: motivating and managing students* 3rd edn, Allyn & Bacon, Boston, MA

——1998 *Comprehensive classroom management: creating communities of support and solving problems* 5th edn, Allyn & Bacon, Boston, MA

Kaplan, J.S. and Carter, J. 1995 *Beyond behavior modification: a cognitive-behavioral approach to behavior management in the school* 3rd edn, Pro-Ed, Austin, TX

Katz, L. 1988 'What should children be doing?' *Rattler* Spring 1988, pp. 4–6

——1995 *Talks with teachers of young children* Ablex, Norwood, NJ

Kauffman, J.M. 1997 *Characteristics of emotional and behavioral disorders of children and youth* 6th edn, Merrill, Upper Saddle River, NJ

Kauffman, J.M., Hallahan, D.P., Mostert, M.P., Trent, S.C. and Nuttycombe, D.G. 1993 *Managing classroom behavior: a reflective case-based approach* Allyn & Bacon, Boston, MA

Kemple, K.M. 1991 'Preschool children's peer acceptance and social interaction' *Young Children* vol. 46, no. 5, pp. 47–54

Kendall, P. (ed.) 1991 *Child and adolescent therapy: cognitive-behavioral procedures* Guilford, New York

Kerr, M. and Nelson, M. 1998 *Strategies for managing behavior problems in the classroom* 3rd edn, Merrill, Upper Saddle River, NJ

Kindsvatter, R., Wilen, W. and Ishler, M. 1992 *Dynamics of effective teaching* 2nd edn, Longman, New York

Kirkby, R.J. and Smyrnios, K.X. 1990 'Child-oriented family therapy outcome research: comparisons between brief family therapy and an alternative treatment' *Australian and New Zealand Journal of Family Therapy* vol. 11, no. 2, pp. 75–84

Knight, B.A. 1995 'The influence of locus of control on gifted and talented students' *Gifted Education International* vol. 11, no. 1, pp. 31–3

Knight, T. 1991 'Democratic schooling: basis for a school code of behaviour' in *Classroom discipline* eds M.N. Lovegrove & R. Lewis, Longman Cheshire, Melbourne

Kohler, F.W. and Strain, P. S. 1993 'The early childhood social skills program' *Teaching Exceptional Children* vol. 25, no. 2, pp. 41–2

Kohn, A. 1993 *Punished by rewards: the trouble with gold stars, incentive plans, A's, praise and other bribes* Houghton Mifflin, Boston, MA

——1996 *Beyond discipline: from compliance to community* Association for Supervision and Curriculum Development, Alexandria, VA

Kounin, J.S. 1970 *Discipline and group management in classrooms* Holt, Rinehart & Winston, New York

Kowalski, K. 1990 'The girl with the know-how: finding solutions to a school problem' *Family Therapy Case Studies* vol. 5, no. 1, pp. 3–14

Kral, R. 1988 *Strategies that work: techniques for solution in the schools* Brief Family Therapy Center, Milwaukee, WI

——1989a 'The Q.I.K. (Quick Interview for Kids): psychodiagnostics for teens and children—brief therapy style' *Family Therapy Case Studies* vol. 4, no. 2, pp. 61–5

——1989b 'After the miracle: the second stage in solution focused brief therapy' *Journal of Strategic and Systemic Therapies* vol. 8, no. 2, pp. 73–6

——1992 'Solution-focused brief therapy: applications in schools' in *The handbook of family-school intervention: a systems perspective* eds M. Fine & C. Carlson, Allyn & Bacon, Boston, MA

Kutsick, K.A., Gutkin, T.B. and Witt, J.C. 1991 'The impact of treatment development process, intervention type, and problem severity on treatment acceptability as judged by classroom teachers' *Psychology in the Schools* vol. 28, no. 4, pp. 325–31

Kyriacou, C. and Newson, G. 1982 'Teacher effectiveness: a consideration of research problems' *Educational Review* vol. 34, no. 1, pp. 3–12

Ladd, G.W. 1985 'Documenting the effects of social skill training with children: process and outcome assessment' in *Children's peer relations: issues in assessment and intervention* eds B.H. Schneider,

K.H. Rubin & J.E. Ledingham, Springer-Verlag, New York

Ladd, G.W. and Mize, J. 1983 'Social skills training and assessment with children: a cognitive-social learning approach' in *Social skills training for children and youth* ed C.W. LeCroy, Haworth Press, New York

Lang, T. and Lang, M. 1986 *Corrupting the young (and other stories of a family therapist)* Rene Gordon, Melbourne

Larner, M. and Phillips, D. 1996 'Defining and valuing quality as a parent' in *Transforming nursery education* eds P. Moss & H. Penn, Paul Chapman Publishing, London

Lattal, K.A. and Neef, N.A. 1996 'Recent reinforcement-schedule research and applied behavior analysis' *Journal of Applied Behavior Analysis* vol. 29, no. 2, pp. 213–30

LeCroy, C.W. 1983 'Social skills training with adolescents: a review' in *Social skills training for children and youth* ed. C.W. LeCroy, Haworth Press, New York

Lee, C. 1993 'Cognitive theory and therapy: distinguishing psychology from ideology' *Australian Psychologist* vol. 28, no. 3, pp. 156–60

Lerman, D.C. and Iwata, B.A. 1996 'Developing a technology for the use of operant extinction in clinical settings: an examination of basic and applied research' *Journal of Applied Behavior Analysis* vol. 29, no. 3, pp. 345–82

Lerman, D.C., Iwata, B.A., Shore, B.A. and Kahng, S.W. 1996 'Responding maintained by intermittent reinforcement: implications for the use of extinction with problem behavior in clinical settings' *Journal of Applied Behavior Analysis* vol. 29, no. 2, pp. 153–71

Lerman, D.C, Iwata, B.A. and Wallace, M.D. 1999 'Side effects of extinction: prevalence of bursting and aggression during the treatment of self-injurious behavior' *Journal of Applied Behavior Analysis* vol. 32, no. 1, pp. 1–8

Lewis, R. 1997 *The discipline dilemma: control, management, influence* 2nd edn, ACER, Melbourne

Lindquist, B., Molnar, A. and Brauchmann, L. 1987 'Working with school related problems without going to school: considerations for systemic practice' *Journal of Strategic and Systemic Therapies* vol. 6, no. 4, pp. 44–50

Lloyd, L. 1997 'Multi-age classes: an option for all students?' *The Australasian Journal of Gifted Education* vol. 6, no. 1, pp. 11–20

Lochman, J.E., White, K.J. and Wayland, K.K. 1991 'Cognitive-behavioral assessment and treatment with aggressive children' in *Child and adolescent therapy: cognitive-behavioral procedures* ed. P. Kendall, Guilford, New York

Lovegrove, M.N., Lewis, R. and Burman, E. 1989 *You can't make me! developing effective classroom discipline* La Trobe University Press, Melbourne

Lusterman, D. 1985 'An ecosystemic approach to family–school problems' *The American Journal of Family Therapy* vol. 13, no. 1, pp. 22–30

MacMullin, C. 1994 *Inclusion: an overview* paper presented to Education Support Principals' Conference, Perth, March 1994

——1998 'Developing a social skills programme for use in school' in *Children's peer relations* eds P. T. Slee & K. Rigby, Routledge, London

MacMullin, C., Aistrope, D., Brown, J.L., Hannaford, D. and Martin, M. 1992 *The Sheidow Park social problem solving program* Flinders University, Adelaide

MacMullin, C. and Napper, M. 1993 *Teachers and inclusion of students with disabilities: attitude, confidence or encouragement?* paper presented to Australian Early Intervention Association (SA Chapter) Conference, Adelaide, June 1993

McCaslin, M. and Good, T.L. 1992 'Compliant cognition: the misalliance of management and instructional goals in current school reform' *Educational Researcher* vol. 21, no. 3, pp. 4–17

McDonald, P. 1993 *Family trends and structure in Australia* Australian Institute of Family Studies, Melbourne

McGrath, H. 1997 *Dirty tricks: classroom games for teaching social skills* Longman, South Melbourne

——1998 'An overview of prevention and treatment programmes for developing positive peer relations' in *Children's peer relations* eds. P. T. Slee & K. Rigby, Routledge, London

McGrath, H. and Francey, S. 1991 *Friendly kids; friendly classrooms* Longman Cheshire, Melbourne

McGrath, H. and Noble, T. 1993 *Different kids, same classroom: making mixed ability classes really work* Longman, South Melbourne

McKim, M.K. 1993 'Quality child care: what does it mean for individual infants, parents and caregivers?' *Early Child Development and Care*, vol. 88, pp. 23–30

McLeod, W. 1989 'Minor miracles or logical processes? therapeutic interventions and techniques' *Journal of Family Therapy* vol. 11, pp. 257–80

Maag, J.W., Reid, R. and DiGangi, S.A. 1993 'Differential effects of self-monitoring attention, accuracy and productivity' *Journal of Applied Behavior Analysis* vol. 26, no. 3, pp. 329–44

References

Mace, F.C. and Wacker, D.P. 1994 'Toward greater integration of basic and applied behavioral research: an introduction' *Journal of Applied Behavior Analysis* vol. 27, no. 4, pp. 569–74

Maples, M. 1984 'Self-concept, locus of control, and self-discipline: valuable constructs for effective classroom management' *Journal of Humanistic Education and Development* vol. 23, no. 2, pp. 80–7

Martin, G. and Pear, J. 1999 *Behavior modification: what it is and how to do it* 6th edn, Prentice Hall, Upper Saddle River, NJ

Matthews, M. 1992 'Gifted students talk about co-operative learning' *Educational Leadership* vol. 50, no. 2, pp. 48–50

Meyers, A.W., Cohen, R. and Schleser, R. 1989 'A cognitive-behavioral approach to education: adopting a broad-based perspective' in *Cognitive-behavioral psychology in the schools* eds J.N. Hughes & R.J. Hall, Guilford, New York

Miller, C.S. 1984 'Building self-control: discipline for young children' *Young Children* vol. 40, no. 1, pp. 15–29

Miller, L.K. 1991 'Avoiding the countercontrol of applied behavior analysis' *Journal of Applied Behavior Analysis* vol. 24, no. 4, pp. 645–7

Mize, J. 1995 'Coaching preschool children in social skills: a cognitive-social learning curriculum' in *Teaching social skills to children: innovative approaches* eds G. Cartledge & J.F. Milburn, 3rd edn, Allyn & Bacon, Boston, MA

Molnar, A. 1986 'A systemic perspective on solving problems in the school' *NASSP Bulletin* vol. 70, no. 493, pp. 32–40

Molnar, A. and de Shazer, S. 1987 'Solution-focused therapy: toward the identification of therapeutic tasks' *Journal of Marital and Family Therapy* vol. 13, no. 4, pp. 349–58

Molnar, A. and Lindquist, B. 1989 *Changing problem behaviour in schools* Jossey-Bass, San Francisco, CA

Montgomery, D. 1996 *Educating the able* Cassell, London

Morgensen, G. 1989 'Act your age: a strategic approach to helping children change' *Journal of Strategic and Systemic Therapies* vol. 8, nos. 2 & 3, pp. 52–4

Mosteller, F., Light, R.J. and Sachs, J.A. 1996 'Sustained inquiry in education: lessons from skill grouping and class size' *Harvard Educational Review* vol. 66, no. 4, pp. 797–842

Murphy, J.J. 1992 'Brief strategic family intervention for school-related problems' *Family Therapy Case Studies* vol. 7, no. 1, pp. 59–71

——1994 'Brief therapy for school problems' *School Psychology International* vol. 15, pp. 115–31

Napier, R. and Gershenfeld, M. 1993 *Groups: theory and experience* 5th edn, Houghton & Mifflin, Boston, MA

Neef, N.A., Mace, F.C. and Shade, D. 1993 'Impulsivity in students with serious emotional disturbance: the interactive effects of reinforcer rate, delay, and quality' *Journal of Applied Behavior Analysis* vol. 26, no. 1, pp. 37–52

Nelsen, J., Erwin, C. and Duffy, R. 1998 *Positive discipline for preschoolers: for their early years—raising children who are responsible, respectful, and resourceful* rev. 2nd edn, Prima Publishing, Rocklin, CA

Nelsen, J., Lott, L. and Glenn, H.S. 1997 *Positive discipline in the classroom* rev. 2nd edn, Prima, Rocklin, CA

Nichols, M.P. and Schwartz, R.C. 1995 *Family therapy: concepts and methods* 3rd edn, Allyn & Bacon, Boston, MA

Nicholson, S. 1989 'Outcome evaluation of therapeutic effectiveness' *Australian and New Zealand Journal of Family Therapy* vol. 10, no. 2, pp. 77–83

Oden, S. 1988 'Alternative perspectives on children's peer relationships' in *Integrative processes and socialization: early to middle childhood* eds T.D. Yawkey & J.E. Johnson, Lawrence Erlbaum Associates, Hillsdale, NJ

Olweus, D. 1993 *Bullying at school: what we know and what we can do* Blackwell, Oxford, UK

Olympia, D.E., Sheridan, S.M., Jenson, W.R. and Andrews, D. 1994 'Using student-managed interventions to increase homework completion and accuracy' *Journal of Applied Behavior Analysis* vol. 27, no. 1, pp. 85–99

Orlick, T. 1982 *The second cooperative sports and games book* Pantheon, New York

Pellegrini, A.D. and Glickman, C.D. 1990 'Measuring kindergartners' social competence' *Young Children* vol. 45, no. 4, pp. 40–4

Pepler, D., Craig, W., Ziegler, S. and Charach, A. 1993 'A school-based anti-bullying intervention: preliminary evaluation' in *Understanding and managing bullying* ed. D. Tattum, Heinemann Educational, Oxford, UK

Perry, D. and Bussey, K. 1984 *Social development* Prentice Hall, Englewood Cliffs, NJ

Perry, R. 1993 'Empathy—still at the heart of therapy: the interplay of context and empathy' *Australian and New Zealand Journal of Family Therapy* vol. 14, no. 2, pp. 63–74

Petersen, L. and Ganoni, A. 1989 *Teacher's manual for training social skills while managing student behaviour* ACER, Melbourne

Peterson, G.W. and Leigh, G.K. 1990 'The family and social competence in adolescence' in *Developing social competency in adolescence* eds T.P. Gullotta, G.R. Adams & R. Montemayor, Sage, Newbury Park, CA

Phelan, P. , Davidson, A.L. and Cao, H.T. 1992 'Speaking up: students' perspectives on school' *Phi Delta Kappan* vol. 73, no. 9, pp. 695–704

Porteous, M.A. 1979 'A survey of the problems of normal 15-year-olds' *Journal of Adolescence* vol. 2, no. 4, pp. 307–23

Porter, L. 1999a *Young children's behaviour: practical approaches for caregivers and teachers* MacLennan & Petty, Sydney

——1999b 'Behaviour management practices in child care centres' unpublished doctoral dissertation, University of South Australia, Adelaide

——1999c *Gifted young children: a guide for teachers and parents* Allen & Unwin, Sydney

Porter, L. and McKenzie, S. in press *Professional collaboration with parents of children with disabilities* Whurr, London

Putallaz, M. and Wasserman, A. 1990 'Children's entry behavior' in *Peer rejection in childhood* eds S.R. Asher & J.D. Coie, Cambridge University Press, Cambridge, UK

Putnam, J.W. 1993 'The process of cooperative learning' in *Cooperative learning and strategies for inclusion* ed. J.W. Putnam, Paul H. Brooks, Baltimore, MD

Raban, B. 1997 'What counts towards quality provision.' *International Journal of Early Childhood* vol. 29, no. 1, pp. 57–63

Reder, P. 1983 'Disorganised families and the helping professions: who's in charge of what?' *Journal of Family Therapy* vol. 5, no. 1, pp. 23–6

Reid, R. and Harris, K.R. 1993 'Self-monitoring of attention versus self-monitoring of performance: effects on attention and academic performance' *Exceptional Children* vol. 60, no. 1, pp. 29–40

Rekers, G.A. 1984 'Ethical issues in child behavioral assessment' in *Child behavioral assessment* eds T.H. Ollendick & M. Hersen, Pergamon, New York

Render, G.F., Nell, J.E., Padilla, M. and Krank, H.M. 1989 'Assertive discipline: a critical review and analysis' *Teachers College Record* vol. 90, no. 4, pp. 607–30

Rhodes, J. 1993 'The use of solution-focused brief therapy in schools' *Educational Psychology in Practice* vol. 9, no. 1, pp. 27–34

Rigby, K. 1993 'Countering bullying in schools' *CAFHS Forum* vol. 1, no. 2, pp. 19–22

——1996 *Bullying in schools: and what to do about it* ACER, Melbourne

——1998 'Gender and bullying in schools' in *Children's peer relations* eds P. T. Slee & K. Rigby, Routledge, London

Rigby, K. and Slee, P. 1992 *Bullying in schools: a video with instructional manual* Institute of Social Research, University of South Australia, Adelaide

——1993 'Children's attitudes towards victims' in *Understanding and managing bullying* ed. D. Tattum, Heinemann Educational, Oxford, UK

Robinson, A. 1990 'Cooperation or exploitation? the argument against cooperative learning for talented students' *Journal for the Education of the Gifted* vol. 14, no. 1, pp. 9–27

Robinson, M. 1980 'Systems theory for the beginning therapist' *Australian Journal of Family Therapy* vol. 1, no. 4, pp. 183–94

Rodd, J. 1996 *Understanding young children's behaviour* Allen & Unwin, Sydney

Rogers, B. 1989 *Making a discipline plan: developing classroom management skills* Nelson, Melbourne

——1994 *Behaviour recovery* ACER, Melbourne

——1995 *Behaviour management: a whole-school approach* Ashton Scholastic, Gosford, NSW

——1997 *The language of discipline: a practical approach to effective classroom management* 2nd edn, Northcote House, Plymouth, UK

——1998 *'You know the fair rule' and much more: strategies for making the hard job of discipline and behaviour management in school easier* ACER, Melbourne

Rogers, C.R. 1951 *Client-centred therapy* Constable, London

——1978 *On personal power* Constable, London

Rogers, C.R. and Freiberg, H. 1994 *Freedom to learn* 3rd edn, Merrill, New York

Roland, E. 1993 'Bullying: a developing tradition of research and management' in *Understanding and managing bullying* ed. D. Tattum, Heinemann Educational, Oxford, UK

Rolider, A., Cummings, A. and Van Houten, R. 1991 'Side effects of therapeutic punishment on academic performance and eye contact' *Journal of Applied Behavior Analysis* vol. 24, no. 4, pp. 763–73

Rose, S.R. 1983 'Promoting social competence in children: a classroom approach to social and cognitive skill training' in *Social skills training for children and youth* ed. C.W. LeCroy, Haworth Press, New York

References

Rosenthal, D.M. and Sawyers, J.Y. 1996 'Building successful home/school partnerships: strategies for parent support and involvement *Childhood Education* vol. 72, no. 4, pp. 194–200

Rubin, Z. 1980 *Children's friendships* Harvard University Press, Cambridge MA

Ryan, R.M. and Deci, E.L. 1996 'When paradigms clash: comments on Cameron and Pierce's claim that rewards do not undermine intrinsic motivation' *Review of Educational Research* vol. 66, no. 1, pp. 33–8

Saifer, S., Clark, S., James, H. and Kearns, K. 1993 *Practical solutions to practically every problem* Pademelon, Sydney

Salmivalli, C., Kaukiainen, A. and Lagerspetz, K. 1998 'Aggression in the social relations of school-aged girls and boys' in *Children's peer relations* eds P. T. Slee & K. Rigby, Routledge, London

Sapon-Shevin, M. 1986 'Teaching cooperation' in *Teaching social skills to children: innovative approaches* 2nd edn, eds G. Cartledge & J.F. Milburn, Pergamon, New York

——1996 'Beyond gifted education: building a shared agenda for school reform' *Journal for the Education of the Gifted* vol. 19, no. 2, pp. 194–214

Sayger, T.V., Horne, A.M. and Glaser, B.A. 1993 'Marital satisfaction and social learning family therapy for child conduct problems: generalisation of treatment effects' *Journal of Marital and Family Therapy* vol. 19, no. 4, pp. 393–402

Schlick, M. 1966 'When is man responsible?' in *Free will and determinism* ed. B. Berofsky, Harper & Row, New York

Schloss, P. J. and Smith, M.A. 1998 *Applied behavior analysis in the classroom* 2nd edn, Allyn & Bacon, Boston, MA

Schmuck, R.A. and Schmuck, P. A. 1997 *Group processes in the classroom* 7th edn, Brown & Benchmark, Madison, WI

Schneider, B.H. 1989 'Between developmental wisdom and children's social skills training' in *Social competence in developmental perspective* eds B.H. Schneider, G. Attili, J. Nadel & R.P. Weissberg, Kluwer Academic Publishers, Dordrecht

Schneider, B.H. and Blonk, R.W.B. 1998 'Children's comments about their social skills training' in *Children's peer relations* eds P. T. Slee & K. Rigby, Routledge, London

Schunk, D.H. 1989 'Social cognitive theory and self-regulated learning' in *Self-regulated learning and academic achievement: theory, research, and practice*

eds B.J. Zimmerman & D.H. Schunk, Springer-Verlag, New York

Schraw, G. and Graham. T. 1997 'Helping gifted students develop metacognitive awareness' *Roeper Review* vol. 20, no. 1, pp. 4–8

Sebastian, P. 1989 *Handle with care: a guide to early childhood administration* 2nd edn, Jacaranda Press, Milton, QLD

Seligman, M. 1975 *Helplessness: on depression, development and death* W.H. Freeman & Co, San Francisco, CA

——1979 *Strategies for helping parents of exceptional children: a guide for teachers* Macmillan, London

——1995 *The optimistic child* Random House, Sydney

Seligman, M. and Darling, R.B. 1997 *Ordinary families; special children* 2nd edn, Guilford, New York

Seymour, F.W. and Epston, C. 1989 'An approach to childhood stealing with evaluation of 45 cases' *Australian and New Zealand Journal of Family Therapy* vol. 10, no. 3, pp. 137–43

Shapiro, E.S. 1984 'Self-monitoring procedures' in *Child behavioral assessment* eds T.H. Ollendick & M. Hersen, Pergamon, New York

Sharp, S. and Cowie, H. 1994 'Empowering pupils to take positive action against bullying' in *School bullying: insights and perspectives* eds P. K. Smith & S. Sharp, Routledge, London

Sharp, S. and Smith, P. K. eds 1994 *Tackling bullying in your school: a practical handbook for teachers* Routledge, London

Sharp, S. and Thompson, D. 1994 'The role of whole-school policies in tackling bullying behaviour in schools' in *School bullying: insights and perspectives* eds P. K. Smith & S. Sharp, Routledge, London

Skinner, B.F. 1989 *Recent issues in the analysis of behavior* Merrill, Columbus, OH

Slaby, R.G., Roedell, W.C., Arezzo, D. and Hendrix, K. 1995 *Early violence prevention: tools for teachers of young children* National Association for the Education of Young Children, Washington, DC

Slee, P. T. 1994a 'Life at school used to be good: victimisation and health concerns of secondary school students' *Young Studies Australia* December, pp. 20–3

——1994b 'Situational and interpersonal correlates of anxiety associated with peer victimisation' *Journal of Child Psychiatry and Human Development* vol. 25, no. 2, pp. 97–107

——1995 'Peer victimisation and its relationship to depression among Australian primary school students' *Journal of Personality and Individual Differences* vol. 18, no. 1, pp. 57–62

——1998 'Bullying amongst Australian primary school students: some barriers to help-seeking and links with sociometric status' in *Children's peer relations* eds P. T. Slee & K. Rigby, Routledge, London

Slee, P. T. and Rigby, K. 1994 'Peer victimisation at school' *Australian Journal of Early Childhood* vol. 19, no. 1, pp. 3–10

Smith, P. K., Cowie, H. and Sharp, S. 1994 'Working directly with pupils involved in bullying situations' in *School bullying: insights and perspectives* eds P. K. Smith & S. Sharp, Routledge, London

Smith, P. K. and Sharp, S. 1994 'The problem of school bullying' in *School bullying: insights and perspectives* eds P. K. Smith & S. Sharp, Routledge, London

Smyrnios, K.X. and Kirkby, R.J. 1989 'A review of brief, child-oriented family therapy outcome research: descriptive reports and single group studies' *Australian and New Zealand Journal of Family Therapy* vol. 10, no. 3, pp. 151–9

——1992 'Brief family therapies: a comparison of theoretical and technical issues' *Australian and New Zealand Journal of Family Therapy* vol. 13, no. 3, pp. 119–27

Smyrnios, K.X., Kirkby, R.J. and Smyrnios, S.M. 1988 'Brief family therapy: a critique of Kinston and Bentovim' *Australian and New Zealand Journal of Family Therapy* vol. 9, no. 3, pp. 139–42

Sokoly, M.M. and Dokecki, P. R. 1995 'Ethical perspectives on family-centred early intervention' in *Working with families in early intervention* ed. J.A. Blackman, Aspen, Gaithersburg, MD

Spradlin, J.E. 1996 'Comments on Lerman and Iwata (1996)' *Journal of Applied Behavior Analysis* vol. 29, no. 3, pp. 383–5

Sprenkle, D.H. and Bischoff, R.J. 1995 'Research in family therapy: trends, issues and recommendations' in *Family therapy: concepts and methods* 3rd edn, eds M.P. Nichols & R.C. Schwartz, Allyn & Bacon, Boston, MA

Stacey, K. and Loptson, C. 1995 'Children should be seen and not heard?: questioning the unquestioned' *Journal of Systemic Therapies* vol. 14, no. 4, pp. 16–31

Stanley, D. 1996 'How to defuse an angry parent' *Child Care Information Exchange* vol. 108, pp. 34–5

Stonehouse, A. 1991 *Opening the doors: child care in a multi-cultural society* Australian Early Childhood Association, Watson, ACT

Strike, K.A. and Soltis, J.F. 1992 *The ethics of teaching* 2nd edn, Teachers College Press, New York

Strohl, T. 1989 'Symptoms: the price we pay to control' in *Control theory in the practice of reality therapy* ed. N. Glasser, Harper & Row, New York

Sulzer-Azaroff, B. and Mayer, G.R. 1991 *Behavior analysis for lasting change* Holt, Rinehart & Winston, Fort Worth, TX

Summers, J.A., Dell'Oliver, C., Turnbull, A.P., Benson, H.A., Santelli, E., Campbell, M. and Siegal–Causey, E. 1990 'Examining the individualised family service plan process: what are family and practitioner preferences?' *Topics in Early Childhood Special Education* vol. 10, no. 1, pp. 78–99

Swetnam, L., Peterson, C.R. and Clark, H.B. 1983 'Social skills development in young children: preventive and therapeutic approaches' in *Social skills training for children and youth* ed. C.W. LeCroy, Haworth Press, New York

Tattum, D. 1993a 'What is bullying?' in *Understanding and managing bullying* ed. D. Tattum, Heinemann Educational, Oxford, UK

——1993b 'Short, medium and long-term management strategies' in *Understanding and managing bullying* ed. D. Tattum, Heinemann Educational, Oxford, UK

——1993c 'Child, school and family' in *Understanding and managing bullying* ed. D. Tattum, Heinemann Educational, Oxford, UK

Tauber, R. 1990 *Classroom management from A to Z*, Holt Rinehart and Winston, Forth Worth, TX

Thompson, C.L. and Rudolph, L.B. 1996 *Counselling children* 4th edn, Brooks/Cole, Pacific Grove, CA

Tinworth, S. 1994 'Conceptualising a collaborative partnership between parents and staff in early childhood services' in *Issues in early childhood services: Australian perspectives* eds E.J. Mellor & K.M. Coombe, William C. Brown, Dubuque, IO

Turnbull, A.P. and Turnbull, H.R. 1990 *Families, professionals and exceptionality: a special partnership* 2nd edn, Merrill, Upper Saddle River, NJ

——1997 *Families, professionals and exceptionality: a special partnership* 3rd edn, Merrill, Upper Saddle River, NJ

Vallerand, R.J., Gagné, F., Senécal, C. and Pelletier, L.G. 1994 'A comparison of the school intrinsic motivation and perceived competence of gifted and regular students' *Gifted Child Quarterly* vol. 38, no. 4, pp. 172–5

Veenman, S. 1995 'Cognitive and noncognitive effects of multigrade and multi-age classes: a best-evidence synthesis' *Review of Educational Research* vol. 65, no. 4, pp. 319–81

——1996 'Effects of multigrade and multi-age classes reconsidered' *Review of Educational Research* vol. 66, no. 3, pp. 323–40

Vollmer, T.R., Iwata, B.A., Zarcone, J.R., Smith, R.G. and Mazaleski, J.L. 1993 'The role of attention

References

in the treatment of attention-maintained self-injurious behavior: noncontingent reinforcement and differential reinforcement of other behaviour' *Journal of Applied Behavior Analysis* vol. 26, no. 1, pp. 9–21

Vollmer, T.R., Progar, P. R., Lalli, J.S., Van Camp, C.M., Sierp, B.J., Wright, C.S., Nastasi, J. and Eisenschink, K.J. 1998 'Fixed-time schedules attenuate extinction-induced phenomena in the treatment of severe aberrant behavior' *Journal of Applied Behavior Analysis* vol. 31, no. 4, pp. 529–42

Walker, J.E. and Shea, T.M. 1999 *Behavior management: a practical approach for educators* 7th edn, Merrill, Upper Saddle River, NJ

Walsh, W.M. and McGraw, J.A. 1996 *Essentials of family therapy: a therapist's guide to eight approaches* Love Publishing, Denver, CO

Waters, J. 1996 *Making the connection: parents and early childhood staff* Lady Gowrie Child Centre (Melbourne) Inc., Melbourne

Watzlawick, P. , Weakland, J. and Fisch, R. 1974 *Change: principles of problem formation and problem resolution* W.W. Norton, New York

Webb, J.T., Meckstroth, E.A. and Tolan, S.S. 1991 *Guiding the gifted child: a practical source for parents and teachers* Hawker Brownlow Education, Melbourne

Westwood, P. 1997 *Commonsense methods for children with special needs* 3rd edn, Routledge, London

Whelan, T. and Kelly, S. 1986 *A hard act to follow: step-parenting in Australia today* Penguin, Melbourne

Wheldall, K. and Merrett, F. 1984 *Positive teaching: the behavioural approach* Allen & Unwin, London

Whitman, T.L., Scherzinger, M.L. and Sommer, K.S. 1991 'Cognitive instruction and mental retardation' in *Child and adolescent therapy: cognitive-behavioral procedures* ed. P. Kendall, Guilford, New York

Whitmore, J.R. 1980 *Giftedness, conflict, and underachievement* Allyn & Bacon, Boston, MA

Whitney, I., Rivers, I, Smith, P. K. and Sharp, S. 1994 'The Sheffield project: methodology and findings' in *School bullying: insights and perspectives* eds P. K. Smith & S. Sharp, Routledge, London

Williams, B.F., Williams, R.L. and McLaughlin, T.F. 1989 'The use of token economies with individuals who have developmental disabilities' in *The treatment of severe behavior disorders: behavior analysis approaches* ed. E. Cipani, The American Association on Mental Retardation, Washington, DC

Wolery, M., Bailey, D.B. and Sugai, G.M. 1988 *Effective teaching: principles and procedures of applied behavior analysis with exceptional students* Allyn & Bacon, Boston, MA

Wragg, J. 1989 *Talk sense to yourself: a program for children and adolescents* ACER, Melbourne

Yong, F.L. 1994 'Self-concepts, locus of control, and Machiavellianism of ethnically diverse middle school students who are gifted' *Roeper Review* vol. 16, no. 3, pp. 192–4

Young, M.E. 1992 *Counseling methods and techniques: an eclectic approach* Merrill, New York

Zanolli, K. and Daggett, J. 1998 'The effects of reinforcement rate on the spontaneous social initiations of socially withdrawn preschoolers' *Journal of Applied Behavior Analysis* vol. 31, no. 1, pp. 117–25

Zarcone, J.R., Iwata, B.A., Mazaleski, J.L. and Smith, R.G. 1994 'Momentum and extinction effects on self-injurious escape behavior and noncompliance' *Journal of Applied Behavior Analysis* vol. 27, no. 4, pp. 649–58

Zirpoli, T.J. and Melloy, K.J. 1997 *Behavior management: applications for teachers and parents* 2nd edn, Merrill, Upper Saddle River, NJ

Index

Index

KING ALFRED'S COLLEGE
LIBRARY